CAMPAIGNS AGAINST WESTERN DEFENCE

CAMPAIGNS AGAINST WESTERN DEFENCE

NATO's Adversaries and Critics

Clive Rose

St. Martin's Press   New York

© Royal United Services Institute 1985

All rights reserved. For information, write:
St. Martin's Press, Inc.,
175 Fifth Avenue, New York, NY 10010
Printed in Great Britain
Published in the United Kingdom by The Macmillan Press Ltd.
First published in the United States of America in 1985

ISBN 0–312–11469–9

Library of Congress Cataloging in Publication Data
Rose, Clive.
Campaigns against western defence.
Bibliography: p.
Includes index.
1. North Atalantic Treaty Organization. I. Title
UA646.3.R6   1985   355'.031'091821   84–18067
ISBN 0–312–11469–9

Contents

Acknowledgements vii

Glossary of Abbreviations viii

PART I   INTRODUCTION

1. Adversaries and Critics 1
2. Western Defence 19

PART II   ADVERSARIES: INTERNATIONAL FRONT ORGANISATIONS AND SOVIET PEACE CAMPAIGNS

3. The Origin of the International Front Organisations, 1919–39 39
4. The International Front Organisations since the Second World War 52
5. The World Peace Council 64
6. The International Department of the Soviet Communist Party and Related KGB Activities 77
7. Campaigns Against NATO 94

PART III   CRITICS: PEACE MOVEMENTS IN THE WEST

8. Origin of the Peace Movement in the United Kingdom, 1930–62 115
9. The Peace Movement in the United Kingdom, 1963–83 137
10. Peace Movements in Western Europe 156
11. The Freeze Campaign in the United States and the Bishops' Letter 188

PART IV CONCLUSION

12	Unofficial Peace Activities in Eastern Europe	213
13	Future Conditional	237

ANNEXES

I	The United Kingdom Nuclear Deterrent	243
II	Profiles of the Principal International Front Organisations	246
III	Estimated Soviet Subsidies to International Front Organisations, 1979	292
IV	Generals for Peace and Disarmament	293
	Notes	295
	Index of Names	303
	General Index	311

Acknowledgements

A number of people have contributed advice and practical help in the preparation of this book and thanks are due to all of them. Four require special mention. First I am indebted to the late Professor Leonard Schapiro, who generously made available to me the results of research undertaken under his auspices when he was chairman of the Institute for the Study of Conflict and encouraged me to take the development and publication of this work through to completion. This provided the basis for Chapters 3 to 7 and also much factual material incorporated in Chapters 10 and 12; it was originally put together in book form by Nigel Clive, who has continued to give me the benefit of his advice throughout. I am also grateful to Rosemary Baker, lately of the Royal United Services Institute for Defence Studies, for the major contribution she made to Chapter 8 and for her help with Chapter 11; and to Brigadier Kenneth Hunt for his valuable advice on Chapter 2. While I gratefully acknowledge their help, I should make it clear that I alone am responsible for the content of the book and the views expressed in it.

CLIVE ROSE

Glossary of Abbreviations

AAPSO	Afro-Asian Peoples' Solidarity Organisation	ICESC	International Committee for European Security and Cooperation
AFSC	American Friends' Service Committee	ICFTU	International Confederation of Free Trade Unions
AGDF	Action Group Service for Peace (West Germany)	ID	International Department of the Central Committee of the CPSU
ASF	Action Group for Peace and Reconciliation (West Germany)		
BPA	British Peace Assembly	IID	International Information Department of the Central Committee
CALC	Clergy and Laity Concerned (USA)		
CND	Campaign for Nuclear Disarmament (UK)	IIP	International Institute for Peace
CPC	Christian Peace Conference	IKV	Interchurch Peace Council (Netherlands)
CPGB	Communist Party of Great Britain	ILF	International Liaison Forum of Peace Forces
CPSU	Communist Party of the Soviet Union	IMEMO	Institute of World Economy and International Relations (USSR)
CPUSA	Communist Party of the USA		
DAC	Direct Action Committee (UK)		
DEMYC	Democrat Youth Community of Europe	INF	Intermediate Range Nuclear Forces
DKP	West German Communist Party	IUS	International Union of Students
END	Campaign for European Nuclear Disarmament	LNU	League of Nations Union
ERW	Enhanced Radiation Warhead	MIRV	Multiple Independently – targetable Re-entry Vehicle
FIR	International Federation of Resistance Fighters		
		OIRT	International Radio and Television Organisation
GLCM	Ground Launched Cruise Missiles	SED	Socialist Unity Party (East Germany)
IADL	International Association of Democratic Laywers	WFDY	World Federation of Democratic Youth

WFSW	World Federation of Scientific Workers	WILPF	Women's International League for Peace and Freedom
WFTU	World Federation of Trade Unions	WPC	World Peace Council
WIDF	Women's International Democratic Federation	WSP	Women Strike for Peace

Part I
Introduction

1 Adversaries and Critics

I

When Sir Winston Churchill wrote the sixth and final volume of his history of the Second World War, he took as his theme: 'How the great democracies triumphed, and so were able to resume the follies which had so nearly cost them their life'. These words were written in 1953: that is to say, in the year Stalin died, six years after the 'Cold War' may be said to have started and seven years after Churchill himself had spoken, in Fulton, Missouri, of an 'Iron Curtain' descending across the continent of Europe. How far has his forecast proved correct? Had the democracies learned nothing from their experience? Since he wrote these words, the democracies have committed plenty of follies: misjudgements, missed opportunities and just plain mistakes. There is nothing very novel or surprising about this. Such follies abounded in the 1920s and 1930s, but the democracies had perhaps learned one thing: the need jointly to devise in advance means for managing, and as far as possible, guarding against, their more serious consequences. The lesson was forced upon them by the circumstances in which they found themselves in 1945. The principal means devised was the North Atlantic Treaty, signed in 1949, by which the North Atlantic Alliance was created.

Every generation probably regards its moment in history as being one of special importance. The Chinese salutation 'may you live in interesting times' is a reflection of this. For the generation which emerged from the Second World War, either from service in the armed forces or having grown up during it, this has seemed particularly true. The war was a watershed, in personal as well as in historical terms. In so far as it is ever possible to draw a line arbitrarily under past events, relegating them, so to speak, to history, this appeared possible in 1945, when the 'post-war era' began. There is a case for saying that it has not yet ended. The world is still living in the aftermath of decisions, policies and attitudes which took shape at the end of the war and in the years immediately following it. The events of those early years have a very direct bearing on the current scene. The next section looks at the principal features of this scene.

II

First and foremost is the overriding shadow of the East–West conflict. Soviet behaviour, which in practice meant Stalin's behaviour, aroused serious misgivings among his wartime Allies. But there was still hope that the cooperation between the Big Three could be maintained; this was seen as a necessary basis for peace and stability, and for the enormous task of reconstruction in the post-war world. So great efforts were made by the Americans and British to preserve it. All too soon, however, it became apparent that this hope was to prove illusory and the efforts fruitless. The fundamental differences which underlay a wartime partnership based on expediency began to reassert themselves. The difference between the East and the West was, and still remains, one between two opposing and irreconcilable forms of society. The difference is both ideological and political. It is as much a difference between two views of the rights of the individual *vis-à-vis* the State as between a power bent on a policy of expansion and those determined to maintain their independence.

In basic terms, the West comprises those countries which profess the values of freedom of speech, political and religious tolerance, democratic representation and respect for individual human rights. More important, for the most part it comprises countries which also try to put these values into practice and are prepared to defend their independence in order to be able to do so. It would be foolish and naive to claim that the countries of the West have always been successful in their efforts, or even that they have all been consistent in making the attempt. There have been and still are plenty of examples of failure. Several Western countries have had, for shorter or longer periods, regimes which have shown scant regard for at least some of these values or have abandoned them altogether. None of them has been without blemish throughout the last 40 years. But the failures, regrettable though they undoubtedly are, give substance to the thesis; they are recognised as such, as lapses from a standard whose generality is accepted in the West. What is more, it is a standard which, because it is expected of the West, often results in a 'double standard' being applied internationally as between the West and the East, with the West being judged more harshly and according to the principles of behaviour which it professes. There are certain safeguards. The effect of pressures and criticisms of partners and allies, expressed both publicly and privately, should not be underrated. The contacts between ministers and officials of the Western countries are close and frequent. On a personal, as well as an official, level it is uncomfortable to have to endure the intimacy of the conduct of day-to-day business under the continuing shadow of disapproval. None of these safeguards can in themselves guarantee that the values will be perpetuated: deeply engrained in the collective Western temperament is a tendency to commit the follies to which Churchill referred. But the freedom to dissent, to demonstrate and to vote, which is the most prized of all Western values provides the best assurance that those who commit follies will in the end be answerable to those in whose name they are committed.

The East means the Soviet Union and those Communist states which comprise its satellites and allies. Over its clients in Eastern Europe the Soviet Union has sought to maintain and has in practice achieved tight control. The Soviet Government has effectively dominated their policies and actions; the physical presence of vast Soviet forces ever since the war has ensured this. Its determination to use these forces if necessary to maintain that dominance has been demonstrated on several occasions during the past 30 years with total ruthlessness: in East Germany in 1953, in Hungary in 1956, in Czechoslovakia in 1968 and in the threat of military intervention in Poland in 1980 and 1981. So it is to Soviet policy that we must look for an explanation of what the East stands for. There are two strands. The first is ideological and has provided the guiding principles from the Bolshevik Revolution onwards. Under this, Soviet policy has been based on a doctrine which ascribes historical inevitability to the ultimate worldwide victory of Communism; on a morality which regards as legitimate anything which is done to promote that victory; and on a philosophy which subordinates the rights of individuals to the interests of the state. Such an ideology does not allow much room for self-doubt, nor has the Soviet Union yet produced any alternative to force and repression as a means of regulating the pressures which the application of these principles engender. The agreement reached between 35 countries, including the Soviet Union and the United States, at the Conference on Security and Cooperation in Europe held in Helsinki in 1975 laid strong emphasis on the observance of human rights and freedoms. It established what was regarded as an international standard for behaviour by the Governments which signed it, and thus a safeguard against abuse. There was some confidence in the West that the Soviet Government would at least make a show of honouring its commitments: its subsequent actions – suppression of a group of Soviet citizens whose intention was to monitor their Government's performance, the arrest of individuals involved and blatant disregard for the Helsinki undertakings both internally and internationally – have shown that Western confidence was misplaced. By hindsight, it may be doubted whether the Soviet Government ever really intended to fulfil what it had agreed, since to do so would have risked undermining the basis on which its power rested.

The second strand of Soviet policy is the traditional Russian sense of insecurity which has often taken the form of a fear of encirclement. In this strand is to be found the historic urge to gain access to warm water ports and to dominate the countries round her frontiers so as to provide a defensive buffer against potential enemies from without. Some may claim that this strand is of greater importance to an understanding of Soviet policies than the ideological strand. Some may even try to use it to justify the invasion of Afghanistan in 1979. But it does not provide an adequate explanation for the aggressive, as compared with the defensive, aspects of Soviet policy world-wide since the end of the Second World War. Whatever weight is given to each of these two strands, their combined effect has produced the imperialist and expansionist foreign policy which the Soviet Government has pursued. It led Dr Henry Kissinger to write in 1979 that: 'to expect the Soviet leaders to restrain themselves from exploiting circumstances they conceive to be favourable is to misread history. To foreclose Soviet options is thus the essence of the West's responsibility. It is up to us to define the limits of Soviet aims'.[1]

The East–West conflict has never been of the West's choosing. It was Winston Churchill again who, as early as 1950, spoke of the need for 'a supreme effort to bridge the gulf between the two worlds so that each can live their life, if not in friendship, at least without the hatreds of war'. This effort has continued ever since. It has achieved some success and suffered many setbacks. It will continue because it responds to the universal urge for genuine peace, despite the misgivings which from time to time beset United States Administrations and occasionally other Western governments and despite the rebuffs which it has constantly received from the Soviet Union.

Another major feature of the post-war era is the nuclear weapon. The explosive power of the only two nuclear bombs to have been used in war – those dropped on Hiroshima and Nagasaki in August 1945 – was equivalent to 14 and 20 thousand tons of conventional explosive (TNT) respectively; 20 thousand tons is two thousand times the power of the largest conventional bomb dropped on Germany in the Second World War. Besides the enormous destructive effect of fire and blast, nuclear weapons bring the additional horror of damage from radiation. Conscious of the awful significance of these new weapons for the future of mankind, the United States initiated, immediately the war with Japan ended in 1945, proposals for the international control of atomic energy, for the elimination of atomic weapons from national armaments and for effective international safeguards to ensure compliance. This initiative was supported by the United Kingdom, which had participated in the wartime development of the bomb. The proposals were elaborated and pursued in the United Nations and resulted in a series of recommendations to the Security Council by the United Nations Atomic Energy Commission, the purpose of which was to establish an international authority with powers of inspection. Unfortunately they foundered on the rocks of Soviet opposition and the efforts to find a basis for agreement came to an end when the Soviet Union conducted its first atomic test in 1949. The largest weapons deployed today – by the Soviet Union – have about one thousand times the explosive power of the first atomic bomb.

It is academic to ask whether it was right – militarily and morally – to develop and use the first nuclear weapons in the 1940s. Anyone who attempts to answer that question must do so against the background of the circumstances and attitudes prevailing at the time when there was a real fear that the Nazis might develop them first. Since then nuclear weapons have become a major factor in all our lives. This does not make them more acceptable or their use any less abhorrent but, whatever anyone may wish, they cannot be disinvented. What is clear is that the existence of nuclear weapons has not only dominated views about war since 1945 but has equally dominated thinking about peace. While no one can be complacent about the 100 or more 'conventional' wars which have taken place in various parts of the world since 1945, involving the deaths of some 10 million people, it is a fact that peace between East and West has been preserved for 39 years. At least since the North Atlantic Alliance was formed, the West has adopted the policy of deterring war – not just nuclear war but any war between East and West. The policy of deterrence is based ultimately on the credibility of the threat that, if necessary, and should deterrence fail, nuclear weapons would be used. The validity of this policy has been questioned, not just on moral but also on practical and strategic grounds. The unquestionable fact is that it has worked. The ultimate disaster of a nuclear holocaust has so far been avoided. This in no way removes the obligation on the governments, of East and West, to pursue vigorously, seriously and continuously, efforts to reduce the levels of accumulated nuclear weapons with at least, as a possible goal, the prospect of their eventual elimination. One who recognised the dangers and whose views are much quoted on both sides of the nuclear argument, the late Earl Mountbatten, gave this wise advice:

> But how do we set about achieving practical means of nuclear arms control and disarmament? To begin with, we are most likely to preserve peace if there is a military balance between East and West. The real need is for both sides to replace the attempts to maintain a balance through ever-increasing and even more costly nuclear armaments by a balance based on mutual restraint. Better still, by reduction of nuclear armaments, I believe it should be possible to achieve greater security at a lower level of military confrontation.[2]

The dilemma remains: how to reduce the dependence on nuclear weapons without at the same time weakening deterrence and thus security? The dilemma is as acute now as it has been at any time since the American nuclear monopoly was broken some 35 years ago. The pace of technological advance on both sides has made it more rather than less intractable, and thus the need to resolve it more pressing. Some may derive some small reassurance from the fact that there have been two areas in which the United States and the Soviet Union have shared a certain measure of common interest – certainly since the Cuban crisis of 1962: their search for ways of reducing the risk that nuclear weapons might be used between them and for controlling their proliferation to other countries. The Hotline and SALT agreements are examples of the former, plus a number of multilateral arms control agreements to which both superpowers are parties. As regard the latter, the Partial Test Ban Treaty (1963) and the Non-Proliferation Treaty (1968), of which the United States and Soviet Union (with the United Kingdom) are joint depository powers, each have more than 100 adherents, and the non-proliferation policy which the two superpowers jointly support has held to the extent that, so far, no new nuclear weapon states have emerged since China joined the two superpowers and Britain and France, in 1964. But the deplorable fact is that no substantive progress has been made on the fundamental problem of reducing the vast accumulation of nuclear armaments by both East and West. By common consensus in the West among governments and publics alike, this remains the most urgent international problem today, despite the divergence of views on how to solve it. But in the East there is no possibility of popular pressures on the Soviet Government to take measures to break the deadlock.

Yet another significant trend is the decline in status of the countries of Europe as a consequence of the Second World War. The devastation of the countries of continental Europe which had been bombed and fought over, especially Germany, was shattering. Britain had suffered enormous damage from German bombing. The destruction of houses, factories and other physical assets and the human casualties were incomparably greater than anything suffered in the First World War. To this must be added the vast expenditure incurred, particularly by the United Kingdom, in the prosecution of the war. To meet this, she had liquidated the bulk of her valuable overseas investments, but even so emerged from the war saddled with a large external debt. From being the world's biggest creditor nation before the war she had become the world's biggest debtor. In comparison, the United States itself and its physical assets on the American continent were untouched: and despite major expenditure on its war effort and the generous wartime aid programme to its Allies known as

'Lend-Lease', the United States emerged from the war in a different economic league from that of any of the European countries. The Soviet Union suffered the highest casualties of all the countries involved in the war and widespread devastation in European Russia, although its territory and resources east of Moscow and Stalingrad remained unaffected.

This decline in Europe's strength was followed by another change which resulted from the liquidation of the Western European colonial empires in the twenty years after the end of the Second World War. The United Kingdom, for example, was in 1946 still the centre of an empire which covered 10 million square miles (18%) of the earth's land surface, with a total population of some 800 millions, about a quarter of the population of the world; by 1983 there remained only 13 small colonial territories scattered around the world, of which the total population, excluding the 5 million in Hong Kong, was less than 200 000. Meanwhile many newly independent countries had emerged, former colonies not only of the United Kingdom but also of France, Belgium, the Netherlands and Portugal. All of them have joined the United Nations, which expanded in size from 50 members, dominated by a built-in Western majority in 1945, to 157 members in 1983, some two-thirds of which describe themselves as 'non-aligned'. Many of these newly independent countries are situated in strategically important positions; some are sources of key raw materials, oil and minerals. The bulk of them are very poor and in urgent need of technical and economic aid from the developed countries, whether East or West. They get virtually no such aid from the East. Many are potentially unstable and therefore particularly vulnerable to Soviet efforts at penetration and subversion, either directly or through Cuban or East German surrogates, and susceptible to Soviet propaganda which may be accompanied by arms sales on favourable terms (the Soviet Union was in 1981 the largest single supplier with 36.5% of the market).[3] Soviet exploitation of this situation, in Angola, Ethiopia, Afghanistan, South Yemen and elsewhere, has shown that it is an illusion to think that non-alignment confers immunity from the East–West conflict.

The changes wrought in Europe by the factors noted above led to another development of the greatest significance: the establishment of the European Communities. The growth of 'Europe', hesitant and turbulent though it has been, may be regarded as the most hopeful feature of the post-war era. Its importance, in relation to the theme of this book, is that it reinforces the cohesion of the West and has effectively made war between its members in future unthinkable.

Affecting all these features of the post-war era has been the way in which the world has, as it were, shrunk in the past 40 years. The speed and availability of air travel has made it possible for statesmen of East and West to meet easily and frequently to an extent inconceivable before 1939; Neville Chamberlain travelled by air for the first time in his life when he flew to Munich to meet Hitler in September 1938.[4] Communications, by radio and by satellite, enable information to be transmitted from one end of the world to another quickly and accurately. Television has meant that the horrors of distant warfare can be brought directly to the homes of non-participants, as in the Vietnam war to American audiences, but not to Soviet audiences in the current fighting in Afghanistan where over 100 000 Soviet troops are deployed. Technological progress has made the concept of 'one world' more of a reality and, with it, has come the growth of interdependence, reflected by a proliferation of international organisations. But one world does not mean a united world; proximity and ease of access have highlighted the divergent, just as much as the shared interests, the points of discord as well as the points of accord. In both cases the contrast has been accentuated by the developments outlined above. It is still as evident as it was in the 1930s that peace with freedom cannot be secured without vigilance, and that the lesson learned then has not lost its force in 1984. For all the emphasis which is rightly put on the importance of dialogue as a means for reducing tension and the risks of confrontation, the continuing need for vigilant and effective defence has in no way decreased.

III

This book is about the defence of the West. It is not primarily concerned with military policies and weapons, although both have a direct bearing on its theme. Its main object is to examine the pressures and influences which tend, indeed are intended, to erode the political support for the strategy on which Western defence is based. Two elements stand out in the account which is given of the events of recent years: abuse of the meaning of the word 'peace' and legitimate fear of nuclear weapons. The exploitation of both these elements by Soviet, and not only Soviet, propaganda and the susceptibility to that propaganda of public opinion in the West has been one cause of erosion. The failure of Western governments to recognise the dangers in time or, when they did recognise them, to take the action needed to counter them has been another.

The main text is divided into two parts. Part II describes what has been done in the past, and is still being done today, under the general direction or close control of the Soviet authorities, to undermine the security and stability of the West. The term 'adversaries' applies to those who are engaged in this activity. No doubt they include – and certainly have in the past included – a fair number of dupes, those who are as much misled by Soviet propaganda as those whom they seek to mislead. But in so far as the latter do this consciously and accept the motivation for it, they must also be classed as adversaries whose actions are inimical to the interests of the Western democracies. Whether they acknowledge it or not, their participation implies at least sympathy with the principles on which Soviet foreign policy is based. When President Brezhnev declared that 'the total triumph of socialism all over the world is inevitable'[5] and that therefore 'everything which serves to build up Communism is moral',[6] he was reaffirming the received Marxist–Leninist view without which the foreign policy of the Soviet Union would collapse like a pack of cards. For from these principles are derived the Brezhnev Doctrine,* the permanent 'struggle against imperialism' and the duty to support 'national liberation movements' which have been the main pillars of Soviet expansionist activities throughout the world. While the adversaries – or many of them – may have reservations about espousing Lenin's endorsement of war as a just means of promoting socialist victory over capitalism, they evidently have no difficulty in accepting the official Soviet view that, whereas 'strength in imperialism's hands is a source of

---

* This asserted (November 1968) that: 'when internal and external forces hostile to socialism attempt to turn the development of any socialist country in the direction of the restoration of the capitalist system, when a threat arises to the course of socialism in that country, a threat to the security of the socialist commonwealth as whole, it already becomes not only a problem for the people of that country but also a general problem, the concern of all socialist countries'. The invasion of Czechoslovakia by Soviet, Polish, East German, Bulgarian and Hungarian forces had taken place three months earlier.

danger of war ... strength in socialism's hands becomes a source of ensuring peace'.[7] More directly relevant to the propaganda role in which the adversaries are engaged is Lenin's dictum that 'the soundest strategy in war is to postpone operations until the moral disintegration of the enemy renders the mortal blow both possible and easy'. Translated into the realities of the nuclear era, this means that 'peace', properly exploited, will provide a way of delivering the mortal blow without recourse to war. Whether under the guise of 'peaceful coexistence' or of *détente*, the objective remains the same as it always has been.

Although the manipulation of international front organisations has acquired particular importance in the promotion of the 'peace campaigns' since 1945, the concept of the front organisation has its origins in the early years of the Soviet regime. Lenin recognised the importance of spreading Communist influence, and of advancing Soviet policy, by the device of using wider organisations which would be under covert Communist control, but which because of their more extensive objectives and ostensibly idealistic nature would attract much greater support than that which would be attracted by any organisation which was avowedly Communist. The idea was taken up by the Third (Communist) International or Comintern, and in the course of the 1920s and 1930s a number of front organisations came into existence with this aim in view. They achieved a considerable measure of success in spreading propaganda for the Soviet regime, as it sought to portray itself, and for Soviet policy through the mouths of prominent people who could not be described as Communist or in some cases even as pro-Communist. This process was much aided by the general ignorance about conditions in the Soviet Union which prevailed in the Western world before 1945.

The situation was different afterwards. Revived international front activities had begun to get into their stride by 1948 with the launching of the Soviet 'peace campaign' from which the World Peace Council emerged in 1950. By that date much of the goodwill which the Soviet Union had been able to win by its huge military effort had been dissipated, or at any rate tarnished, by Stalin's post-war policies and by the much more extensive knowledge in the West of the nature of the Soviet regime. This resulted from the enlightenment provided by many former Soviet citizens who had remained in the West after the war. Soviet efforts to penetrate the West were intensified and Soviet control over these international front organisations became much more thorough than it had been in the pre-war period. This was achieved by the transfer of control of these organisations from the Comintern, which was dissolved in 1943, to the International Department of the Central Committee of the Soviet Communist Party (CPSU). Control of the front organisations was ensured by placing Soviet officials or trusted non-Soviet Communists in key positions in each. In practice this has proved effective; on virtually no issue has the policy decision taken by an international front organisation differed from the position adopted by the Soviet Union (or at least not for very long).

Although the World Peace Council remains the principal international front organisation, the system devised after 1945 has enabled other fronts to be established rapidly to meet new situations or requirements, with Soviet nominees ready to fill key appointments. Post-war front organisations have two main functions. First, the traditional one, originating with Lenin, of propagating Soviet policies, normally under some such emotive headings as 'peace', 'racial equality' or 'liberation from colonialism', to a much wider public than is available to members of foreign Communist parties. Secondly, they provide a valuable means of improving the image of the Soviet Union. International reactions to Soviet policies from Stalin's time onwards have increased the need to present 'socialism with a peaceloving and democratic face' and to be able to do so from a base of assured sympathisers.

Indeed the principle that 'peace' is inseparable from 'socialism' and thus from the spread of Soviet influence is central to Soviet propaganda which, in practice, is indistinguishable from Soviet policy. Anything therefore that serves to advance Soviet foreign policy aims, which are invariably presented as unchallengably dedicated to the furtherance of peace between nations, can be subsumed under the broad umbrella of 'peace'. Thus the front organisations which are devoted to the 'liberation struggle' of Africans, Asians, Arabs or Latin Americans serve the 'cause of peace', in Soviet parlance, because they undermine the 'enemy of peace', Western imperialism and in particular the United States. International front organisations devoted to the campaign against racialism are also part of the 'struggle for peace', and it is the United States and its 'imperialist' allies which are represented in Soviet propaganda as being the supporters of racialism, for example in South Africa. Similarly, support for 'liberation movements' has paid off in the United Nations where it has won support for many Soviet policies among Third World countries which form the majority in the General Assembly.

It would be a mistake to underestimate the international front organisations' success. The many non-Communists who participate in them often appear undismayed or unaware that the cause they support, though praiseworthy enough in itself, is used to promote Soviet influence through the world or that the respectability which their presence gives has enabled some of the organisations to achieve recognition and status in the specialised bodies of the United Nations. Nor does it seem to perturb them that the policies advocated have invariably been at the expense of the West. Disarmament has always had high priority, through successive variations on the 'peace campaign' theme; in terms of Soviet rhetoric it is always the aggressive NATO bloc which is required to disarm, while the primary purpose of Soviet arms is portrayed as being to make the world safe for 'socialism'. Similarly 'liberation' has always meant liberation from 'Western imperialism' and 'colonialist oppression', but has been indignantly rejected as having no relevance to Hungary, Poland or Afghanistan, to the annexation of the Baltic States by the Soviet Union in 1940 or to the peoples incorporated into the Russian Empire by 19th century Tsars (who are now on the point of becoming a majority of the population of the Soviet Union).

The international front organisations are an important instrument of Soviet foreign policy. They complement and reinforce other 'active measures' such as disinformation, and official government propaganda which provides much of the raw material on which their activities are based. In some cases success can be measured directly by the result. For example, there can be little doubt that President Carter's decision in 1978 to suspend manufacture of the 'neutron bomb' was strongly influenced by the pressure of Western public opinion, originally generated by the massive campaign against this weapon then mounted by these organisations. But in general their activity must be seen as part of the continuous Soviet efforts to soften up the West, to divide peoples from their governments and one country from another, especially the United States from Europe, all with the purpose of undermining the West's morale and its will to resist the spread of Soviet influence. This is, in effect, a continuation of the Soviet policy established in the earliest period, when Lenin realised that the liberty prevailing in the Western democracies offered an exceptional opportunity for exploitation by Soviet propaganda and subversion. The Soviet Government's recent handling of the campaign against NATO's plans for deployment of Intermediate-Range Nuclear Forces (INF) has provided ample evidence of this.

The activities described in Part III are of a very different kind. Today, revived peace movements in the West owe their existence to the very liberties which the international front organisations have been set up to undermine. In the case of the United Kingdom many of the roots of the present peace movement can be seen in the period following the First World War. In other countries of Western Europe the indigenous peace movements are generally of more recent origin than in the United Kingdom. At any rate their roots are not so deeply grounded in the pre-war political scene. Their origins and motivations are directly related to their countries' historical experience and to individual national circumstances. The leaders of these movements and their supporters are the 'critics'.

Those who are opposed to the current aims and activities of the British peace movement frequently compare the situation today with the disastrous consequences of the widespread pacifist and anti-militarist influences on government policies in the 1930s. This lesson from history provides a warning which it would be perilous to disregard. But there is no strict parallel between the present and the pre-nuclear era, or between the nature and aims of the Soviet regime and those of Hitler's Germany. In terms of brutality there may often be little to choose between them, but the dangers and, in particular, the consequences of renewed conflict, are infinitely greater than in the 1930s. Many, perhaps most, of the critics in the United Kingdom and their counterparts in other countries of Western Europe are motivated by a sincere desire to find a basis for lasting peace and a genuine conviction that present Western policies are not conducive to that end. That they may be misguided over the alternative policies they advocate, often naive in their expectations and sometimes violent in the methods they use to convey their message is not the point. All these factors are inherent in the democratic environment which the critics, and those who are the object of their criticism, wish to preserve. What is more serious is that by their manner of operation they lay themselves open to penetration and exploitation by adversaries whose aims have been discussed above and are very different from their own.

In the United States the critics, at least those who are of real significance, are operating on a different plane from the various peace movements in Western Europe. Some of the advocates of the proposed nuclear arms' 'freeze' claim to find common cause with members of the European movements. But although there are several versions of the 'freeze' concept, some more simplistic and extreme than others, it represents not so much a radical reversal of existing policy as a seriously argued and comprehensively elaborated variation of policies which have been pursued by previous United States Administrations.

In contrast to the adversaries, there is no central direction of the activities of the critics. The basis of the shared policies and objectives of the Western peace movements is entirely pragmatic. The campaign for European Nuclear Disarmament (END), with its European Appeal, has succeeded in providing a common platform, a forum for exchanging and comparing views and experiences, and out of these has emerged a consensus of ideas about what is seen to be needed. But there is, and can be, no attempt by any central authority to impose policies on the supporters of END. The risk the critics run is of getting burned by operating in too close proximity to the fire of the adversaries – participation in events sponsored by front organisations and close collaboration with Communist or Communist-controlled groups – so that the distinction between their objectives and the objectives of those who owe their allegiance to Moscow is no longer readily perceived.

Part IV of the book contains a chapter on unofficial peace initiatives in Eastern Europe. This has been included partly to demonstrate the differences between the freedom in which peace movements in the West are able to operate and the severe restrictions and penalties to which any independent movements in the East are subject, and partly because of the role these movements play in the thinking of members of the END. The scale of their activities is miniscule by comparison with the rallies and demonstrations mounted in the West. They are little interested in the unilateralist aspects of the Western peace movements. While their chances of securing any modifications in current Soviet and Warsaw Pact policies are negligible, the fact that they have managed to survive at all is important.

The purpose of this book is to expose some of the facts and dispel some of the illusions about the aims and activities of both adversaries and critics. As the starting point for this task, Chapter 2 is devoted to a brief account of the origins and development of Western defence policy since the Second World War.

2 Western Defence

The Second World War ended in Europe when the armistice came into effect at midnight on 8 May 1945. Two months later the leaders of the three principal victorious powers, the United States, the Soviet Union and the United Kingdom, met at Potsdam near Berlin to decide, as they hoped, how the post-war world should be ordered. Nearly four years later, on 3 April 1949, the North Atlantic Treaty was signed in Washington, signalling the collective will of the West to resist the advance of communism. This swift change needs elaboration.

Stalin's immediate objectives in 1945 were never deeply concealed. He was determined to impose Soviet control over the countries of Eastern Europe and to keep Western influence out of the Balkans. Soviet ambitions for further expansion were less obvious until the war was over. The way in which Stalin pursued his objectives was calculated and successful. To understand why it was successful, it is necessary to recall two things. First, the priority which all the war-time allies shared was to defeat Nazi Germany. Second, despite their differing interpretation of Soviet policy, the United States and the United Kingdom were fully agreed on the need to secure Soviet cooperation in maintaining peace in the post-war world. The compromises which they felt compelled to make in order to achieve this were frequently the source of subsequent difficulties.

A foretaste of these emerged at the conference at Yalta, in the Crimea, three months before the armistice. Stalin arrived at Yalta with the knowledge that the Soviet army was already in control of most of Eastern Europe; Warsaw had fallen and the Russians were within 50 miles of Berlin. In the West, the American and British forces had not yet succeeded in crossing the Rhine. This military background was an important factor in the political discussions. Nevertheless, the Americans and British did secure a commitment from Stalin to promote free elections in the countries of Eastern Europe leading to the establishment of broadly-based democratic governments, although they were obliged to accept the incorporation into the Soviet Union of one-fifth of the area of pre-war Poland, which had already in practice taken place. Whatever reservations they had, Roosevelt and Churchill both stuck to their determination to try to make cooperation with the Soviet Union work. They were quickly disillusioned by two events: the imposition, by Soviet ultimatum, of a Communist Government on Rumania, and the imprisonment of 13 Polish democratic politicians on a visit to Moscow to discuss the establishment of a broadly-based Government for Poland.

When the Potsdam conference took place, Germany had been defeated. Russian troops had been the first to enter Berlin; the American and British forces, in accordance with arrangements agreed for the occupation, had stopped west of the River Elbe. The main purpose of the conference was to settle the principles for joint administration of Germany as a single political and economic unit. Stalin demanded exorbitant reparations from the Soviet zone, thus putting its economic viability in question; and he presented his colleagues with a further *fait-accompli* over Poland, into which he had already incorporated a large slice of pre-war Germany (about 18%) in compensation for territory the Poles had been forced to cede to Russia in the East.

Yalta did not produce a blueprint for the division of Europe between East and West. Nor did Potsdam provide the authority for a divided Germany. If the agreements reached at these two conferences had been adhered to by the Soviet Government, there might still have been a chance of creating a post-war Europe on the basis of cooperation rather than of conflict. But Soviet policy, backed by Soviet military presence, determined otherwise. One by one, between 1946 and 1948, in the countries of Eastern Europe, communist-controlled Governments were established and independent political parties were eliminated. The pattern varied according to local circumstances; elections were accompanied by terror and intimidation of non-communist candidates. The outcome, by the first half of 1948, was that the whole of Eastern Europe was under tight Soviet political as well as military control.

Western protests at these developments were ignored and attempts to make progress in the Council of Foreign Ministers (established at Potsdam to prepare the post-war settlement) on future plans for Germany were frustrated by the Russians. Yet the growing disillusionment and fears about Soviet conduct were, at least until the end of 1947, confined to a relatively small minority in Europe and America. To the generality of people on both sides of the Atlantic, the situation was still seen in simple terms: Germany was the defeated enemy, who must never again be allowed to become a threat to world peace; Russia had been the loyal ally, whose role in bringing about Germany's defeat had been crucial, as also was Soviet cooperation in maintaining the peace.

In the United States, the United Kingdom and Canada pressure was high for rapid demobilisation and the return home of men serving overseas. The need to restore industry to peacetime purposes and, in the case of the United Kingdom, to rebuild bomb-shattered cities were powerful factors. So the run-down in strength of the Western forces in Europe was rapid – from a total of 5 million at the end of the war to less than 900 000 a year later. The scale of the American withdrawal from Europe was particularly striking, from more than 3 million down to 400 000 in 1946 and to 200 000 by mid 1947. The Soviet Union followed a different course. The strength of the Soviet forces in 1946 was still 6 million; Soviet industry remained fully organised on a war-time basis; and there was no 'public pressure' for its return to peace-time purposes.[1]

THE ATLANTIC ALLIANCE

Nevertheless, 1947 saw the beginnings of American awakening to the dangers in Europe. In March, President Truman took a major initiative when he announced American support for Greece and Turkey. In June, the American Secretary of State, General Marshall, responding to the dire economic situation in Europe, launched the offer of economic aid to Europe known as the 'Marshall Plan'. Under French and British leadership, the countries of Western Europe responded immediately to this lifeline. The Russians withdrew unceremoniously from the Paris meeting called to discuss it, and the countries of Eastern Europe were forbidden by Moscow to take up the offer. The subsequent breakdown in December of the London meeting of the Council of Foreign Ministers, led to the initiative by Ernest Bevin, British Foreign Secretary, which resulted, 16 months later, in the North

Atlantic Treaty. Bevin saw the need to mobilise the 'moral and material force' of Western Europe in a union which would inspire confidence in the West and stem the advance of Soviet communism, and the importance of gaining American support without which such a union could not hope to survive.[2] France and the BENELUX countries responded enthusiastically; the United States, reluctant at first to break with tradition by accepting any permanent defence commitment in Europe, was cautious. However, American hesitations were finally overcome, first by the example of European 'self-help' given by the conclusion of the Brussels Treaty in March 1948, and second by the evidence of Soviet intentions provided by the Prague coup in March and the blockade of Berlin which began in June. In 1949, the North Atlantic Treaty had 12 founding members. Greece and Turkey joined in 1952, the Federal Republic of Germany in 1955 and Spain in 1982. Its purpose, in 1984 as in 1949, is to provide for collective action against threats to the territorial integrity or political independence of any of its members.

In 1949 the threats from the Soviet Union were seen as both political and military. More precisely, it seemed clear that the Soviet Union was ready to use the overhanging threat of its vast military strength in Europe to back its aim of extending Communist power and influence. This policy had succeeded most recently and most flagrantly in Czechoslovakia in 1948; with first British and then American help, it had been thwarted in Greece and Turkey; and the Atlantic Alliance came just in time to save Norway from the sort of pressure to which Finland had been forced to succumb. Since 1949 the Soviet Government, directly and through its agencies and proxies, has pursued an unremitting campaign of hostile propaganda against the Atlantic Alliance, its policies and its activities. At various times, as it has suited Soviet tactical purposes, the campaign has alternated between warnings and blandishments, between threats of dire consequences and offers of cooperation. The Peace Campaign, described in later chapters, has been in marked contrast to the facts of the almost wholly unrestrained Soviet military build-up. Throughout the 35 years of NATO's life, however, Soviet objectives with regard to the Alliance have remained constant. They are: first, to create divisions between the European members and the United States, with a view to undermining and ultimately destroying the American commitment to Europe; second, to disrupt the cohesion of the European members in support of Alliance policies, with a view to reducing the strength of resistance to the Soviet threat; and third, to exploit fears and doubts about Alliance policies among Western populations, with the object of weakening the will of Alliance Governments to fulfil those policies. The main focus of the Soviet campaign during the past four years has been the NATO Double-Track decision of 12 December 1979 on Intermediate Nuclear Force (INF) Modernisation and Arms Control.* In the massive campaign they have waged against this decision, the Russians may have hoped not only to discredit and overturn it, but also, by doing so, to make real progress towards all three of their objectives with regard to the Alliance. By the end of 1983 they had failed in both endeavours. Deployment of the new missiles had begun in the United Kingdom and Germany, despite the vociferous opposition of the peace movements; and the Alliance had reaffirmed its support for both tracks of the decision and its determination to maintain the dialogue with the Russians, despite their abrupt withdrawal from the START and INF arms control talks in Geneva. The reasons for the Double-Track decision and the Soviet attacks on it must be seen against the background of NATO's strategy and the current state of the East–West military balance.

NATO's STRATEGY

From the start, NATO's strategy has been based on deterrence. The proposition is a simple and obvious one: it is to impress on any potential agressor that, whatever he might hope to gain from aggression, the price he would have to pay, in terms of loss and damage to himself, would be much too high to make the aggression worthwhile. Provided he is convinced of this, he will be deterred from initiating aggression. The same logic applies to the

---

* The description of these forces in use at the time of the Double-Track decision was Long-Range Theatre Nuclear Forces (LRTNF). It was changed in 1981 to Intermediate range Nuclear Forces (INF), as being a more accurate description both of NATO's systems and of the corresponding Soviet systems. These are systems whose range is shorter than that of intercontinental systems, for example. Intercontinental Ballistic Missiles (ICBM's), which are included in the former SALT (Strategic Arms Limitation Talks) and current START (Strategic Arms Reduction Talks) and longer than that of Battlefield or Short-range Nuclear weapons (formerly described as Tactical Nuclear Weapons) whose purpose is to affect the conduct of the tactical battle. INF is normally used in this book.

more probable situation of blackmail or intimidation by the threat of aggression. If the threat is not likely to be carried out, it loses its force. Since it is central to the Alliance's philosophy, and has been publicly stated on many occasions, that NATO's weapons will never be used except in response to attack, this strategy provides a firm basis for the prevention of war. Despite the efforts of its detractors, who exist among both adversaries and critics, no rational case has been made against its validity, which is supported by the experience of the past 35 years. But the credibility of deterrence depends on three conditions: first, the Alliance must have the capability to respond effectively in the event of aggression; second, the Alliance must have the will to use this capability, should deterrence fail; and third, the Alliance must be perceived by the Soviet Government to have both the capability and the will, if necessary, to use it.

From its inception, the Alliance had to devise a strategic doctrine under the shadow of vast Soviet superiority in conventional forces, very little room for manoeuvre in depth and the prospect of a developing Soviet nuclear capability following the first Soviet atomic test of August 1949. It had barely started on this task when the Communist invasion of South Korea took place in June, 1950. This was taken by the Alliance as an indication of what might happen in Europe. There were only 200 000 poorly-armed Allied occupation forces in Western Germany, and in all no more than 14 Allied divisions and 1000 aircraft in Western Europe, compared with between 175 and 200 Soviet divisions and 20 000 aircraft. The Americans sent over 4 more divisions, making a total of 6.[3] These Allied forces could not hope to do more than fight a delaying action and fall back to defensive positions behind the Rhine until a counter-offensive could be launched with the support of nuclear weapons of the United States Strategic Air Command. As this was patently unsatisfactory as a basis for either deterrence or defence, a study was put in hand of the conventional forces needed to deter, and resist, aggression as far to the East as possible. The original military estimate of 96 divisions and 9000 aircraft was clearly unattainable. A reduced level of 50 divisions and 4000 aircraft was approved in 1952 (the Lisbon Force Goals). In military terms this was not enough. In the words of one well-qualified observer, 'the Alliance turned consciously to nuclear weapons as a substitute for the financial and manpower sacrifices which would have been necessary to mount an adequate conventional defense'.[4] By 1954 tactical (battlefield) nuclear weapons were already being deployed in Europe. Yet even the Lisbon Force Goals were proving too high; they were further reduced to 26 divisions, which would include the 12 to be contributed by Germany, and 1400 aircraft. This is approximately the level of the ready forces in place on the Central Front in 1984. The role of tactical nuclear weapons and of the Intermediate Range Ballistic Missiles (IRBM) which were to be deployed in Europe was formally defined in the new strategic concept of 'Massive Retaliation' which the Alliance adopted in 1957 (contained in NATO document MC 14–2). This was based on the firm intention that, should deterrence fail, nuclear weapons would be used at an early stage. The conventional forces would not, because of their limited size, be expected to defeat a determined attack but rather to act as a 'trip-wire' to allow time for nuclear retaliation to be implemented. In a later refinement, they would 'force a pause' which would give the Soviet leaders time to reflect whether to continue the attack and incur the risk of nuclear strikes against their forces and their cities. The Alliance endorsed the policy of 'Forward Defence', involving a commitment to resist any Soviet attack at the eastern frontier of West Germany, which remains an essential element in NATO's current strategic concept.

'Massive Retaliation' was already coming under criticism by the time it was formally approved by the Alliance. Few people doubted the need for a clearly distinguishable 'fire break' between conventional and nuclear weapons. But there were two problems. One was that, if battlefield weapons ever had to be used, especially when the Russians had them too, their use would be likely to cause devastation in West Germany and possibly other NATO countries. This made a doctrine involving the automatic early use of such weapons by NATO highly unattractive to its European members. The other objection was that a massive nuclear strike by IRBM's against targets in the Soviet Union was seen as an inappropriate response to what might be a relatively small-scale conventional attack with limited objectives, and thus too inflexible. Moreover both superpowers were developing delivery systems of intercontinental range. By the early 1960s this raised the prospect that for the first time American territory would be vulnerable to Soviet nuclear attack; for this reason the Americans were concerned at being dependent on a strategic doctrine which relied exclusively or almost exclusively on the use of nuclear weapons in the event of aggression. Moreover, it was recognised that the time would come when the capability for 'Assured Destruction', the ability in all circumstances to retaliate with a massive nuclear strike even after being attacked by nuclear weapons, which was the ultimate deterrent against Soviet aggression, would also be achieved by the Russians. This aroused European fears that the advent of strategic parity between the two superpowers would result in the decoupling of the American strategic deterrent from Europe. One outcome was the emergence of the theory of 'Mutual Assured Destruction', developed by the American Secretary of Defence, Robert McNamara, which, in effect, postulated a choice, at the strategic level, between national suicide and nuclear stand-off.

At this level a full-scale strategic nuclear exchange was unthinkable, and at the same time incredible as a deterrent to anything but a massive Soviet nuclear attack. Subsequent developments in American targetting policy were aimed at providing greater flexibility in the role of the strategic forces in order to improve their credibility, by strengthening the belief on the part of the potential aggressor that the United States would actually do what it threatened to do. Thus the 'selective options' introduced in 1980, which in effect codified plans which had long existed for strikes against a variety of military targets as more credible alternatives to Soviet cities and industry, were designed to strengthen deterrence against all kinds of Soviet attack and were not in any sense a move towards a nuclear war-fighting policy. But none of these developments alters the fact that it is still the mutual threat of destruction which ultimately assures the delicate balance of deterrence between the two superpowers.[5]

FLEXIBLE RESPONSE

So far as NATO was concerned, these problems led to a thorough review by the Kennedy Administration of the doctrine of 'Massive Retaliation' in the early 1960s. The Cuban crisis had underlined the urgency of this. The outcome was an American proposal to replace it by the concept of 'Flexible Response' involving much greater reliance on conventional forces to defeat a conventional attack. The Americans argued that this was a feasible goal and that the Soviet conventional strength had been overestimated. The Europeans were not convinced. McNamara has recalled that this proposal met with strong opposition from European members of the Alliance on the grounds that the United States was seeking to 'decouple' itself from the defence of Europe, that the primary factor deterring Soviet aggression was the danger of rapid escalation to the strategic level from the early use of tactical nuclear weapons under the 'Massive Retaliation' concept, and that the Alliance would not be willing to support the increased conventional forces which would be required.[6] The fact was that the Europeans did not wish to move towards reliance on a purely conventional defence, with the possibility of a long-drawn out conventional war on European soil, and believed that the Russians would only be deterred from fighting such a war by the threat of the early use of nuclear weapons. The debate continued for five years before a compromise was reached in December 1967 (contained in NATO document MC14–3).

The new concept involved:

(i) intention to meet aggression at any level with whatever forces were needed to defeat it and restore deterrence;
(ii) the aim of placing on the aggressor the onus for deciding whether to escalate the conflict, ie to use nuclear weapons, or abandon his attack;
(iii) reserving full political control over all decisions concerning the use of nuclear weapons;
(iv) ensuring that there was no gap in the continuum of deterrence between conventional and theatre nuclear forces and between theatre nuclear forces and United States strategic nuclear forces (the 'triad')*; and
(vi) providing forces in all three legs of the 'triad' which would be adequate for these purposes.

The concept did not imply automatic first use of nuclear weapons, as is sometimes alleged, although under (i) the option of first use was envisaged as a last resort. While Soviet forces did not have to be matched on a one-for-one basis, it presupposed a considerable strengthening of NATO's conventional forces. For all the problems associated with this concept it did represent the most thorough attempt so far made to take account

---

* Not to be confused with the American use of the term triad to mean the land, sea and air components of their strategic nuclear forces.

of the rapid advances of technology on both sides and to provide criteria for planning the best mix of nuclear and conventional forces for credible deterrence. To a greater extent than any of the previous attempts, it provided a coherent approach to the conduct of defence in a situation of inherent uncertainty. The measure of its success is that, 16 years later, 'Flexible Response' still remains the basis for NATO's defence planning. The trouble is that the conventional force requirements, which have increased with the Soviet build-up, have not been fully met, with the result that in the event of aggression, NATO would have to face an early decision whether to use nuclear weapons. Moreover, the Alliance's plans to provide adequate theatre nuclear forces to support the concept have aroused public opposition in the West.

THE MILITARY BALANCE

These plans must be seen against the background of developments in the East–West military balance in Europe. Writing in June 1981, the Supreme Allied Commander Europe, General Bernard Rogers, drew attention to 'the unabated growth of Soviet military power over the past 15 years'.[7] Whereas in the 1960s the West could rely on their advantage in technology and nuclear weapons to compensate for Soviet numerical superiority in conventional forces, the Russians had recently succeeded in eliminating much of their qualitative disadvantage while maintaining their quantitative lead. After quoting examples both of the Warsaw Pact's quantitative superiority and of the impressive range of new missiles, tanks, aircraft and other equipment deployed by the Russians during the previous decade, General Rogers concluded:

> The relentless growth and modernisation of Soviet military power has resulted in an increasingly adverse force balance between the Warsaw Pact and NATO. In my opinion, NATO has now been surpassed – or soon will be – in all categories of forces necessary to implement its strategy, ie strategic nuclear, theatre nuclear and conventional.

SACEUR's assessment of the balance was endorsed in an authoritative study approved by all NATO Governments and published in May 1982.⁸ This provided a comparison of forces on each side in Europe which showed, in the principal categories, Warsaw Pact superiority of 173 divisions to 84; 42 500 main battle tanks to 13 000; 31 500 guns and mortars to 10 750; and 7240 combat aircraft to 2975. In INF the NATO comparison showed a balance in favour of the Soviet Union and its allies of 3:1 in aircraft and of 1200:0 in missile warheads deployed. Only in short-range (battlefield) nuclear forces did NATO still have a slight edge, by 1100 to 950 systems deployed. Three examples illustrate the scale of the Soviet military build-up: Soviet production of main battle tanks in the 5 years from 1978 to 1982 averaged 2800 a year (the figure for 1981 was 2000 compared with production by the whole of NATO of 760);⁹ Soviet strategic nuclear missiles deployed have increased from 2203 in 1973 to 2378 in 1983, compared with a decline in American deployments from 1710 to 1613 during the same period (the figure for 1983 with British and French strategic missiles included is 1775);¹⁰ following the introduction of the SS-20 in 1977, Soviet deployment of INF missile warheads doubled in the 4 years to 1981 (and has continued to increase since then despite the Geneva negotiations), while NATO had no comparable systems deployed.¹¹ None of these figures are, in themselves, conclusive; as with any statistics it is possible to produce figures which still show areas of NATO advantage and there are some compensating factors not reflected by numbers. But they are indicative of the trend to which General Rogers drew attention and led him, in a lecture in September 1982, to re-emphasise his view that 'today's imbalances, including present and imminent [Warsaw] Pact qualitative advances in equipment, have grown so serious and the trends so adverse, that we can no longer rationalise away the ever-widening gap'. Underlining his assessment of the military threat which the Soviet build-up represents, he continued:

> It is preposterous in my judgement to dismiss the threat posed by Pact capabilities by claiming that its growth of military power is directed solely at defence, reflecting no more than traditional Soviet insecurity. The size, type and location of Pact forces go far beyond the requirements for defence. The offensive nature of numerous Pact manoeuvres demonstrate both the capability and readiness for aggression.¹²

This is the spectre of Soviet military might facing NATO in Europe. The willingness of the Soviet leaders to make direct use of their military power to serve political ends has been demonstrated in action taken against their Eastern European allies on at least three occasions in the past 30 years and more recently in the invasion of Afghanistan in 1979. There have been numerous examples of Soviet and Soviet-inspired intervention in other parts of the world. On this experience, no Western Government can afford to calculate on any other basis than that, given the opportunity, the Soviet Union would not hesitate to use this same power, for blackmail if not for direct military action, against Western interests if these were perceived as conflicting with its own political aims. This is why NATO has constantly to ensure that the opportunity does not arise.

STRENGTHENING NATO's DETERRENCE

The problem is not so much that NATO's capability has declined in absolute terms but that Soviet military capability has increased at a much faster pace. Measures agreed by the Alliance in 1978, for example, the Long Term Defence Programme and acceptance of the target of 3% real annual increases in defence spending, have resulted in a genuine strengthening of NATO's forces. But, first, they have not proved enough to maintain the relative balance and, second, for a variety of reasons, many of the commitments have not been met. This applies particularly to the conventional leg of the triad, the strengthening of which was the starting point of the Flexible Response strategy. As a result NATO's present posture has been described as a 'delayed tripwire' and SACEUR has remarked that NATO has 'mortgaged our defence to the nuclear response'. In other words NATO cannot be sure of fulfilling the purpose of the Flexible Response strategy by 'meeting aggression at any level with whatever forces are needed to defeat it' except by threatening the very early use of nuclear weapons with the risk of escalation that that would entail.

To meet this problem, two separate, but not necessarily incompatible, proposals have emerged. One is that NATO should formally adopt a policy of 'No first use' of nuclear weapons, matching the declaration made by the Soviet Government in 1982. This policy is favoured by some distinguished and highly qualified authorities on both sides of the Atlantic. Although expressed in various ways, the main ground for it is that since no Government would contemplate the act of suicide involved in engaging in a strategic nuclear exchange, no rational Government would ever initiate a process, the escalatory consequences of which it could have no certainty of controlling. This policy is not acceptable to the Alliance or advocated by any of its members. This is not so much because the premise is disputed, as because it is precisely this premise which is at the heart of NATO's deterrent strategy. This is why the Alliance Heads of Government, at their Summit meeting in June 1982, firmly restated that NATO policy is based on no first use of *any* weapons, conventional or nuclear. The second course is to strengthen the Alliance's conventional forces so as to make it possible to meet the full requirements of Flexible Response. This implies giving NATO the capability to resist and defeat conventional attack by conventional response, thus clearly placing on the aggressor the onus for deciding whether to escalate. No one believes that the Soviet Government would take such a decision, so long as they are deterred from doing so by the prospect of nuclear retaliation. If this posture is achieved, the effective role of NATO's nuclear weapons should be to deter Soviet use of nuclear weapons; in practice a position of 'No First Use' or at least 'No Early Use' will apply. When this point is reached the prospects for genuine mutual reductions in nuclear weapons should be greatly improved.

This second course has increasingly gained ground both within the Alliance and widely among expert opinion. It is supported by many of those who have favoured a 'No first use' declaration. The possibility of realising it may be said to depend on four conditions: fulfilment by all NATO Governments of their existing force goals; improvement of the effectiveness of NATO's conventional forces by means of new and emerging technologies; adaptation of NATO's plans, making use of these technologies, to take full advantage of vulnerable points in the Warsaw Pact's concept of operations; and willingness of Governments to make available the financial and other resources needed. At their meeting in June 1982, the Heads of Government put in hand an Alliance study of American proposals on the use of emerging technologies; so far no official conclusions have been made public. But General Rogers has explained how, given the improved means of identifying targets, better communications and more accurate conventional weapons which would result from the application of new technologies, it should be possible to stop an initial attack at or near the Eastern frontier of the Federal Republic while at the same time executing deep strikes against Warsaw Pact follow-on forces so as to prevent them from reinforcing those in the front line. Thus, if the Alliance is prepared to fulfil the four conditions mentioned above, the result, in his view, will be that 'we can reduce the possibility of a Pact attack by establishing the credible prospect that our conventional defence will succeed'.[13] A broadly similar conclusion was reached in a major study completed in 1983 by a group of prominent individuals from the United States, United Kingdom, Germany and Norway, which included recently retired senior NATO commanders, former leading officials and academic specialists in strategic studies.[14] As regards costs, their estimate was that the improvements recommended could be met by expenditure of approximately an extra 1% on top of the target of 3% real annual increase agreed in 1978, but that this level of expenditure would need to be sustained beyond the expiry of the current 3% commitment in 1986. There is thus an emerging consensus on what needs to be done to 'raise the nuclear threshold'. The Alliance's collective approach has so far been cautious, as regards both military benefits and financial implications.

Much greater public anxiety, has been aroused by the measures taken by the Alliance to ensure the credibility of the Long Range Theatre Nuclear Force (now INF) leg of the 'triad'. These were announced in the NATO Double-Track decision of 12 December 1979 which provided, first, for the deployment in Europe of 572 American ground-launched missiles and, second, for the offer by the United States to negotiate with the Soviet Union agreed mutual limitations on long-range theatre nuclear forces. The sustained Soviet onslaught on this decision has already been referred to above; much of the rest of this book will be concerned with the opposition to it in the West as well as in the East. It is therefore important to understand why, within the context of NATO's strategy as already explained, the decision was necessary.

The Soviet Union began to deploy the SS-20 missile system in 1977. This system has a range (5000 km) which enables it to reach targets anywhere in Western Europe even when based to the East of the Ural mountains. Being below the intercontinental missile range of 5500 km (i.e. it cannot reach the United States), it is not subject to the limitations in the SALT agreement. Not only has it a longer range but it is also more accurate (by a factor of 3) than the SS-5 for which it was assumed to be intended as a replacement; it carries three independently targettable warheads (known as MIRVs), compared with the SS-5's one; and it is mobile. Its introduction was viewed by European Governments as representing a major increase in the threat to their countries compared with the 100 or so SS-5s and 600 shorter range SS-4s which had been operational since the early 1960s. By December 1979, 120 SS-20s had been deployed. Deployment continued at the rate of more than one SS-20 a week until, by end of November 1983, 378 had been deployed, of which 252 (armed with 756 MIRVs) were targetted against Western Europe, the remaining 126 being in Soviet Asia. Andropov said in October that all the SS-5s had been phased out and that only 200 SS-4s remained. Throughout this period there were no United States land-based missiles deployed in Europe capable of reaching the Soviet Union, the last IRBMs having been withdrawn in 1963. Both sides have nuclear strike aircraft in the INF category. Various figures for these have been quoted by the Russians with the object of showing that parity exists – in 1983 just as they claimed it did in 1979 – over the whole category of INF systems. The results of any calculation vary according to what is included and what is left out. The Russians achieve 'parity' by omitting from the Warsaw Pact side of the balance categories which they include on the NATO side. The balance of land-based INF aircraft at the end of 1981, including comparable types on each side, was 2500 for the Warsaw Pact against 800 for NATO.[15] Over and above this Warsaw Pact figure, there were 135 Backfire bombers. But of the NATO aircraft only about a quarter were capable of carrying out strikes against the Soviet Union itself. Some of these have since been phased out (the United Kingdom Vulcans and Buccaneers) and, on military grounds, there was by 1979 a pressing need to plan for the most suitable system to succeed the remainder (principally American F111s in the United Kingdom).

These figures show that by the end of the 1970s, NATO was faced with a serious imbalance at the INF (Theatre Nuclear Force) leg of the triad. Moreover, as events were to prove, this imbalance was increasing. The main concern was with the SS-20. The European members of the Alliance feared that the Russians might believe they could threaten all of Western Europe from bases in the Soviet Union, without incurring the risk of retaliatory strikes against their own territory. With no comparable United States INF missiles in Europe, they might calculate that the Americans would have no credible means of retaliation since they would not, in response to strikes against Western Europe, threaten to use their strategic nuclear forces for fear of retaliation against United States territory. In these circumstances the Russians would be operating from a 'sanctuary' and would have succeeded in 'decoupling' Western Europe from the American strategic deterrent. Thus the Europeans – especially the Germans (whose then Chancellor, Helmut Schmidt, was the first to draw attention to this problem) – would be vulnerable to Soviet pressures. The Alliance therefore recognised an urgent need to 'ensure that there was no gap in the continuum of deterrence'. The 1979 decision gave equal weight to plans for deployment of new missiles in order to fill this emerging gap and to proposals for arms control negotiations which, by 'constraining the Soviet build-up', would 'modify the scale of NATO's INF requirements'. The decision involved deployment of 108 Pershing II missiles in Germany and 464 Ground Launched Cruise Missiles (GLCM) in the United Kingdom (160), Italy (112), Germany (96), Belgium and the Netherlands (48 each), spread over a period of five years starting in December 1983. (In the case of the Netherlands, acceptance of basing is still subject to confirmation – see page 166.) Both missiles can reach targets in the Soviet Union, but the range of the GLCM is only half that of the SS-20, while that of the Pershing II (1800 km) is insufficient to reach Moscow from West Germany. To reach its targets the Pershing II would take 14 minutes, approximately the same time as the SS-20 would take to reach London, Paris, Bonn etc. The cruise missile would take 3 hours. Both missiles carry a single warhead; their deployment will not increase the number of NATO nuclear weapons in Europe since the existing stockpiles will be reduced on a one-for-one basis as the new missiles are deployed. Moreover NATO also announced in December 1979 the unilateral withdrawal of an additional 1000 US nuclear warheads from Europe and, in October 1983, of a further 1400. Since the warheads may each have an explosive yield of anything up to tens of kilotons, these withdrawals represent a significant unilateral reduction in NATO's nuclear weapons, to which the Soviet Union has made no response.

To some, the complexity of this rationale may seem esoteric or even arcane. But its actuality demonstrates the extent to which nuclear weapons have introduced into international relations a new dimension of political calculation. However abhorrent this dimension may be there is no possibility of ignoring it. This is why the political case for deploying Pershing II missiles and Ground Launched Cruise Missiles in Europe is every bit as compelling as the military case, and many would argue that it is more so. The decision did not mean, as some people have claimed to believe, that the United States planned to confine nuclear war to Europe; on the contrary, it was taken, as explained above, with the deliberate intention of reassuring the Europeans and making clear to the Russians that the United States would be directly involved in the response to any Soviet nuclear threat against Western Europe. This is one reason – though it is not the only one – why the Soviet proposal for an arms control agreement based on a balance between a reduced number of SS-20s and the total of French and British strategic missiles is unacceptable, since it would involve zero American deployments while some 480 SS-20 warheads continued to threaten Western Europe. (The background of the United Kingdom nuclear deterrent is summarised in Annex 1.) The NATO aim in the bilateral United States-Soviet negotiations, which started in November 1981, is still to achieve the original position announced by President Reagan of zero deployment of INF missiles applying equally to both sides. But NATO is prepared to accept an interim agreement based on partial implementation of the 1979 decision provided Soviet INF systems are reduced to an equal level.

The very violence of the Soviet reaction to the NATO decision in itself went far towards substantiating NATO's rationale. The whole thrust of Soviet policy on this issue since 1979 has been aimed at securing the cancellation of the plans for deployment of the American missiles in Europe and, by doing so, to weaken NATO's collective will to carry out decisions taken in the interests of its security. From the start of the arms control negotiations in November 1981 until they withdrew in November 1983, the Russians made no advance from their initial position of refusing to accept any NATO deployments, although they continued, throughout the negotiations, to deploy SS-20s at the rate of at least one missile, with three warheads, a week. Since November, not only have the SS-20s been further increased but the Russians have also begun to deploy in East Germany and Czechoslovakia a new INF system, the SS-22, which with a range of 900 kilometres, is capable of reaching London and many parts of England. The Soviet propaganda campaign against the NATO decision has continued unabated since the decision was taken in 1979, with scant regard for accuracy or attempt at rational argument. It is this issue above all others which has exercised the minds and engaged the activities of both adversaries and critics in recent years. With the start of deployments of cruise missiles in the United Kingdom and Italy and of Pershing IIs in Germany it was the hope, unanimously affirmed by NATO Ministers at their meeting in Brussels in December 1983, that the Russians would in 1984 get down to serious negotiation. This hope was, however, frustrated by the totally negative attitude adopted by the Soviet government.

Part II
Adversaries: International Front Organisations and Soviet Peace Campaigns

3 The Origin of the International Front Organisations, 1919–39

The Communist front organisations owe their origin to Lenin. In January 1919 he invited left-wing groups in England, Ireland, France and the United States to attend the founding Congress of a new Third (Communist) International, the Comintern. This took place in Moscow in March, five years after Lenin had originally decided to launch it.[1] The appeal made at this First Comintern Congress to workers everywhere to rally to the support of the new Soviet régime in Russia was a successful propaganda operation which helped to stimulate industrial unrest in a disorganised Europe still suffering from the consequences of the First World War. That national Communist parties were expected to conform to Moscow's instructions emerged from Lenin's 'Left-wing Communism, An Infantile Disorder', published in April 1920, which gave details about the tactics to be followed by the new-born parties in their own countries. Lenin's main theme was condemnation of the kind of ultra-revolutionary attitude which so often failed to exploit the opportunities offered by genuinely democratic institutions: Communist parties were to abandon their sectarian exclusiveness and instead pursue power by working through and within such democratic organisations as trade unions, which were controlled by their opponents. British Communists, for example, should 'if necessary, use every trick, cunning, illegal means, concealment of the truth or prevarication', in order to establish themselves inside the trade unions and should learn to support the Labour Party, by their votes, 'as the rope supports the hanged man'. There were similar injunctions to other foreign Communists. Lenin's motives in condemning 'Leftism' were readily understandable, given the spread of that 'infantile disorder' within the Communist Party of the Soviet

Union (CPSU); consequently it was important for him to discredit the 'leftists' in those foreign Communist parties from which the Soviet Party might in future seek support. Bourgeois society had to be undermined, and this called for the emergence of a breed of proletarian politicians who could beat the democrats at their own game.

'Every sacrifice must be made', Lenin wrote, 'the greatest obstacles must be overcome, in order to carry on agitation and propaganda systematically, stubbornly, insistently and patiently, precisely in all those institutions, societies and associations to which proletarian or semi-proletarian masses belong, however ultra-reactionary they may be . . .'.[2] He added that 'inexperienced revolutionaries often think that legal methods of struggle are opportunist, because in this field the bourgeoisie, especially in peaceful, non-revolutionary times, deceived and fooled the workers, and they think that illegal methods of struggle are revolutionary. But this is not true. . . . Revolutionaries who are unable to combine illegal forms of struggle with every form of legal struggle are very bad revolutionaries'. Moreover, 'To conquer an opponent who is stronger than you is only to be achieved . . . by the most meticulous, careful, thoughtful and skilful exploitation of every "crack", even the smallest one between our enemies . . . and also every opportunity, even the slightest, of winning over a mass ally, even if this ally is temporary, unreliable, insubstantial or conditional . . .'. Lenin envisaged this strategy as applicable not only to trade union and other democratic working class groups: influential middle class groups should also be formed or penetrated, and turned to Moscow's advantage.

At the Second Comintern Congress in July and August 1920, Zinoviev, who had become President of its Executive Committee on its foundation, attempted to transform it from a loose federation into a 'single world communist party' of which the national parties would be merely constituent sections. The Congress also adopted resolutions on policy towards colonial and semi-colonial territories, to which Lenin attached great importance, regarding them as the weakest point in the imperialists' armour. In accordance with this policy, Communists should aim to bring about 'a close alliance of all national and colonial liberation movements with Soviet Russia', and should support 'national revolutionary movements' (the 'national liberation movements' of modern Communist jargon).

By 1921, however, the prospect of further revolutions was receding and attempts to foment them in Poland, Hungary, in the Baltic States and in Germany had failed. Lenin saw that the immediate need of the fledgling Soviet state was for normal trade relations with and, possibly, financial backing from the capitalist powers. Consequently, at the Third Comintern Congress in June and July 1921, Lenin sounded the retreat from world revolution. But he still envisaged that ostensibly democratic youth organisations, cooperatives and trade unions, once captured by Communists, would serve as 'transmission belts' for the Soviet cause. He recognised that, for Communism to advance in the West, there was a need for organisations of this kind, which provided protective cover for the enlistment of a wide range of sympathisers, to back up openly Communist parties. In a memorandum probably dictated at this time to Chicherin, the Soviet Commissar for Foreign Affairs, Lenin expressed his belief that in general 'the so-called cultured strata' of Western Europe and America 'were incapable of understanding either the present position of things or the real state of relative power'. The Bolsheviks must therefore be prepared to exploit the gullibility and idealism of the 'deaf mutes in the West', who, he believed, would 'work hard in order to prepare their own suicide'.[3]

Thus Lenin laid down the guiding principles for what were to become the first Communist front organisations. However, these original Leninist ideas were soon refined in important ways. As the concept developed, Moscow considered that front organisations should, as a matter of tactics, be separated administratively from the workings of the national Communist parties. While the primary aim of Communist parties was to achieve and then retain political power, the role of front organisations was one of disguised manipulation and agitation in support of the Party's eventual goals. While national Communist parties could, of course, help the broader-based bodies locally, the connexion between them was better hidden. Given this division of responsibility, the work of the front organisations was envisaged primarily as a long-term operation designed to weaken non-Communist societies generally. But these organisations should also play an important role in defence of the Soviet Union. Lenin laid down that both legal and illegal forms of struggle were to be exploited. It was in line with these general ideas that Otto Kuusinen, the Finnish Communist leader, during the meeting of the Executive

Committee of the Comintern in March 1926, suggested the creation of 'a whole solar system of organisations and smaller committees around the Communist Party ... smaller organisations working actually under the influence of the Party, although not under its mechanical control'.[4]

Although the term 'front organisation' is an accurate description of Communist practice, it is not itself Marxist–Leninist jargon. The nearest that Lenin himself came to using some such phrase was when describing the relationship of trade unions to the masses under socialism as 'transmission belts'; the nearest that modern Communists come to using such a term is when they use the phrase 'sympathising mass organisation'. In the 1930s, Willi Münzenberg, the German Communist, referred to such organisations as 'Innocents' Clubs'. Thus, although very well understood by all concerned, 'Communist front organisation' is not a term which Communists themselves employ.

The fact is that the Leninist stratagem of the 'united front' – which is Marxist–Leninist terminology – implies the creation of 'front organisations'. It was Lenin himself who decreed that Communists, while preserving their own identity, should establish contact with the masses either by temporary collaboration with social democratic or trade union leaders (the 'united front from above') or by appealing over their heads to the rank-and-file (the 'united front from below'). Membership of a front organisation did not, and does not today, necessarily imply commitment to Communism; from the start the intention has been to attract and exploit support of non-communists for communist purposes. This policy led to the Communists' 'united front' tactics of the 1920s and, indeed, of the present day. In the 1930s and 1940s it also led to the more broadly-based 'Popular Front against fascism' of the inter-war period, by no means confined to those on the left, and to the later 'national front' with all parties, not excluding conservatives or monarchists. In pursuit of such a 'national front' British Communists actually urged their supporters in 1945 to work for a 'Government of National Unity', representing *all* British parliamentary parties, to take office after the General Election of that year.

As early as the 1920s there were in being Communist front organisations created to buttress the general strategy of the 'united front'. A leading British instance was, and still is, the Labour Research Department (LRD). This had originally been founded in 1912 by Sidney and Beatrice Webb as a serious research organisation to support the Fabian Society. By the end of the First World War, the conversion of its able young secretary, Robin Page Arnot, to Communism had led to Communist domination of the organisation as a whole. What is interesting is not merely that LRD still exists and is still able, despite its Communist background, to pass itself off in the eyes of the media as 'an independent body' concerned with trade union affairs, but that as long ago as 1925 the Communist Party regarded it as its creature. In April of that year a British representative, Tom Bell, reported to the Comintern, in a classic definition of what is meant by the term 'Communist front organisation', that

> ... in Great Britain, we already have a kind of information department – the Labour Research Department. This Department is not a Party concern but it is under the control of the Party.[5]

By the 1930s there were already so many bodies of this kind that the Labour party introduced its proscribed list of organisations with aims incompatible with its own. At the height of the Cold War in the 1950s, this list included all the major international front organisations (such as the World Peace Council) and all the main British front organisations (such as the British Soviet Friendship Society and the British Peace Committee). The Labour Party decided to abolish its proscribed list in 1972. Most of the organisations formerly listed, especially those active internationally, remain active.

THE FELLOW TRAVELLERS

The Anglo-Saxon 'fellow-traveller', the French 'compagnon de route', the German 'Sympathisierender auf den Weg' of the 1920s and 1930s had little in common with the native Russian 'poputchik', criticised by Trotsky in 1923 for his inadequate understanding of the Revolution. The non-Russian fellow-travellers were in fact to make a most significant contribution to promoting the image of Soviet Russia between the two world wars, particularly after Hitler came to power in 1933 and during the subsequent Popular Front era. They included some of the most prominent writers, artists and scientists in Europe and America. The consequence was to give intellectual respectability to the causes which they championed. Both the fellow-travellers and the 'political pilgrims'[6] to the Soviet Union showed a critical stance towards Western values, especially after the depression had caused widespread unemployment and after the rise of Nazism. Sympathy with 'socialism' seemed a logical consequence of their estrangement from the contemporary scene. The Nazi menace, in particular, encouraged the drift towards communism and the Soviet Union: as the fellow travellers argued, nothing else could match the monstrosity of Hitler, Mussolini and Franco in view of the supine attitudes towards them of most Western Governments. By contrast, the Soviet Union projected the image of fascism's most determined opponent. Hence the stream of impressive literary names who associated themselves with the Soviet call for action against fascism, including Malraux, Gide, Aragon, Hemingway, Dreiser, Shaw, Auden, Spender and Silone.

In their carefully stage-managed visits to the Soviet Union, the political pilgrims found what they wanted to find: the irremediable defects of capitalism highlighted against the merely ephemeral problems of the Soviet Union. Western political freedom was seen as only the freedom to witness the contrast between affluence and poverty. To Sidney and Beatrice Webb, the OGPU (the Soviet security police, now known as the KGB) had not only performed a constructive feat of social engineering by inducing the convicts of labour camps to enter into 'socialist competition' but had also achieved triumphs of human regeneration. The Webbs also detected a greater sense of purpose, reflecting higher values, in the Soviet leadership: Stalin, no dictator, did not even have such extensive power as Congress had conferred on President Roosevelt. The American critic Edmund Wilson similarly considered the Soviet Union to be a purposeful society devoted to constructive sacrifice. The British academic, Harold Laski, found prisoners welcoming the chance to be remade into model citizens. Dr Hewlett Johnson, then Dean of Canterbury, considered Russia the most moral country he had known. Bernard Shaw took off his hat to Stalin for delivering the goods. D. N. Pritt used his legal expertise to claim that punishment in the Soviet Union was 'social correction'; André Malraux declared that 'just as the Inquisition did not affect the fundamental dignity of Christianity, so the Moscow trials have not affected the fundamental dignity of communism'. None of them realised, in the words of Vladimir Nabokov, that had they 'been Russians . . . they would have been destroyed . . . as naturally as rabbits are by ferrets and farmers'.[7]

If these and many other distinguished names were available to support the front organisations from the twenties, it was not until the thirties that their maximum impact was felt. The first international front organisation got off to an uncertain start. When *Clarté* was founded in Paris in 1919, with branches abroad, its original appeal was to intellectuals disillusioned by the aftermath of the First World War.[8] It acquired notoriety when Henri Barbusse, author of *Le Feu*, lent his name to it. Its first Directing Committee soon included Georges Duhamel, Anatole France, André Gide, Thomas Hardy, Upton Sinclair, H. G. Wells and Stefan Zweig. But when Barbusse, an open convert to Communism, applauded the foundation of the Comintern and the French section of *Clarté* agitated for a Communist take-over of the French Socialist party, the foreign affiliates first withdrew and then withered away, although many of *Clarté*'s intellectual recruits were later to return to the fold.

The lesson of this incident – that non-Communist intellectuals were more likely to lend their names to a Communist cause if its organisers did not parade their affiliations – was well learned by the most skilful manager of front organisations in this period, Willi Münzenberg. One of the founders of the German Communist Party (KPD), Münzenberg became its leading propaganda expert, a member of its Central Committee and a deputy in the Reichstag. Previously, in Zurich, he had come in contact with Lenin and other leading Bolsheviks and after 1916 was among Lenin's strongest supporters.[9] When, in 1920, the Communist Youth International held its first World Congress in Moscow, Willi Münzenberg became its first President, at the age of thirty-one. In 1921, while Russia was in the throes of famine, an appeal for help was launched by the Comintern and, in September of that year, Münzenberg founded the *International Workers Aid* (IWA), another Communist organisation, and indeed the first international 'front', to attract support from non-Communist writers and other intellectuals. It set the classical pattern for the many other such organisations that were to follow. Under Münzenberg's guidance, the IWA had succeeded by 1926 in collecting some two million dollars' worth of commodities. By 1931, long after the Russian famine of 1921 had been forgotten,

Red Aid – as IWA came to be known – claimed over a hundred thousand supporters in Germany, had offered assistance during the British General Strike in 1926 and had organised support for Sacco and Vanzetti (two left-wing extremists condemned to death in the USA in 1927). With the help of many German newspapers and by using its influence in the emerging motion picture business, the Münzenberg Trust (as it became known) found sponsors, not only within, but outside the German Left. Within the left, his flexible approach to the problem of broadening support for his many diverse projects allowed Willi Münzenberg to make allies of those very same 'social fascists' which his own Party, the KPD, was then, in response to Stalin's 'Class against Class' directive, still reviling. His greatest achievement during the depression years of 1929–33 was to engineer the *International League Against War and Fascism*, also known as the Amsterdam-Pleydel Movement, which gained the support of among others Edo Fimmen, the secretary of the International Transport Union, and Ellen Wilkinson, a leading member of the British Labour Party. Its Organising Committee, formed in 1932, included Barbusse, Gorky, Shaw, Dreiser, Upton Sinclair, Albert Einstein, Heinrich Mann and Madame Sun Yat Sen; the treasurer of the British group was John Strachey. The ensuing Congress produced a manifesto denouncing aggressive capitalism; it also denounced such 'so-called' peace-keeping organisations as the League of Nations until the Soviet Union itself became a member of the League in 1934.[10]

Münzenberg's initial success with the International League Against War and Fascism was followed by the *World Committee for the Struggle Against War*, supported by Bertrand Russell and Havelock Ellis. In September 1932, Münzenberg's influence had spread across the Atlantic with the launching of the *American League Against War and Fascism*. Münzenberg escaped from Germany on the night of the Reichstag fire and subsequently set up his headquarters in Paris. In 1935, when the Popular Front policy replaced 'Class against Class' and was organised in France and throughout the world, Münzenberg exploited the opportunity to expand his activities and to arrange the publication of *Ce Soir* edited by Aragon, in Paris and of *PM* in New York, in the pages of which social democrats and liberals jointly voiced a diluted version of the Stalinist line.[11] In the same year, the first '*International Congress of Writers for the Defence of Culture*' was held in

Paris. The French and German delegations included André Malraux, Aragon, Gide, and Bertolt Brecht and Mann. The British delegation was led by E. M. Forster and included J. B. Priestley and Aldous Huxley. In his speech, Forster said: 'I am not a communist, though perhaps I might be one if I was a younger and a braver man, for in communism I see hope. It does many things which I think evil, but I know that it intends good. Fascism does evil that evil may come.' Gide had a warmer reception from the Congress when he referred to Russian communism as 'an unprecedented experiment . . . which fills our hearts with hope . . . an impetus capable of carrying forward in its stride the whole human race.' Although soon to break with Communism at this time he still looked forward to the day when, under communism, 'great literature could be made, not as till now out of men's sufferings but out of their joy'.[12]

In July 1937, the Second Congress in this series moved from Valencia, Madrid and Barcelona to Paris. Gide was by now no longer available, following the publication of *Retour de l'URSS* which led to his denunciation in the Soviet and Communist press.

The League of American Writers (LAW)[13] was set up in New York in 1935. It was a counterpart to the *Association des Ecrivains et Artistes Révolutionnaires* (AEAR), founded in Paris three years earlier. Earl Browder, on behalf of the US Communist Party, assured the delegates that the party did not intend to instruct distinguished writers how or what they should write. At the League's Second Congress in 1937, the liberal Waldo Frank was elected chairman, Hemingway made a speech and President Roosevelt was elected an honorary member. The Münzenberg role of stage management was handled by the Party's cultural organiser, Alexander Trachtenberg.

The main front organisation for German writers living in Paris was the *Schutzverband deutscher Schriftsteller* (SDS), refounded after its dissolution by the Nazis, which matched the AEAR in France and the League of American Writers. Its Communist members included Anna Seghers and Alfred Kantorowicz who was general secretary; according to what had become standard practice, a fellow traveller, Rudolf Leonhard, was elected its first president. The SDS attempted to counter Nazi propagandist events, such as the Nuremberg Rally of 1936, and attracted wide support among writers, actors and academics in its presentation of another Germany different from Hitler's.[14]

In England, the most effective instrument of the Popular Front was the Left Book Club, launched in 1936 by Victor Gollancz with the help of John Strachey and Harold Laski.[15] By 1939 its membership was about fifty-seven thousand, indicating an average estimated readership for each book of a quarter of a million. The Club soon established informal links with the Labour Party, the Independent Labour Party, the Liberal Party, the Socialist League and the Communist Party. It organised Russian language classes, showed Eisenstein's and Pudovkin's films, set up discussion groups, sponsored poetry readings, formed a Theatre Guild and organised tours by such pro-Communist scientists as J. B. S. Haldane and J. D. Bernal. To maintain some illusion of balance, the Club also published George Orwell's *Road to Wigan Pier* and Clement Attlee's *The Labour Party in Perspective*, but these works were accompanied by instructions to group conveners to contrast them unfavourably with orthodox Marxist works on similar themes. It has been estimated that about a third of the Club's choices before the War were written by such prominent Communists as Thorez and Palme Dutt, while the list of optional choices included many other Communist authors, such as John Gollan, J. R. Campbell and Emile Burns. At a mass meeting of the Club in London in April 1939, Dr Hewlett Johnson spoke of the Soviet Union's provision of equal educational opportunity and of the effective democratic franchise enjoyed by Soviet citizens. As a fellow-travelling enterprise directed at a Popular Front audience, the Club achieved greater success than the more short-lived *Left Review*, founded and edited by Communist intellectuals. But the Left Book Club, like its counterpart in the US, the League Against War and Fascism, by then known as the League for Peace and Democracy, was soon to fall victim to the Nazi–Soviet Pact.

THE ANTECEDENTS OF THE NAZI–SOVIET PACT

At the Comintern's sixth Congress in 1928, the Russians carried out one of those characteristic reversals of policy which reflected the extent to which the Comintern was a battlefield for Russian domestic quarrels – in this case, Stalin's campaign against Bukharin.[16] The policy of alliance with non-Communist parties, which had brought Stalin under such heavy fire from Trotsky with regard to China and to Britain, was not jettisoned, but the more moderate elements in the foreign parties, who had served their turn as the supporters of the campaign against Trotsky, now became enemies. The main targets of the Comintern were the 'reformists' inside the Communist parties and the left-wing social democrats, who were now branded as the most dangerous enemies of Communism and the dictatorship of the proletariat. This was patently not an ideological environment favourable to the creation of the new solar system of front organisations envisaged by Kuusinen in 1926: but in these lean years, when even the Comintern seems to have feared that the 'action of the revolution was hanging fire', it was Münzenberg, as already described, who 'extended the base under cover of the united front slogan'.[17] For example, during the final years of the Weimar Republic, 1930–33, the German Communist Party worked in concert with the Nazis to destroy successive centrist and social democratic institutions and administrations in the belief that a Nazi victory in Germany would pave the way for Communist revolution.[18] This all changed with the advent of Hitler. 'Class against Class' was hurriedly abandoned. Stalin's German policy lay in ruins. The Soviet Union, undaunted and unashamed, next began to proclaim itself the leading international opponent of the Third Reich and the new policy was formally unveiled by Georgi Dimitrov at the Seventh Comintern congress in Moscow in 1935. He called for a broad, world-wide 'united front' against Nazi Germany. Communists and social democrats and others were exhorted to work together. Thanks to Münzenberg, however, even before the Congress, between 1932 and 1935, a whole new galaxy of front organisations had emerged in Western Europe and America, as has already been noted.

To promote the immediate tactic of organising resistance to Nazi Germany, without abandoning his ultimate objectives, Stalin had to steer a devious course. If during the 1930s he used Litvinov, the People's Commissar for Foreign Affairs, to present the Soviet Union at the League of Nations as the leading champion of the resistance to Hitler – a role in which, incidentally, Litvinov wholly believed – he was, to use a phrase of Lenin's, 'keeping a stone up his sleeve'.[19] This was to pursue his alternative plan of an alliance with Hitler. Indeed, one of the functions of the international and national front organisations, during the 1930s, was to divert Western attention from Stalin's overtures to Berlin. In July 1934, while negotiations for the

Franco-Soviet pact were in progress, the French claimed to have reliable information that Moscow was exploring the possibilities of a pact with Hitler. During 1936–37, the Soviet trade representative in Berlin, Kandelaki, put out feelers for an agreement, which were rebuffed. If it was true that the European powers never fully trusted or welcomed the Soviet Union as an ally, it was also true that the Soviet Union never regarded its improved relations with these powers as more than a stratagem, the ultimate objective being to consolidate Soviet power. When Litvinov, the architect of the policy of collective security, was replaced by Molotov in May 1939 a further step was taken towards the achievement of Stalin's grand design, culminating in Ribbentrop's visit to Moscow on 22 August and the signature of a Treaty of Non-Aggression between the Soviet Union and Germany the following day. Thereafter, world war was no longer in doubt.

The conclusion of this Pact caught the Communist Party of Great Britain (CPGB) off balance. Its initial reaction, on 2 September 1939, was to describe the war as 'a war on two fronts – against Hitler abroad and against the imperialist Chamberlain government at home'. Its General Secretary, Harry Pollitt, publicly committed the party in support of the war, 'believing it to be a just war which should be supported by the whole working class and all friends of democracy in Britain'. The CPGB was however quickly called to order by Moscow. After a hurried visit for consultation by a leading member of the central committee, D. F. Springhall, written instructions were received from the Comintern which were repeated almost verbatim in a resolution adopted by the Central Committee on 3 October, at the strong urging of Palme Dutt, the party's leading theoretician. This was followed by the issue of a manifesto on 7 October declaring that 'the continuance of this war is not in the interests of the people of Britain, France and Germany. . . . The responsibility for the present imperialist war lies equally on all warring Powers. . . . The struggle of the British people against the Chamberlains and Churchills is the best help to the struggle of the Germans against Hitler'. The policy of 'revolutionary defeatism' was maintained until Hitler's attack on Russia in June 1941, which resulted in yet another *volte-face*, this time devised rapidly to avoid once again being out of step with Moscow.[20]

The effect of the Nazi–Soviet Pact on the fellow travellers and the front organisations was however both immediate and damaging.[21] On 29 August 1939, the *Union des Intellectuels Francais* issued a statement, signed by a number of prominent fellow-travellers, including Fréderic and Irène Joliot-Curie, expressing stupefaction at the pact. Heinrich Mann's heresy was to consider that it was the Battle of Britain which in 1940 decided the fate of Europe. One-third of the officers of the League of American Writers' resigned (the League did not meet again until June 1941) and by the end of 1939 the League for Peace and Democracy was dissolved, as well as the American Friends of the Soviet Union. In Britain the Left Book Club, although not formally disbanded until 1948, swiftly changed course and balanced the Dean of Canterbury's *The Socialist Sixth of the World* by publishing Leonard Woolf's *Barbarians at the Gate*, an attack on the Soviet Union. For Gollancz and Laski, for Strachey, Day Lewis and Spender, the anti-imperialist war line adopted by the Comintern in September 1939 led to their final break with Communism, although others, such as the Webbs, Shaw, Hewlett Johnson and D. N. Pritt remained apologists of the Soviet Union to the end of their lives.

The death of Willi Münzenberg in the summer of 1940 was the final postscript to this period. His operational independence from the German Communist Party had already earned him bad marks from his former colleagues, Ulbricht and Pieck, who had blackened his reputation within the Comintern:[22] he had been summoned to Moscow in 1936 and had not come well out of his interrogation. By 1938, he was already an outcast, in spite of personal appeals to Stalin and Dimitrov which went unanswered. In March 1939, he was expelled from the German Communist Party; after the Nazi–Soviet pact, he accused the Soviet Union of having betrayed the peace of Europe. In May 1940, he was interned together with all the other German nationals in France. A month later, he and two others escaped as the German Army was approaching the camp in which they were held. A few miles away, near Grenoble, his body was found hanging from a tree. The Stalinists spread the story that he had committed suicide.[23] But this, in itself, obviously raised doubts about the true cause of his death. Revolutions notoriously consume their own: it was widely believed that he was a victim of agents of the Soviet secret police.[24]

4 The International Front Organisations since the Second World War

The success in the 1930s of what Münzenberg cynically called his 'Innocents' Club'[1] had shown the potential use of those latent forces in Western public opinion that could be mobilised to Soviet advantage. This source of support was greatly increased by Russia's military performance after Hitler's invasion of the USSR and by the legitimate admiration widely evoked for the major part ultimately played by the Soviet armed forces in Hitler's defeat. There was therefore an obvious need and an opportunity, after 1945, for new permanent international front organisations adapted to post-war conditions. It was, moreover, realised that in spite of earlier successes, the front organisations of the 1930s had often been improvised, however brilliantly, and their coordination had often been haphazard. Nor was the need for new front organisations due only to their relatively elementary structure in the 1930s. During the war, the techniques of mass communication had made significant advances and these were soon harnessed to a new and more comprehensive 'solar system' of Soviet-controlled international front organisations, designed to match the emergence of the USSR after 1945 as the world's second power. A wide spectrum of professional and specialised groups was involved in this process, and an attempt was made to impose a coherence of technique and structure which has lasted to the present day. (Chapter 6 describes how the CPSU's International Department, as successor to the Comintern, has been responsible for directing their work.)

By the Cold War period of the late 1940s, the Soviet Communist Party exercised controlling influence in four leading international front organisations which have retained their primacy ever since. The first and still the most important is the

World Peace Council (WPC), now based in Helsinki, which was formed in 1949 and which has succeeded in virtually expropriating the word 'peace', equating it with 'struggle' and attaching it to the so-called 'World Peace Movement'. The WPC's aims, which sound irreproachable, go well beyond the 'prohibition of all weapons of mass destruction' and the 'elimination of all forms of colonialism and racial discrimination' in the fight against 'imperialism' to advocacy of 'peaceful coexistence' on Soviet terms. The second is the *World Federation of Trade Unions* (WFTU), with headquarters in Prague, which was set up in 1945 originally on a non-Communist basis 'to consolidate and unite the trade unions of the world, irrespective of race, nationality, religion or political opinion'; by 1949, British, American and other democratic trade unions had withdrawn because of the Communists' domination of the fledgling organisation. The third, the *World Federation of Democratic Youth* (WFDY), with headquarters in Budapest, claims to work 'with due regard for differing political tendencies and religious beliefs, for closer international understanding and cooperation among all international and national youth organisations ... for the achievement of ... democracy, friendship and world peace'; but the WFDY has, in practice, been under Soviet Control since 1950. Similarly, the *International Union of Students* (IUS), set up in Prague in 1946, aims to promote 'the struggle for economic and social progress, democracy and ... security of all people against imperialism, colonialism ... and racial discrimination', but had lost its non-communist support by 1951. The WPC, the WFTU, the WFDY and the IUS have been continuously active in the promotion of Soviet policies from their inception in the post-war period until the present day, both in the Third World and through associated national organisations in Western countries. They have given full support to Soviet policy in Europe, in the Near and Middle East, in Vietnam and elsewhere in the world, and have organised numerous conferences in furtherance of this purpose. Some examples of these other activities are the supply of aid and funds to 'national liberation movements' in such countries as Angola, Guinea-Bissau, Mozambique, the Cape Verde Islands, Namibia and South Africa, and the sponsoring of delegation visits to Soviet-occupied Afghanistan.

A rare instance of open opposition to the management of a WFDY conference was provided by the Democrat Youth Community of Europe (DEMYC), representing European Christian Democrat and Conservative Youth Organisations, at the meeting in Helsinki of the World Forum of Youth and Students for Peace, Detente and Disarmament in January 1981. WFDY's insistence on hearing a pro-Babrak Karmal Afghan delegate was opposed, at the instigation of DEMYC, by the non-Communist West European organisations and the Forum's collapse was only averted by Soviet acceptance in the communique of a demand for the withdrawal of all foreign forces from Afghanistan.[2]

Three other post war international front organisations also play a significant role. The *Women's International Democratic Federation* (WIDF), originally founded in Paris in 1945 by the Communist-dominated *Union des Femmes Francaises* and now based in East Berlin, ostensibly aims 'to unite women of all races ... religions and political opinions ... to defend their rights as citizens, mothers and workers ... and to ensure peace, democracy and national independence'; it has been under Soviet control since its inception. The *International Association of Democratic Lawyers* (IADL) was founded in Paris in 1946 at an International Congress of Jurists held under the aegis of the communist controlled *Mouvement National Judiciaire*; by 1949 most non-Communist lawyers had left and it is now based in Brussels with the apparent objective of 'promoting understanding and fraternity among lawyers ... and support for democratic principles favourable to international peace and cooperation'. The *World Federation of Scientific Workers* (WFSW), like the IADL, was founded in 1946 and has offices in both London and Paris. Officially it aims 'to link organisations concerned with safeguarding scientific rights ... and to promote the use of science for peaceful purposes'. It has, however, consistently taken a strong pro-Soviet stance on all foreign policy issues, for example the invasion of Czechoslovakia in 1968 and of Afghanistan in 1979.

Of less importance than those seven international front organisations are three others also dating from the post-war period. They are the *International Radio and TV Organisation* (OIRT), founded in 1946 and influential in the Third World: the *International Federation of Resistance Fighters* (FIR) was set up in 1951 to mobilise pro-Soviet sentiment among ex-servicemen and to support Soviet disarmament initiatives and the *International Organisation of Journalists* (IOJ), was established in Prague in 1946 'to defend the freedom of the press ... and support the struggle against war psychosis and . . . fascist propaganda'. The IOJ has been effective in propagating Soviet attitudes and techniques in Third World countries where there is a receptive audience for its view that 'the mass media cannot be divorced from the overall socio-political structure of a country' and for its advocacy of the development of State-owned media. Over 500 Third World journalists have attended courses at the IOJ's training centres in East Berlin, Budapest and Sofia.

Subsequently, in the 1950s, three more such organisations were formed. First and most important was the *Afro-Asian Peoples' Solidarity Organisation* (AAPSO), set up in Cairo in 1957, 'to unite and coordinate the struggle of the Afro-Asian peoples against imperialism and colonialism . . . and to ensure their economic, social and cultural developments'. AAPSO was originally under joint Soviet-Chinese control but the subsequent Sino-Soviet dispute led to China's withdrawal in 1967. The second, the *International Institute for Peace* (IIP), was established in Vienna in 1957 to provide legal cover for the WPC secretariat after the World Peace Council had been expelled from Austria for 'activities directed against the interests of the Austrian State'.[3] The third was the *Christian Peace Conference* (CPC), with headquarters in Prague, formed in 1958 'to be a forum at which Christians from all over the world will meet together and search for God's will concerning current political, social and economic problems'. CPC ran into trouble when its Czech founder and first President, Professor Hromadka, a Lenin Peace Prize winner, was forced to resign after his open letter opposing the Soviet invasion of Czechoslovakia in 1968.

Detailed information on the membership, organisation, leading officials and staff secretariats of these organisations is contained in Annex II. This demonstrates clearly the extent to which all of them are interlocked and have close connections with the World Peace Council. All obediently follow the Soviet line on such foreign policy issues, as anti-nuclear movements, Afghanistan or disarmament, whether their members be churchmen, journalists, scientific workers, lawyers, students or trade unionists; many share 'solidarity days' and a major aim, which some have achieved, is to acquire the image of respectability by gaining differing forms of recognition within the United Nations family of organisations, including ECOSOC, FAO, UNESCO and UNIDO.

The subsidies paid from official Communist sources to the thirteen leading front organisations have been estimated by American sources at over $63 million (in 1979) of which the lion's share, or nearly $50 million, went to sustain the operations of the WPC.[4] A breakdown of the estimated Soviet funding of the principal international front organisations is at Annex III. The WPC claims that it is funded by contributions from national peace committees and donations to its World Peace Fund. In fact, it is both overtly and covertly subsidised by the USSR and other Communist countries. The open subsidy is in the form of subventions from Communist parties and from sources such as the Soviet Peace Fund. The late Boris Polevoi, when chairman of this Fund, stated in the Soviet Peace Committee publication, *XXth Century and Peace* in April 1980 that it was voluntarily supported by 'millions of Soviet citizens': but he also explained that the Fund was close to the Soviet Peace Committee which aimed 'to render financial aid to the organisations, movements and personalities fighting for stronger peace, national independence and freedom' and that his clients included 'the leaders of the international democratic organisations working for peace'. In a letter to *The Times*, in 1976, the late Lord Noel-Baker and Monsignor Bruce Kent, now general secretary of the Campaign for Nuclear Disarmament, stated that the WPC was 'financed by contributions from the Communist Parties of the countries of the world'.[5] And in a letter to the *New Statesman*, in October 1980 Ruth Tosek, a former senior interpreter at front organisations meetings, wrote to say that 'all the funds of these organisations, in local and hard currency, were provided above all by the Soviet Union, but also by other East European satellite countries, on the basis of set contribution rates, paid by the governments of these countries through various channels'.[6]

The development of this interlocking system of front organisations, of which in practice only three date from after Stalin's death in 1953, each with professional secretariats (unlike their more primitive counterparts of the 1930s) trained to make the best use of modern publicity techniques has given the Soviet Union two long-term advantages: first, of being able to create the impression of wide-ranging popular and intellectual support for Soviet policies; and, second, of coordinating its campaigns and of being able to concentrate on specific issues. In this way, the post-war front organisations have become and have remained major instruments of Soviet foreign policy.

GENERAL AND SPECIFIC OBJECTIVES

In analysing the objectives of the international front organisations, it should be remembered that orthodox Marxism–Leninism regards the prosecution of the 'international class war' until all non-Communist power centres are eliminated not only as legitimate but also as a duty. This 'world revolutionary process' – which includes 'national liberation struggles' – will only be completed with what *Pravda* has called 'the complete and final victory of communism on a world scale'.[7] Only then will 'peace', in the Marxist–Leninist sense, be possible. Indeed, there is striking continuity between Stalin's statement to the 19th CPSU Congress in 1952 that 'the fight for peace' can turn into 'the fight for socialism' and Brezhnev's version at the 25th CPSU Congress in 1976 that 'socialism and peace are inseparable'. Andropov said much the same thing when he addressed the plenum of the CPSU Central Committee in June 1983: 'the threat of nuclear war impelled us to place a new value on the basic purpose of the activity of the whole Communist movement. Communists have always been fighters against the oppression and exploitation of man by man, and today they are struggling for the preservation of human civilization, for the right of mankind to life'. Hence Soviet policy, in a fundamental sense, stands for permanent conflict with the democracies: this is 'the road to peace' as seen from Moscow, rather than peace in the sense in which the word is generally understood by non-Communists.

The purpose of the international front organisations is to project in the non-Communist world a favourable image of the Soviet Union and its policies, and to influence foreign public opinion in its support. Front organisation propaganda is consequently directed towards the fostering of a climate of opinion in which the apparent objectives of Soviet policy can be accepted by all men and women of goodwill. Thus 'peace' is preserved by the Soviet Union and threatened only by the 'imperialists'. In pursuit of these general objectives, the main task of the front organisations is to undermine the Western alliance, rather than directly to promote Soviet communism. Individual adherents may, of course, be drawn into more active commitment to Soviet causes but in the first instance these organisations' role is aimed at generating opposition to Western policies. Increasingly, therefore, their work is to promote anti-American, anti-NATO opinion among those who may be generally disaffected or critical of Western policies rather than specifically to encourage any section of society inclined to unconstitutional revolutionary action. A particular target is those who are impatient with or disillusioned by the slow and protracted process of multilateral disarmament by all the powers, including the Soviet Union, and who claim to see in unilateral policies by the West alone the key to further progress.

Boris Ponomarev, whose leading role as head of the International Department of the CPSU is analysed later, wrote in 1979 that '... it is impossible to understand how people who are objectively, and one would suppose also subjectively, committed to bridling the arms race and ending the threat of a world war, can pay tribute to, even tend to support the so-called theory of two superpowers which equates the United States and the Soviet Union, the military power of imperialism and of socialism. There is nothing wrong about strength. What matters is who has it and for what purpose it is used. Strength in imperialist hands is a source of war danger. Strength in the hands of Socialism has become an instrument for ensuring peace and lessening the war danger. This was so in the past and is also true today'.[8]

This position was further illustrated in an article on nuclear weapons in a Moscow journal in October 1980 by Major-General A. S. Milovidov, a leading authority on military doctrine. In the 'class analysis' of war and peace, Milovidov considered nuclear armaments as 'fearsome weapons of war' when in the possession of 'imperialism', but a 'protective shield of peace' when owned by socialist states. For this reason, he rejected 'abstract pacifism' and unilateral disarmament by the Soviet Union: 'the Soviet Union cannot undertake the unilateral destruction of its nuclear weapons (and indeed has no right to do so, as it is responsible to the peoples of the world for peace and progress). To do so, would mean disarming in the face of the forces of war and reaction. While speaking out against the use of nuclear weapons, the Soviet Union does not exclude the possibility of using them in extreme circumstances ... Marxist–Leninists decisively reject the assertion of certain bourgeois theorists who consider nuclear missiles unjust from any point of view . . .'.[9]

Three specific objectives emerge from an analysis of front organisation activities in the past generation. The first is to isolate the United States from its NATO allies as the 'main enemy' politically, strategically and morally. To this end, the role of the US in Western Europe is attacked by the front organisations as hostile to *détente* and its policies as a threat to peace. In the Third World the US is portrayed as a superpower inimical to anti-colonial aspirations and as an opponent of the 'national liberation struggle', although the Third World's overwhelming condemnation of the Soviet invasion of Afghanistan, as shown by the UN General Assembly resolutions of 1980, 1981 and 1982 and 1983 somewhat undermined these efforts. (In November 1983, the voting was 116 to 20, with 17 abstentions, the largest vote against the USSR since 1980.) Above all, the front organisations exploit any latent divisions within NATO. They have seized on such issues as differing approaches on Southern Africa, Latin America and the Middle East and the whole field of disarmament to provide material for this purpose.

The second objective, closely allied to the first, is to reinforce the Soviet military aim of securing strategic advantage. Propaganda themes have varied according to the requirements of the military balance; sometimes they have concentrated on a single issue which the Soviet Union has seen as being important in relation to its strategic interests at the time; at others they have involved a broad effort to promote measures which will lead to a weakening of NATO's relative strategic position. An early example of the former was the Stockholm Peace Appeal, launched in March 1950, which called for prohibition of nuclear weapons. This was at a time of clear Soviet nuclear inferiority (the first Soviet test had taken place only six months earlier) but overwhelming conventional superiority. Signatures totalling 500 million were claimed for the Appeal, whose theme paralleled the official Soviet line at the time on disarmament at the United Nations. But as the Soviet Union began to develop a more sophisticated nuclear capability after the Soviet thermonuclear weapon test in 1953, the Appeal was suspended. Other themes on such subjects as the dismantling of foreign military bases, the abolition of 'aggressive' military pacts, the establishment of 'nuclear free zones', a 'freeze' on nuclear weapons, reductions of military budgets have also been exploited with the same purpose in view. Recent examples are the campaign against Enhanced Radiation Weapons (ERW, the so-called 'neutron bombs') in 1977 and 1978, which the Russians counted as a success, and the current campaign against NATO's INF modernisation plans. It is irrelevant, for this purpose, that in official negotiations, it is Soviet intransigence which has blocked progress.

The third objective is to perform a diversionary role in the general interests of Soviet foreign policy. Front organisations concentrate the attention of international public opinion on the shortcomings of Western societies, thereby diverting attention from the realities of life in the Soviet Union. In this way, a more favourable background is created for the projection of Soviet policy. Indeed, one of Münzenberg's functions in the 1930s had been to disguise the implications as well as the facts of Stalin's collectivisation programme and of the great purges of 1936–38 which culminated in the Moscow trials. Similarly during the early 1950s the Stockholm Peace Appeal, orchestrated by the World Peace Council, was designed to divert the attention of the world from the developing Soviet nuclear weapons programme and to concentrate on the dangers of the nuclear predominance then enjoyed by its main adversary. This was also the period of the internal Soviet campaign against 'cosmopolitanism' in the arts and sciences, of Lysenko genetics, of the liquidation of the Yiddish writers and of the alleged 'Doctors' Plot' against Stalin. In Eastern Europe, there were the show trials of the 'Titoist' leaders, after Tito's excommunication in 1949 which was itself a severe blow to Communist solidarity. An important subsidiary role of the 'peace campaign' waged by the front organisations during Stalin's final years, was to divert attention from these events. A similar function has been performed by the current anti-NATO campaign which has served the purpose of diverting attention from the Soviet Union's military build-up and massive levels of military expenditure, from its military occupation of Afghanistan, from the problems in Poland and from its disregard for the human rights provisions of the Helsinki Final Act. But the comprehensive basis for positive action by the front organisations in promoting Soviet foreign policy interests is contained in the periodic 'Programmes of Action' adopted by the WPC, which contain a vast compendium of detailed items, sometimes in conflict with one another, for activities on a world-wide scale. These are considered in Chapter 5.

Finally, there have been suggestions that front organisations perform an ancillary service for Soviet intelligence. According to a United States Congressional committee in July 1978,[10] 'front gatherings serve as agent enlisting grounds for Soviet and bloc intelligence services. Front meetings in the USSR and Eastern Europe are ideal for this purpose, because bloc intelligence officers can control the circumstances of their meetings with likely recruits, with no fear of surveillance by, or interference from, non-Communist security services. Most of the agents enlisted by communist bloc intelligence services over the years were targeted while on visits to the Soviet bloc, some while in attendance at front meetings or on free vacations in the bloc offered in connection with these gatherings'. The report adds that front organisations also act as cover for Communist parties and organisations in countries where conditions are not ripe for open Communist activities or for the establishment of Communist parties; they have also helped to channel training and arms to insurgents and hostile political groups.

METHODS AND TECHNIQUES

Congresses and conferences are the primary means by which the leading international front organisations rally support and project their message so as to influence a maximum audience. These are attended by representatives of the national 'peace committees' or comparable highlighted organisations which are the local instruments of the WPC or other front organisations (see Chapter 5). In this, as in other matters, the WPC takes the lead. In recent years, the tempo of the 'peace congress' technique has increasingly concentrated on the theme of disarmament – which means in Soviet parlance only NATO's nuclear disarmament. Modern communications mean that the work of mass congresses, such as those organised by the WPC in Warsaw in 1977 and the 'World Parliament of People for Peace' in Sofia in September 1980, can be quickly supplemented by frequent meetings of particular organisations without the elaborate preparations needed for larger gatherings. In this development, the WPC again set the lead, as is shown by the fact that when its Presidential Bureau met at Antananarivo, Madagascar, in 1981, there were no fewer than 105 peace movements and international organisations represented.[11] The chief theme of the meeting, despite its African setting, was opposition to NATO's nuclear modernisation and, more pertinently, to the projected US Rapid Deployment Force (RDF) for the Indian Ocean.

The major front organisations also control a number of subsidiaries – fronts, as it were, for fronts. The managements are interlinked in such a way that dominant influence is maintained in Soviet or pro-Soviet hands. The way in which this is achieved and the wide range of activities and interests covered by these subsidiary bodies world-wide is illustrated by the example of the WFTU.

The WFTU has organised a cluster of international commissions covering such diverse subjects as trade union education, multinational companies and the environment, in addition to solidarity committees with the peoples and workers of Africa, Palestine and Korea. It has also set up eleven Trade Union Internationals with a comprehensive coverage of industrial and agricultural workers, as well as the World Federation of Teachers Unions, better known by its French initials FISE, whose purpose is to combat the influence of non-Communist rivals in bodies affiliated to the International Confederation of Free Trades Unions (ICFTU), formed by Western trade unions after their withdrawal from WFTU in 1949. Likewise, the AAPSO, in association with the WPC, set up in 1977 the International Committee against Apartheid, Racism and Colonialism in Southern Africa, which has held conferences in London, Paris and Stockholm. It has also controlled, since 1978, the International Commission of Enquiry into Crimes of the Racist Regimes in Southern Africa. This is based in Brussels, and its chairman, the Irish lawyer and politician, Sean MacBride, holder of both the Lenin and Nobel Peace Prizes, is in addition vice-chairman of the WPC subsidiary, the International Liaison Forum of Peace Forces (ILF). The ILF's Executive Secretary, the Russian Oleg Kharkhardin, is an official of the International Department of the CPSU, and the vice-chairman of the WPC-affiliated Soviet Peace Committee. Sean MacBride was joined at the ILF as vice-president by Arthur Booth (UK), Knud Nielsen (Denmark), president of the non-Communist Association of World Federalists, and Mrs Edith Ballantyne (Canada), the Czech-born general secretary of the Women's International League for Peace and Freedom (WILPF). Another influential WPC subsidiary is the Brussels-based International Committee for European Security and Cooperation (ICESC), the secretary of which is the veteran Belgian cleric, Canon Raymond Goor, who is a WPC Presidential Committee observer. Also in the same category of 'sub-fronts' created in order to penetrate the network of Non-Governmental Organisations (NGOs) at the United Nations in Geneva is the 'Special NGOs Committee on Disarmament' and related organisations. This group was organised by the WPC during 1978 as part of the campaign against NATO's modernisation proposals. Its creation was assisted by the WPC-affiliated Swiss Peace Committee and by Warsaw Pact diplomatic representatives accredited to the agencies of the United Nations based in Geneva.

A further technique, dating from the Münzenberg era, is the use for propagandist purposes of the names of prominent personalities. During the World Peace Congress in Vienna in 1952, sponsors included some familiar pre-war names, including Brecht, Aragon, Jean Paul Sartre and Hewlett Johnson. The tradition continues today, as evidenced by use of the names of Pastor Martin Niemöller, active in the current anti-NATO campaign (he died on 6 March 1984), and of Rev. Ralph Abernathy (US), both of whom, with Hortensia Allende (Chile), Sean MacBride and Yasser Arafat, are Presidents of Honour of the WPC.

A recurrent practice of front organisations is, wherever possible, to use the resources of local Communist parties in their campaigns. Provided that the local situation does not render this practice counterproductive, local parties can often provide support disproportionately large in relation to their membership. An example of this technique was to be seen in Holland, after the launching of the Soviet campaign against US proposals to deploy Enhanced Radiation Weapons in Europe, when the Dutch Communist Party swiftly helped to set up an 'Initiative Group' of activists to 'Stop the Neutron Bomb' (see Chapter 10).

There is no doubt that the elaborate structure of front organisations described in Annex II will remain an important element in Soviet foreign policy projection world-wide. But their use for this purpose in individual countries will vary according to the tactical advantages which they are seen by Moscow to offer.

5 The World Peace Council

Before examining exactly how Soviet control is exerted over these front organisations by the CPSU's International Department, it is necessary to define the role of the WPC as the largest and most effective of them.

The WPC acts as the flagship, directing and coordinating the pro-Soviet components of the international peace movement. Its origins go back to the World Congress of Intellectuals for Peace held at Wroclaw (Breslau) in Poland in August 1948, subsequent conferences in New York and Paris and the 'World Committee of Partisans for Peace', established in Paris in 1949. Its present name was adopted in November 1950. It has been based in Helsinki since 1968, having been expelled from Paris in 1951 and from Vienna in 1957 by the French and Austrian governments, on both occasions for activities against the interests of the host State.

All has not been plain sailing. In Stalin's last years, the aggressive tone of the international front organisations tended to alienate even those few potential sympathisers in the West who were still inclined to accept the Soviet view. Yugoslavia was expelled from all the international front organisations after Tito's break with Stalin in 1948. After Stalin's death in 1953, further problems arose with the Soviet suppression of the Hungarian revolution in 1956, the growing Sino-Soviet schism in the early 1960s which led to China's withdrawal from the international front network, and the invasion of Czechoslovakia in 1968. None of these problems proved insuperable, mainly because the CPSU's International Department was able to maintain its administrative control of front organisation activities unimpaired (see Chapter 6); but they had serious repercussions on Communist parties in the West, many of whose members were alienated by the hardline Soviet actions. The effect of these tensions will be considered later.

The secretary-general of the WPC since 1966, and its President since 1977, has been Romesh Chandra, a member of the Central

Committee of the pro-Soviet Indian Communist Party. His long association with the WPC dates back to his appointment as a member of the secretariat and its executive committee in 1953. This continuity of experience, together with his Indian nationality, has enabled Chandra to maximise the WPC's influence in the Third World and helps to explain its close links with the AAPSO, with which Chandra has been involved since its creation in 1957. AAPSO was particularly active at the time of the Vietnam War; its subsequent involvement in the political, financial and military support of 'national liberation movements' in the Third World has been controlled by the International Department of the CPSU, working through the Soviet Afro-Asian Solidarity Committee.

Recent examples of joint WPC–AAPSO ventures have been International Conferences 'Against Apartheid' in New Delhi and 'For Afro–Arab Solidarity against Imperialism and Reaction' in Addis Ababa, both held in September 1978, and 'Solidarity with the Struggle of the People of Namibia' held in Paris in September 1980. Some 90 Solidarity Committees and Liberation Movements are affiliated to AAPSO.

Chandra's obedience to the Soviet line has been undeviating for the past 30 years, surviving the invasions of Hungary in 1956, Czechoslovakia in 1968 and Afghanistan in 1979. When the treatment of dissidents in the USSR and Czechoslovakia was raised by the pacifist and non-Communist War Resisters' International at the World Congress of Peace Forces in Moscow in 1973, Chandra declared that peace organisations which adopted an anti-Soviet stance 'ceased to be genuine'. In 1975, he said in Moscow that the WPC 'positively reacts to all Soviet initiatives in international affairs'. In January 1981 he wrote: 'In the hands of Socialism [military] force has for the first time in human history become an instrument for safe-guarding peace and social progress. So much for the "Soviet threat". If it does exist, it is, figuratively speaking, not a threat to peace but a threat of peace in the name of peace.'[1]

The WPC's structure is a model for the other international front organisations. The Council, which has 1600 members, meets only once every 3 years. It elects a Presidential Committee, whose function is to run the organisation between Council sessions. The Presidential Committee appoints a Bureau, consisting of the President, Vice-Presidents and national peace movement representatives. The Bureau meets 3 or 4 times a year and is responsible for planning and carrying out decisions. This body, supported by a Secretariat also appointed by the Presidential Committee, effectively runs the WPC. The Soviet element at all levels is crucial since it ensures control by Moscow. Until his death in December, 1981, E. K. Federov, an alternate member of the CPSU Central Committee, was a vice-president and also thus a member both of the Presidential Committee and of the Bureau. The Soviet Vice-President is now E. M. Primakov, First Deputy Chairman of the Soviet Peace Committee. G. A. Zhukov, President of the Soviet Peace Committee and a member of the CPSU Central Committee, and Vitaly Shaposhnikov, a deputy head of the CPSU's International Department is also a member of the Presidential Committee, and the Soviet Union is represented on the Secretariat.

The WPC's coordinating role among the various fronts is ensured by the membership of the Presidential Committee of the leading officials of most of the other front organisations. The president of the WIDF, Freda Brown (Australia), the secretary-general of AAPSO, Nuri Abdul Razzaq Hussain (Iraq), the president of the CPC, Karoly Toth (Hungary), the secretary-general of the IOJ, Jiri Kubka (Czechoslovakia), the president of the IUS, Miroslav Stepan (Czechoslovakia) and the secretary-general of the WFDY, Miklos Barabas (Hungary) are all members. Thus six leading front organisations are represented at the highest level of the WPC. The Council has also formed commissions to deal with a wide range of subjects and has a well organised information network with centres in Helsinki, Havana, Addis Ababa and New York. It produces the monthly *Peace Courier* in English, French, Spanish and German and a bi-monthly journal, *New Perspectives*, in the same languages, plus Japanese.

CONGRESSES AND PROGRAMMES

As the most heavily subsidised of the front organisations (see Annex III) the WPC has been able to hold 13 World Peace Congresses since 1949 and some 16 conferences of peace committees, limited to representatives of national affiliates, in the past decade. With four exceptions, all these 29 gatherings have been held in the USSR, in Eastern Europe or in Havana. In supporting 'liberation movements' in Africa, Asia and Latin America, the

WPC claims that the Soviet Union is the 'natural ally' of Non-Aligned and other Third World countries, whose 'anti-colonialist struggle' is second only in importance to the 'struggle for peace'; it also campaigns on behalf of a 'New International Economic Order' which is to replace the 'economic exploitation of the Third World' by 'imperialist countries', principally the US. In addition the WPC exploits such issues as 'Solidarity with the Arab People and their Central Cause – Palestine' against 'Israeli aggressors' who are the 'tools of US imperialism', and exposes the 'crimes of the racist regimes in southern Africa'. While other front organisations are designed to appeal to sectional groups, these are all subsumed within the WPC's universal appeal in directing the international peace movement. China, not surprisingly, has other views: in May 1977, a Chinese spokesman at the UN referred to the WPC as 'the highest tool of a certain superpower'.

In laying down detailed programmes of action in recent years, the WPC has listed its principal military objectives as the strengthening and broadening of national movements for a world-wide network of peace organisations (all mainly directed at lobbying for disarmament on Soviet terms and opposing the deployment of new US missiles in Europe), the ending of the 'arms race' and halting of the imperialist military build up in the Persian Gulf, the Middle East, the Mediterranean and the Caribbean; the establishment of a Nordic nuclear free zone, and cooperation with the UN Disarmament Commission and their affiliated Non-Governmental Organisations (NGOs) on disarmament questions. Emphasis has also been laid on cooperation with the intergovernmental organisations of the United Nations, in particular UNCTAD, UNESCO, UNIDO, ILO, UNEP and FAO, in 'the struggle against the damaging activities of transnational corporations . . . and the imperialist policy of destabilisation in the field of information and culture'.

Action to secure peace in Asia has included 'the campaign against the conspiracies of the Washington-Peking-Tokyo axis and international solidarity campaigns to expose the Peking hegemonists who are working in collusion with US imperialism for the destabilisation of Vietnam, Laos and Kampuchea'. Likewise, solidarity has been pledged with African 'liberation movements' and with campaigns 'against the agreements with the US and the governments of Egypt, Kenya, Somalia and Oman for the use of their military bases by US troops and the creation of reactionary military alliances, such as the Inter-African Military Force planned by France'.

There has also been a call for solidarity with the Palestine Liberation Organisation (PLO) and with the Arab peoples in their struggle to liquidate the military and political consequences of the Camp David accords; with Libya against threats of aggression from Egypt and the US: with the people of Algeria against the imperialist policy of destabilisation in North Africa and with the people of the Western Sahara and their movement the Polisario Front. In Latin America, eight countries whose peoples live under tyrannical regimes that violate human rights have been contrasted with the Cuban people (whose human rights were assumed by implication not to have been violated) 'in their just demand for an end to the economic blockade illegally imposed by the US and the dismantling of the US base in Guantanamo'.

Indeed human rights have been a standard item on the agenda of most WPC conferences, although it is scarcely surprising that the violation of those very rights in Communist countries is never mentioned. It was one of the Polish members of the WPC's Presidential Committee, Wieslaw Gornicki, who appeared at a WPC Bureau meeting in Copenhagen in January 1982 as General Jaruzelski's spokesman, to assure the assembled company that the Polish people were in good hands (he had acted as chief press spokesman in Warsaw after the imposition of martial law in Poland on 13 December 1981).

The WPC's 1983 Programme of Action, adopted in Lisbon in November 1982, followed closely the guidelines laid down in preceding years. Pride of place was given to preparations for the World Assembly for Peace and Life, against Nuclear War (which was held in Prague in June 1983) and to support for the Summit of the Non-Aligned Movement held in New Delhi in March 1983. Increased cooperation was urged with the United Nations and its specialised bodies, particularly UNESCO, ECOSOC, UNCTAD and UNIDO. Among the 30 countries selected for 'Solidarity' Campaigns, the theme for Argentina was, unsurprisingly, 'support for the demands of the Argentine people for sovereignty over the Malvinas', but mention of Afghanistan was reduced to no more than 'the observance of a solidarity week'. Lengthy, and often repetitive, sections on economic cooperation and political solidarity contained slogans, sometimes contradictory, designed to present every international and domestic issue in an 'anti-imperialist' and anti-United States context and to identify the WPC fully and indiscriminately with every aspect of the supposed aims of the Third World countries, irrespective of their merits or practicality.

The introduction of the 1983 Programme noted that 'never has the danger of a nuclear conflagration – and the consequent destruction of all that is most precious on this Earth, of life itself – been so great as it is today'. In line with current priorities of the Soviet leadership, the introduction continued: 'The Reagan Administration presses on relentlessly with its efforts to deploy Pershing II and Cruise missiles in Western Europe in 1983. If these plans are not halted, the world will enter a qualitatively new period which may well make it virtually impossible to halt the arms race. The US Defence Secretary has proudly declared that the US is spending billions on a project for a "protracted" nuclear war with the Soviet Union. The Pentagon Generals are welcome to their lunacy, but the thinking behind this "project" can lead to the nuclear annihilation of all peoples. The world has understood better than ever the perils of the arms build-up, after the genocidal war waged by Israeli ruling circles, backed by Washington, against the Lebanese and Palestine peoples.' The significance of the 'anti-war movement' was highlighted and, in contrast to the 'war makers and war profiteers', who were 'unable to halt the growth in numbers of the participants in peace marches, demonstrations, rallies and other actions' and 'seek desperately to divide the anti-war organisations, to blunt the edge of the peace movement', the WPC expressed 'its readiness to cooperate with all forces fighting against nuclear war and for disarmament'. The sections on disarmament and security contained no original ideas. They were in effect a compendium of familiar proposals from earlier propaganda campaigns. Many of them may seem, in the simplistic form in which they are presented, desirable in principle. But they are put forward with complete disregard for their security implications, for the state of current negotiations on many of the proposals and for the position adopted by the Soviet Union in these negotiations, which is so often the reason for the lack of progress. The absence of realism or balance in the proposals shows that they can be intended to serve no other purpose than to provide a platform for anti-Western propaganda.

The WPC's professional skill at global coordination of the

Soviet peace movement was shown in its management of the World Parliament of Peoples for Peace, held in Sofia in September 1980, and (despite an apparent attempt by the Czechs to keep the WPC in the background) of the 'World Assembly for Peace and Life, Against Nuclear War', held in Prague in June 1983. It was claimed that at Sofia '330 political parties were represented – Socialist and Social Democratic parties, Christian Democratic, Communist and Liberal parties, Agrarian, Radical and Centre Parties, as well as national parties from all continents'.[2] Similarly, at Prague, there were said to have been '3625 delegates from 132 countries and 119 international organisations . . . 20 per cent from socialist countries, 40 per cent from developing countries and 40 per cent from advanced capitalist countries'.[3] The Prague Assembly ended with an Appeal which predictably highlighted the threat of nuclear war and emphasised the acute danger 'posed by plans to deploy new first strike nuclear weapons in Western Europe' which it was 'utterly essential' to stop. The assistant secretary of the British Peace Assembly, Florence Croasdell, was warmly applauded when she declared that the Soviet Union was working for peace '24 hours a day' and went on to say that 'the only social order that is going to bring any progress for our children is socialism, and real socialism is in the Soviet Union. Nevertheless the Soviet Union does not impose its system on anybody, but America is out to dominate the world'.[4] But this, the thirteenth major international WPC conference since 1949 was less successful from its organisers viewpoint than the Sofia meeting three years before. Of the distinguished visitors invited to attend as guests of honour only Yasser Arafat appeared for the later sessions and, in general, the event did not attract the publicity overseas that had been expected. It was clear that it did not live up to its advance billing as the most significant of Congresses ever called on the initiative of the WPC.[5]

That this was so was made clear in an article in the *World Marxist Review*, the Soviet-controlled monthly magazine published in Prague, which appeared in December 1983. It was by the Czech peace activist, Tomas Travnicek, who had served as one of the World Assembly's three 'co-chairpersons'. Travnicek began by conceding that the 'bourgeois mass media' in the West had 'paid scant attention' to an Assembly widely stigmatised as a 'communist event . . . organised with Moscow's money'. He loyally rebutted this charge, asserting that 'all expenses connected with it were covered not by Moscow's propaganda service, but by volunteer contributions from citizens of the CSSR, who gave more than 60 million crowns to the Peace and Solidarity Fund'. Travnicek, for good measure, tried to turn the tables by counterclaiming that the Second Convention of European Nuclear Disarmament (END), held in Berlin the previous May (see Chapter 9), had been 'financed by US special services through the special "working group" set up under the US President'.[6] Significantly, in a five page article, Travnicek mentioned the WPC only once (on the fourth page and in a throwaway context), thereby seeking to perpetuate the last minute pretence that the Assembly had not in fact been a WPC event.

The Soviet-controlled peace movement has not yet fully recovered the momentum lost as a result of Prague's lack of impact overseas. Follow-up conferences in the trade union and disarmament field which were foreshadowed at Prague have been duly held in Sofia and London. The most important international meeting held to discuss the new Soviet peace and disarmament propaganda moves took place in Vienna on 14–17 November 1983. This, the second meeting of the Vienna Dialogue on Disarmament and *Détente*, was held at WPC instigation but under broader sponsorship, including that of the Austrian Peace Council, and was as widely attended as any previous Soviet front meeting of this kind. Its immediate aim was, of course, to direct West European public opinion to the danger allegedly posed by the stationing of NATO's new cruise and Pershing II missiles. Its most significant long-term aim was to call for the international preparations needed to ensure Communists exploitation of the UN Peace Year to be held in 1986. Western peace activists are likely to hear more of the Vienna Dialogue on Disarmament and *Détente* in future, as the WPC has clearly invested heavily in its success.

THE WPC AND THE UNITED NATIONS

At the UN session in 1981, the WPC's application for higher consultative status with ECOSOC was put before its Committee on Non-Governmental Organisations (NGOs). During the Committee's hearings the WPC's application was withdrawn; the reasons why were explained in two important statements by the

UK and US delegates, which were published in the Committee's report on 16 March 1981, the UK delegation noted that 'resolution 1296 (XLIV) required that non-governmental organisations should make a full and accurate declaration of their financial situation. However, the representative of the WPC has said that his organisation's accounts are not submitted to an independent audit. He also admitted under questioning that the financial statement submitted to the Committee covered only a fraction of the WPC's actual income and expenditures. In other words, the WPC has presented to the Committee a false statement of its accounts . . . and also stated that it does not receive contributions from any Government. But its representative . . . carefully avoided answering specific questions . . . on that point. It is clear, however, that the WPC has received large-scale financial support from government sources and has gone to great lengths to conceal that fact'.

This was not all. The delegation continued by stating that '. . . the WPC claims to support the principle of non-interference in the internal affairs of nations. Yet its own Programme of Action for 1981 contained policies which are in direct contradiction of that principle. One example is that organisation's support for the People's Front for the Liberation of Oman, whose objective is the overthrow of the sovereign government of a Member state of the United Nations. The WPC's history suggests that activities of this kind are part of a pattern rather than mistaken aberrations. The WPC was expelled from Paris . . . and from Vienna, for activities directed against the interests of the State. . . . The WPC claims also to support the replacement of the policy of force by that of negotiation. But there are numerous examples in the WPC's own literature of discrepancies between this objective and the policies pursued . . . for example its attitude to the situation in Kampuchea and Afghanistan, condemned in the General Assembly resolutions . . . as a blatant case of foreign armed intervention'.

There was more to come: 'ECOSOC . . . demands that organisations in consultative status should be of a representative character. The spokesman for the WPC has said that his organisation represents hundreds of millions of people. The World Parliament of Peoples for Peace is presented as a kind of rival to the United Nations itself. However the grand facade of the WPC is no more substantial than a Hollywood film set. The great majority of delegates at . . . the World Parliament came from a very small group of countries, whose governments share the same political complexion; in many countries the ... membership amounts to no more than a handful of individuals on the fringe of the political spectrum of their own country. Delegates at the WPC's congresses who hold independent views find that they are given little opportunity to air those views. . . . There is a curious inconsistency in the way the WPC pursues (its) objectives of disarmament and detente. It vigorously attacks the defence policies of the United States and of its allies in Europe and elsewhere, as for example in its campaign against the deployment by NATO of Theatre Nuclear Forces in Europe. But the literature makes no reference . . . to the steady build up of missiles targetted on Europe, which has made that policy necessary. The WPC campaigns for the reduction of military budgets. But it makes no mention of one country among the major military powers which spends a higher proportion of its resources on armaments than any other. The reason for this selectivity lies in the nature of the WPC's relationship with that major power. As Romesh Chandra, president of the WPC, has stated: 'the Soviet Union invariably supports the peace movement. The WPC in its turn positively reacts to all Soviet initiatives in international affairs.'

The British delegation concluded by declaring its belief 'that the true objective of the WPC is a one-sided effort to promote disarmament in those countries ... where public opinion is capable of affecting defence policies and expenditure levels, while Governments which are immune from public pressure continue to build up their military strength. The WPC is a disguised instrument of one country's foreign policy. It is a wolf in sheep's clothing and its clothing has begun to look threadbare. . . . The UK delegation considers that the withdrawal by the WPC of its application amounts to an admission'.[7]

Commenting on the same resolution 1296 (XLIV), the US delegation added that 'the WPC, as a Non-Governmental Organisation, in plain language, is a sham. . . . It claimed to be an organisation with a structure, but cannot control itself. It admitted to have deceived this Committee by not declaring vast amounts of financial resources from various sources. . . . Its "audited" budget was audited by the organisation itself. . . . The organisation claims to be committed to laudable aims and goals of the United Nations while at the same time it ignores the serious decisions of the United Nations in many areas of its concern, e.g.

its President is reported in one of its publications as having conferred upon Mr Heng Samrin an award saying: "The conferment of this award is the recognition by the world of the existence of the State of Kampuchea" – this in direct contradiction of the United Nations decisions. In summary, the WPC . . . has all the characteristics and complete profile of a propagandistic extension of a particular government or group of governments'.

One year later the UN was preoccupied by the Argentine invasion of the Falklands Islands and its grave international consequencies. It only took one month after the Argentine invasion of the Falklands Islands in April 1982 for the front organisations, unabashed by previous rebuffs at the UN, to go into action. In the first week of May, the WPC gave the lead by calling on the UN to promote a peaceful settlement of the dispute reflecting the UN's stand on decolonisation and based on the return of 'the Malvinas' to Argentina, as urged by the Non-Aligned countries and supported by the WPC's so-called World Parliament of the Peoples for Peace in Sofia in 1980. Immediately thereafter, the WFTU appealed to workers to act resolutely 'to stop British imperialism's colonial war adventure in the South Atlantic'. On 14 May, the IADL said that 'the dispute . . . should be resolved by recognising Argentina's sovereignty while safeguarding the islanders' interests'. On 24 May, the Czech newsagency reported a statement from the International Organisation of Journalists in Prague condemning the 'dangerous imperialist conspiracy which aimed to establish a military pact in the South Atlantic as an extended arm of NATO'. In June, Romesh Chandra, the WPC President, cabled the secretary-general of the UN 'to prevent the further deterioration of the situation . . . and to guarantee a peaceful solution through negotiations on the basis of relevant UN resolutions on the Malvinas'. And in a subsequent statement the WPC declared that the British Government was seeking through the use of military power to 'revive the days of gunboat diplomacy and the imposition of its colonial rule by force'.

THE WIDER INFLUENCE OF THE WPC

The WPC also influences a number of bodies which are not in themselves front organisations – or even 'fronts for fronts' – but which play an important part in the formation of world public opinion. This influence is exercised by leading WPC members who secure key appointments in these other bodies.

One such body which is not an international front organisation is the Generals for Peace and Disarmament, originally launched in 1981. Certain retired senior officers who recently held high level appointments in NATO countries support this body (see Appendix IV). Of the nine retired officers originally associated with it, one, da Costa Gomes (Portuguese President 1974–76) is a WPC Vice-President, another, Koumanakos (Greece), was elected to the WPC Presidential Committee in 1983, and two others, Pasti (former president of the superior council of the Italian Armed Forces) and Sanguinetti (former Deputy Chief of the French Naval Staff) are WPC officials.

In May 1981, five generals (da Costa Gomes, Meyenfeldt (Netherlands), Koumanakos, Bastian (West Germany) and Pasti) issued an appeal in Bonn urging the leaders of 33 European nations and of the US and Canada – in other words of the countries that had signed the 1975 Helsinki Declaration – 'to stop the arms race and convene a new European conference to discuss disarmament measures'.[8] Admirals Lee (US) and Sanguinetti, General von Baudissin (West Germany) and Brigadier Harbottle (UK) issued separate statements called for an end to the arms race and 'urging NATO's present chiefs to return to sanity and negotiations to ensure security and peace'. In November 1981, a memorandum also demanding an end to the arms race and nuclear confrontation was issued in the Hague by seven former senior officers excluding Admiral Lee and General von Baudissin but including a new name, General Johan Christie (Norway).

On 4 June 1982, three more names were listed as members of this group. In a joint memorandum issued in Bonn on the eve of the Second United Nations Special Session on Disarmament, Generals Antonios Papaspirou and Michaelis Tombopoulos (Greece), and Günter Vollmer (FRG) joined nine others to assert that 'peace can only be maintained, and the level of military confrontation be reduced, if agreements on limitation and a reduction in nuclear arms are effected'.[9] After a meeting in Vienna in January 1983, attended by six of the 13 members of the Group, the Generals published a booklet entitled *10 Questions Answered* giving the views of those present on the NATO plans for INF deployment. The case made against these plans contained many of the inaccuracies and much of the dubious argumentation familiar from Soviet propaganda.

At a press conference on 24 January, after their Vienna meeting, the generals made a strong collective attack on NATO's decision to station cruise and Pershing II missiles in Western Europe. They welcomed the Declaration issued by the Warsaw Pact Summit meeting in Prague on 5 January and the disarmament proposals contained in it.[10] They claimed that the US was 'trying to make Europe a front line in a war against Communism, and thereby avoid the direct destruction of America'. A further conference in Vienna, in May 1984, was held, for the first time, jointly with eight Warsaw Pact generals. After the conference, Vladislav Kornilenko, the Secretary of the Soviet Peace Committee, who was also present, commented that 'the aims of the group [generals for Peace and Disarmament] . . . are identical to those of the Soviet Peace Movement'.[11]

6 The International Department of the Soviet Communist Party and Related KGB Activities

Despite the diversity of their propaganda, the basic thrust of any campaign mounted by the international front organisations is decided in a centralised manner at the summit of Soviet policy making. To understand the role of these organisations in Soviet foreign policy, some knowledge is required of the Soviet control mechanisms as exercised through the International Department of the Central Committee of the CPSU. In this connection, it should be remembered that policy-making takes place at the highest levels of the CPSU. The Soviet government itself, including the Soviet Ministry of Foreign Affairs, is no more than the most important 'transmission belt' (in the Leninist sense). The Party is supreme in all matters. Furthermore the propaganda and political work of the international front organisations is but one part of an intricate and highly coordinated effort involving senior levels of the Soviet Party, the Soviet Government, and the Soviet intelligence services. It is thus in the context of the highest Soviet foreign policy formulation that these organisations' work must be seen. Subject only to the Politburo itself, the CPSU's International Department is principally responsible for the formulation of this policy.

As one of the more than 20 departments of the Central Committee which service the Politburo and represent the most influential of the permanent policy-making staff, it is commonly believed to be the department responsible for relations with non-ruling communist parties. In fact it has much wider responsibilities.[1]

The International Department (ID) is one of the lineal

descendants of the Third International – the Comintern whose foundation by Lenin in 1919 was described in Chapter 3 and which, after directing the international Communist movement as Stalin's most powerful overseas instrument throughout the 1930s was dissolved by the latter, as a gesture of goodwill towards his wartime allies, in 1943. In practice, Soviet control over national Communist Parties was by then so complete that the organisation's continuance was unnecessary. With the coming of the Cold War and with the CPSU reverting to many of its older exclusive slogans, the Comintern was in effect revived as the Communist Information Bureau (or Cominform) on 6 October 1947. Its purpose was to reassert Moscow's firm ideological control and to ensure coordination of all political activities in the struggle against imperialism, of which the American offer of economic assistance to Europe (the Marshall Plan) earlier in the year was seen as the latest manifestation. Its original members were the Communist parties of the USSR, Poland, Czechoslovakia, Bulgaria, Hungary, Romania, Yugoslavia, France and Italy. Its original headquarters were in Belgrade, but they were moved to Bucharest after the expulsion of Yugoslavia from the organisation in June 1948. Subsequently in the changed political climate the Cominform was itself dissolved in 1956. Its functions reverted to the powerful Foreign Affairs department of the CPSU Central Committee which had been founded after the dissolution of the earlier Comintern in 1943.

After assuming a variety of overseas activities, the position of the Foreign Affairs Department was rationalised in the mid-1950s by splitting it into three separate departments, two of them with a distinct technical function: a department for relations with the Communist Parties of the Soviet Bloc, and a department for Cadres Abroad (closely linked to the Committee for State Security – the KGB) which is responsible for cells inside foreign missions, and for supervising party discipline. After the establishment of these two new departments of the Central Committee, the core of the Foreign Affairs Department remained with a third, the International Department. Its head, Boris Ponomarev, described by Khrushchev as 'that relic of the Comintern' (he worked on its Executive Committee from 1937 to 1943), has been continuously in charge of the department since its inception.

Ponomarev headed the group of academics who produced the official textbook on the *History of the CPSU* in 1959 and the *History of the Foreign Policy of the USSR* in 1976. He wrote a long article for *Pravda* in April 1950 on the 30th anniversary of the publication of 'Left-wing Communism, An Infantile Disorder', pointing to the continued relevance of Lenin's 'principles of strategy and tactics which demanded that, in carrying out their policy, Communists should combine the strictest fidelity to the ideas of communism with a readiness to use roundabout ways of achieving their objectives'.[2] This was the context in which the postwar international front organisations were established.

Effective CPSU control over all branches of Soviet policy is primarily achieved by the 24 departments of the Central Committee, which work under the aegis of the Secretariat, and hence of the General Secretary (Chernenko). Each of them is headed by a senior party official. They prepare the briefs and assess information for the Politburo, in theory the executive body of the Central Committee but in practice the centre of all political power in the Soviet Union. The General Secretary, who controls the activities of the Central Committee's departments through his subordinate secretaries, is chairman of the Politburo. A complete system for the effective exercise of CPSU control over policy is thus provided by the combination of a general secretary, secretaries (most of whom are themselves members or candidate members of the Politburo) and heads of departments and their staffs. Although Government ministers, with their own departments, participate in the formulation of policy, the influence of the party organisation on policy is much greater than that of the corresponding departments of the government machine headed by the Council of Ministers. This is true of the ID, and was reinforced in 1973 when Gromyko, as Minister for Foreign Affairs, became a full member of the Politburo and thus was able to pull senior party rank over the head of the ID, Ponomarev, who had become only a candidate (non-voting) member of the Politburo in 1972. But even then Mikhail Suslov, who was considerably senior to Gromyko in Politburo ranking, was in overall charge of foreign policy and propaganda (including the work of the international front organisations) at the Politburo level. Suslov had been head of *Agitprop*, the CPSU department responsible for laying down the party line and for publicising it, from November 1947 to July 1948. He was one of the five Central Committee Secretaries in 1947 and was one of the three Soviet delegates who signed the declaration expelling Tito from the Cominform. He became a member of Stalin's last Praesidium (Politburo) in 1952 and was, until his death in January 1982, the senior member of the Politburo by length of service.

The status of the officials of the ID indicates that its functions extend well beyond the supervision of relations with non-ruling Communist parties. Ponomarev himself has collected many important appointments. He has been a secretary of the CPSU since 1961 and a full member of the Academy of Sciences since 1962 and it is perhaps significant that he became a candidate member of the Politburo in 1972. He has been for many years chairman of the Foreign Affairs Commission of one of the chambers of the Supreme Soviet. His first deputy is Vadim Zagladin, a Western European specialist who had editorial experience on *New Times* and has worked at the Institute of World Economy and International Relations (IMEMO). His other deputies include Vitaly Shaposhnikov (see Chapter 5), R. A. Ulyanovsky, a former professor and deputy director of IMEMO who is an expert on 'liberation movements'; and specialists on the Middle East and Latin America (K. N. Brutents), on Africa (P. I. Manchka), on the English speaking countries (A. S. Chernyaev) and on Japan and South East Asia (I. I. Kovalenko).

This variety of specialist interests among Ponomarev's deputies corresponds to the different areas of the world to which the officials of the ID devote their time. They extend much more widely than would be required by mere liaison duties with non-ruling Communist parties. A study of their activities in recent years as reported in the Soviet press, such as visits abroad and meeting foreign delegations at home, show that their interests extend to Europe, USA, Africa and the Near and Middle East, to countries in which no Communist party exists, and to circumstances where relations with a local Communist party are irrelevant.

The ID is distinctive in its authority and its power as well as its leadership. It has consultants and can call on the services of the various research institutes attached to the Soviet Academy of Sciences, such as IMEMO, headed by Alexander Yakovlev, and the Institute for the US and Canada, headed by Georgi Arbatov. Both were elected full members of the CPSU Central Committee at the 26th Party Congress in February 1981 and both work closely with the ID. Arbatov's institute has a department dealing with military, political and disarmament problems, while

IMEMO has a 'European Security Sector', headed by Professor Daniel Proektor, another frequent 'peace emissary' who has often visited London and Paris. During late 1979, as the campaign against NATO's new nuclear weapons was gathering momentum, Professor Proektor addressed a foreign affairs study group in Hamburg, emphasising Soviet concern over the proposals to install GLCMs in Western Europe. Georgi Arbatov has also made frequent and often important appearances on American, West German and British television and given press interviews, arguing the case against NATO nuclear modernisation. He is a regular visitor to and lecturer in Western countries, including the United Kingdom. On 16 March 1981 he was in Bonn for a press conference to launch his book *The Soviet Standpoint: the USSR's Policy Towards the West*, at which he denied assertions that the USSR was seeking military superiority over the West. Arbatov was also a member of the Olaf Palme Commission on Disarmament and Security Issues, whose report was published shortly before the UN Special Session on Disarmament in June 1982.

The ID is also responsible for the *World Marxist Review*, the official mouthpiece of Soviet ideology abroad which is published in Prague. By contrast, the Ministry of Foreign Affairs cannot match the International Department in its prestige, access to research equipment and – most of all – its political muscle; this is particularly evident in the ID's control, with the Cadres Abroad Department, over appointments and promotions in the Soviet foreign service, as well as in the fact that it maintains its own representatives in important Soviet embassies abroad. Because of their function of liaison with local Communist parties and pro-Soviet organisations, these representatives enjoy a virtually independent status.

Working in close coordination with the ID is the CPSU's International Information Department (IID), formed in 1978. The IID is headed by the former *Tass* Director-General, Leonid Zamyatin, a full member of the CPSU Central Committee. Its first deputy head was Valentin Falin, former Soviet Ambassador to Bonn who became a political commentator on *Izvestiya* in 1983. The IID supervises *Tass* and the Soviet features agency *Novosti*, as well as all foreign affairs news in the Soviet press, Moscow Radio's external services, 'non-official' Soviet radio stations mainly aimed at Third World countries (e.g. *Radio Peace and Progress*) and clandestine 'black' radio stations operating from the Soviet

Union, such as the *National Voice of Iran*, and *Radio Ba Yi*, which poses as a Chinese station representing Chinese political dissidents.

Apart from the ID and the IID, the KGB is also involved in Soviet 'peace' campaigning through its *Service A*, or Disinformation Department, which is part of the KGB's First Chief Directorate (Foreign Intelligence). Service A has the responsibility for those covert special operations which are termed 'Active Measures'. This work includes the circulation of forgeries, including disinformation aimed at foreign governments and their decision-making process, and sometimes more open propaganda deception aimed at public opinion in the target country.[3]

To the Russians, 'disinformation' has long been an established technique. They are its leading exponents, as reflected in the recent adoption into English of the word, which derived from the Russian word *dezinformatsia*. *Dezinformatsia* is defined in the Soviet Shorter Political Dictionary as 'the deliberate dissemination of false and provocative information'. It includes the use of true information in a tendentious way, with malign intent, and the exploitation of the fruits of other subversive activities such as provocation and compromise operations. Soviet diplomacy is conducted on a basis quite different from that of Western countries. In some Soviet missions intelligence officers may out-number their diplomatic service colleagues by as much as two to one; the emphasis is on intelligence gathering and subversion, in which disinformation plays a considerable part.

Disinformation operations are therefore part of Soviet activities directed against the non-Communist world, and are coordinated with such other techniques as diplomatic negotiations, economic and military aid, press and radio propaganda and subversion through Communist parties and front organisations.

The range of disinformation operations is wide. Its principal aims are to undermine confidence between non-Communist countries and to weaken the cohesion of NATO, especially the ties between the United States and its European allies; to create misleading impressions of the intentions of the Soviet Union, which are not consistent with their real policies as demonstrated by their actions; to channel the activities of genuine Western critics of their government policies into directions which best serve Soviet purposes; and to discredit Western individuals and groups considered harmful to Soviet interests.

What is certain is that the Russians think it valuable, and are giving it even greater priority now than previously. With the increase of regular contacts between individuals and organisations in the West and their putative counterparts in the Soviet Union and its Communist allies, disinformation has become less readily detectable, easier to spread and more likely to be believed.

Two historic examples which illustrate the early use of these techniques are worth recalling. One belongs to the period of the Second World War, when the Russians succeeded in keeping the considerable army of Soviet deserters led by General Vlasov out of active service in the German army by planting on the Germans, through a high-level double agent in the confidence of the German High Command, the false information that Vlasov was under Russian control. To establish confidence in the double agent they went to the length of feeding through him to the Germans genuine military intelligence, which led to the loss of thousands of Russian troops, particularly in the Ukraine.

The second example, from the 1920s, concerns The Trust, a spurious opposition movement which the Russian authorities successfully launched and which built up extensive contacts with Western diplomatic and intelligence circles and with emigré groups. Once these channels were established they were used primarily to neutralise emigré opposition, but they were also useful for obtaining intelligence from the West, influencing the West into believing that Bolshevism no longer constituted a serious threat and luring several Western agents and emigré Russians to their deaths in the Soviet Union. It has been estimated that in the early twenties one in four of Russia's emigrés were controlled by the OGPU, forerunner of the KGB. Though successful, The Trust was eventually exposed and was wound up in 1926.

Subsequently the OGPU made alternative arrangements for maintaining contact with its opponents in exile. These continued throughout the 1930s and beyond; indeed the KGB carries on the work to this day, most notably by its longstanding attempts to infiltrate the emigré organisation known as the NTS (*Narodnoi Turdovoi Soyuz* or Popular Labour Alliance). NTS, which has its headquarters in Frankfurt (West Germany) and representatives throughout the West, is very active and dedicated in its attempts to influence developments inside the Soviet Union. In practice, the KGB try to use it as a listening post inside the groups in the

West which are engaged in fomenting opposition to Soviet Communism.

There are many other examples of Soviet disinformation activities since 1945. Detailed accounts of several of them are contained in a recent book on the KGB.[4] A frequent ploy is to circulate among Western journalists and others forged documents, purporting to be purloined secret NATO correspondence or US Government documents of various kinds, with the object of confusing and, if possible, sowing dissension among NATO members. A recent example was a letter purporting to have been written by General Alexander Haig, then Supreme Allied Commander Europe, to the NATO Secretary-General, Dr Joseph Luns, on 26 June 1979. After rehearsing the importance of countering Allied hesitation over the forthcoming NATO decision on INF missile deployment and emphasising the relevance of this decision to plans for the 'first use' of nuclear weapons by NATO, the forged letter continued: 'If argument, persuasion and impacting the media fail, we are left with no alternative but to jolt the faint-hearted in Europe through the creation of situations, country by country as deemed necessary to convince them where their interests lie. This would call for appropriate and effective action of a sensitive nature which we have frequently discussed. ... To this end your authority and your active assistance, especially in the Netherlands, can hardly be overestimated.' Following several months' circulation of the continent of Europe during 1982, this letter was reproduced in facsimile by London's Young Communist League in February 1983 as part of the campaign to stop INF deployment,[5] even though it had been officially denounced as a forgery nine months earlier by NATO. Another case was the attempt, by means of forged cables purporting to have been sent by the US Embassy in Rome in August and December 1982, to demonstrate that the accusation that the Bulgarian secret service (and behind them the KGB) was responsible for the assassination attempt on the Pope in May 1981 was fabricated by the CIA. The forged documents, attributed to reputable but anonymous sources, were published in the Rome left-wing weekly, *Pace e Guerra*, on 21 July 1983. The US Embassy immediately pointed to major errors in the format of the published versions of the cables as evidence that they were forgeries. They were nevertheless used as the basis for a report in the London *Morning Star*, 21 September 1983, which claimed that the CIA were responsible for the fabricated charges brought against the Bulgarian agent, Sergei Antonov.

An example of another type of deception propaganda used by the USSR in the context of 'peace' campaigns was the surfacing during 1980 of alleged 'US war plans' based on contingency documents. These had been stolen by an American KGB agent in Paris in the early 1960s. The Soviet press reported these as evidence of a US *decision* to launch nuclear war. These documents, circulated in several West European countries, illustrate the extent to which the campaigns of the international front organisations have to be seen in the context of the Soviet propaganda effort as a whole.

In order to allow Service A of the KGB's First Chief Directorate the fullest opportunities to pursue its objectives, it is given right of access to files on all KGB agents and operations abroad. This means that agents, particularly those at a high level, can be used not only to provide secret information but also to act as agents of influence in propagating ideas or promoting policies. Western journalists writing on Communist affairs include some individuals whose connections with the Soviet intelligence are so close that, even if they do not take an openly pro-Soviet line, Soviet control over them often seems likely. The Russian drive to recruit new agents for disinformation purposes is intense and continuous. Particular attention is paid to diplomats and journalists resident in Moscow and to politicians, scientists, arms control and disarmament experts, businessmen and students who visit the Soviet Union. The attempt to subvert Western nationals in the Soviet Union, where conditions are most favourable to the Soviet intelligence, is supplemented by the efforts of the thousands of Soviet intelligence representatives operating in the non-Communist world. Apart from those filling appointments in Embassies and other recognised 'official' bodies, the news agencies such as Tass and Novosti are represented abroad very largely by intelligence officers.

There is also recent evidence that KGB officers have been identified as infiltrating 'peace organisations'. In October 1981, Vladimir Merkulov, a Second Secretary at the Soviet Embassy in Copenhagen, and Valentin Kuznetsov, the Cultural Attaché, and other colleagues were expelled from Denmark for their involvement with the Cooperation Committee for Peace and Security, founded in Copenhagen in 1974 after a WPC Congress in Moscow in 1973. The Cooperation Committee had invited Soviet lecturers to address Danish schools and teachers training colleges on such themes as opposition to Denmark's membership of NATO and support for a 'Nordic nuclear-free zone'. In January 1981, Merkulov's predecessor, Stanislav Chebotok, who had been transferred to Oslo, was publicly named as a KGB agent in the newspaper *Verdens Gang*. (Subsequently in January 1984, Chebotok was expelled from Oslo with four other Russians. The Norwegians described the senior of those expelled as generally regarded as running the embassy and 'outranking even the ambassador'). In June 1981 it became known that a Norwegian 'peace' organisation, Art for Peace, had also organised a meeting at the People's House in Oslo, using funds from the Soviet Embassy. In April 1981, the Netherlands Government expelled the *Tass* representative, Vadim Vasilyevich Leonov, subsequently identified as a KGB officer on 15 July in *Reformatorisch Dagblad*, which claimed that his main assignment had been to maintain contact with the leaders of the Dutch anti-nuclear movement.

This activity has not been confined to NATO countries. In April 1983, the Swiss Government expelled the Novosti (Soviet news agency) correspondent in Berne, Alexei Dumov, and closed the local Novosti Office, on the grounds of repeated and serious interference in Swiss internal affairs. The case against Dumov was his close involvement in the Swiss peace movement, including the organisation of demonstrations, drafting appeals and collection of signatures. A KGB officer, Leonid Ovchinnikov, serving as a First Secretary in the Soviet Mission in Geneva, who was said to be responsible for supervising Dumov's activities, was expelled at the same time.

THE DOCTRINAL FRAMEWORK

In order to meet the requirements of Soviet foreign policy, the international front organisations have to adapt themselves to evolving Soviet doctrine. Hence the significance of the ideological pronouncements of Ponomarev and his first deputy, Zagladin, who have played a key role in Soviet foreign policy and, particularly, in the policy of *détente*. This became apparent in the early 1970s with the rapid decline of Soviet authority over the

Communist parties of Italy, France and Spain when these parties attempted to efface their past subservience to Soviet interests.

Signs of trouble first became visible at the international conference of Communist parties held in 1969 in Moscow. Although the Soviet Union was generally successful in this motley assembly in securing broad agreement for its policies, a certain amount of criticism was expressed over its invasion of Czechoslovakia in 1968 and it completely failed to obtain any condemnation of China. The principal theme of the document finally adopted was the need for unity in the face of 'imperialism'. Three of the main elements in the basic doctrine closely followed the traditional Soviet line: 'proletarian internationalism', which since Stalin's day had meant one thing only, putting the interests of the Soviet Union first; unity with socialists, provided they renounced adherence to class collaboration – that is, for practical purposes, became Communists; and 'peaceful coexistence', which in no way inhibits either Soviet support for 'liberation movements' abroad or the development of the class struggle. But, reading between the lines, it was already clear in 1969 that many Communist parties were resistant to the dominant role which the Soviet Union was trying to maintain.

In an analytical article in *Kommunist*, September 1971, Ponomarev listed the main sins of revisionism from which, according to him, some parties still suffered. These were the 'right deviations' – denial of the importance of the class struggle or of the dictatorship of the proletariat; denial of the leading role of the working class (i.e. the Communist Party); emphasis on parliamentary as against mass struggle, and hostile criticism of the Soviet Union. The sins of 'the left' were rejection of the need for a broad, democratic programme; the isolation of Communists; adventurism; too much stress on armed struggle and repudiation or distortion of the principle of peaceful coexistence. He also attacked 'one-sided' stress on independence without due regard to 'proletarian internationalism'. At that time, the full meaning of the Soviet policy of peaceful coexistence was not yet apparent even to some Western Communists. At that stage few of them suspected that their expectation of Soviet support for revolution abroad was likely to be sacrificed to immediate Soviet interests in its dealings with the West. But it was a different matter when the agreements with the US were announced with much publicity in 1972. Hence the need for Brezhnev's assurance in June 1972 –

following the signing of the SALT I agreement – that *détente* with the West 'in no way signified the end of the ideological struggle . . . on the contrary, we should be prepared for its intensification'.

During 1974, however, it became apparent that the Soviet policy of *détente* and in particular what was understood to be its underlying purpose – the urgent Soviet need for US and Western European technology, credits and grain – was causing grave suspicion of Soviet motives, notably in the Spanish Communist party. This explained the attack against Azcarate, the leading Spanish Communist ideologist, in the official journal of the Central Committee of the CPSU for alleging that there was a contradiction between the state interests of the socialist countries and the interests of the revolutionary movement; for refusing to recognise that peaceful coexistence created a better environment for advancing revolution than the Cold War; for opposing the forthcoming conference of European Communist parties, and for stressing the independence of individual Communist parties without recognising the overriding importance of proletarian internationalism.

The same year Ponomarev published a key article in *Problems of Peace and Socialism* on 'the World Situation and the Revolutionary Process' which was directed at Western Communist parties. He argued that *détente* was advantageous to revolutionary prospects because it also undermined the militaristic preparations of 'the imperialist powers' and strengthened 'realistically minded elements within the bourgeosie'. The article emphasised the duty to combat anti-Sovietism and to show complete loyalty to proletarian internationalism. At the same time, Zagladin was emphasising the importance of resisting the illusion that *détente* meant class peace.

Despite these efforts, by the time the much delayed conference of European Communist parties met in June 1976, the disagreements between the CPSU and its major European partners had not been resolved. In particular, it was evident that the latter would not follow the lines laid down for the conference by Ponomarev. He had suggested, at a preparatory meeting in Warsaw in 1974, that the Conference should adopt a document stressing that the progress of socialism in Europe was due to Soviet foreign policy and especially the policy of *détente*; the need to combat the main tool of 'imperialism', which was anti-Sovietism; and active resistance to Chinese attacks on proletarian internationalism, 'our unique weapon in the struggle against imperialism'. In the *World Marxist Review*, January 1975, he had argued that the 'world correlation of forces' had made it possible to shift the main thrust of action from the Third World to Europe. This was 'due to *détente*'. At a further preparatory meeting in Budapest in December 1975 he had stressed that economic relations between the Soviet Union and the capitalist powers did not strengthen the latter; that there was no incompatibility between *détente* and the class struggle, and that proletarian internationalism had grown even more important when so many divergent international situations existed in the different countries of the Western world. Zagladin later declared that the Helsinki Conference on Security and Cooperation in Europe, 1975, was a triumph of Soviet foreign policy which made the West realise that the Cold War was no longer possible. Even on the eve of the 25th Congress of the CPSU, at which the French and Italian delegates reasserted their claims to pursue independent policies, Zagladin could write that 'we are for diversity . . . but in a way which precludes any possibility of the essentials being discarded'.

In the event the essentials were discarded when the European Communist parties' conference finally met in Berlin in June 1976. It produced a document which contained no mention of the vital Soviet formula, proletarian internationalism; no condemnation of anti-Sovietism; no acceptance of the Soviet demand for the hegemony of the Communist party in alliances with socialist parties; and an almost unqualified endorsement of the human rights resolutions of the Helsinki Final Act, without the customary Soviet qualification about non-interference in internal affairs.

The ID had plainly faltered in its control over the major Western European parties. It had notably failed to remove their fears that the Soviet Union was ready to sacrifice their revolutionary prospects to its short-term economic requirements of credits, technology and grain. If, however, *détente* and proletarian internationalism had been hard to sell to Berlinguer in Italy, to Carillo in Spain and to Marchais in France, no such problems arose with Romesh Chandra. During a Latin American tour in December 1976, the president of the World Peace Council stated that '*détente* means essentially a change in the balance of forces in the world in favour of peace and against imperialism. . . . There is a wrong idea that *détente* means lessening the struggle against imperialism: *détente* means the intensification of the struggle'.[6]

International front organisations are used to exploit what Ponomarev has described as the 'new forms of struggle with greater possibilities', for example in their campaign against NATO's nuclear modernisation. In an article in *Kommunist* in 1977, he set out his plans: 'International developments of the past few months have shown that the development of *détente* is grounded in powerful objective tendencies, that *détente* has sunk deep roots in present day international life and that in this area there are now considerable reserves of strength. The wave of mass protests against the production of the neutron bomb has demonstrated the hollowness of the imperialist propagandists' calculation that people have 'grown used' to living with a nuclear sword of Damocles hanging over their heads and that alarm over the threat of nuclear war seems to have diminished. ... Realistically-minded circles in a number of capitalist countries acknowledge the peaceful character of the foreign policy pursued by the socialist countries and are prepared to oppose the cold war demagogues. ... It must be emphasised that words alone cannot halt the production of neutron bombs or cruise missiles. Words will not stop the spread of nuclear weapons. What is needed is vigorous, militant and determined action.'[7]

At one time it looked as if the failure of the ID to enforce its control over those Western Communist parties which had asserted their independence might not matter very much. One of the principal rebels – the French Communist Party – has in effect lost interest in the Eurocommunist argument. Evidently the CPSU still retained sufficient means of control over it to ensure that result. On questions of foreign policy, too, all Communist parties tend to support the Soviet line, even if they remain critical over its policy in Afghanistan and Poland. But by 1982 a more serious rift appeared between the Soviet Union and some Western Communist parties, especially the Italian. The danger was the intention of the so-called 'Euro-Communist parties', led by the Italians, to urge nuclear disarmament in the Warsaw Pact countries as well as in the NATO area. This was not at all in line with Soviet policy, which is to put the blame squarely on the West for the arms race and therefore to insist that the primary responsibility for disarmament does not lie with Moscow.

MECHANISMS OF CONTROL

Such is the institutional and doctrinal framework of the International Department. How is its detailed, tactical control exercised over the international front organisations? First, such 'mass organisations' as the Soviet Peace Committee and national 'peace committees' (or their equivalent) in most countries of Eastern and Western Europe, are affiliated to the World Peace Council or some other international front organisation. These bodies then send large delegations to each congress, conference or executive meeting of the front organisation in question. The predominance of 'mass' Soviet membership inside each of the major international front organisations determines the outcome of any 'democratic election' of officials and thus ensures Soviet influence on the attitude of each front organisation. Thus, although the WFTU, for example, claims a membership of over 190 million, some 107 million come from the USSR, and about 90 per cent of the total represents trade union organisations from countries within the Soviet sphere. The same applies to the WFDY, which claims a membership of 150 million in 110 countries, with the bulk of the members from Communist countries, and to the IUS, which boasts of 10 million members in 118 member organisations, the great majority of them being in Communist countries. (The WPC, which claims affiliates in some 135 countries, does not publish membership figures.)

A second means of control is by seconding officials of the ID to the headquarters of the various front organisations. For some years, for example, ID representatives have worked closely with the WPC secretariat. Those of its members playing key roles within the WPC include Vitaly Shaposhnikov, and Oleg Kharkhardin, vice-chairman of the Soviet Peace Committee, who is also general secretary of the ILF of Peace Forces, a WPC subsidiary based in Helsinki.

These officials were named in a report on Soviet propaganda quoted by a US Congressional committee in July 1978.[8] Referring to the relationship between these officials and the WPC president, Romesh Chandra, the report noted that an unnamed 'representative of the International Department of the Soviet Communist Party has for years sat at Chandra's side, in a background role, but holding ultimate control'. The report also noted that 'by maintaining control over key WPC officials, the USSR commands the content of the communiques, resolutions and statements which issue from WPC events, and directs the final decision on WPC projects and activities'.

Although opposition to Soviet domination erupts on occasions, trusted leaders are usually able to confine it to private meetings of commissions or sub-commissions. At several meetings in 1977, beginning with the World Forum of Peace Forces in Moscow in January, non-Communist participants embarrassed Soviet representatives by asking pointed questions about human rights violations in the USSR. But opposition views seldom emerge at large-scale public gatherings. Dissenting views, if they exist, are ignored; for example, the Soviet human rights activist, Andrei Sakharov, sent a message to a WPC-sponsored 'forum on disarmament' held in York in 1976, but it was not read to delegates, as requested, because, according to the organisers, it was too long, too late and of a 'different nature' from other messages. Two Soviet delegates threatened to walk out if it was read.[9]

Visits by senior officials of the International Department provide a third means of control. Between 1970 and 1973, Ponomarev's foreign engagements took him repeatedly to the Near and Middle East, France, West Germany, Canada and the United States. He was received by the President in Washington and attended a dinner for the United States President in Moscow. He visited Britain in October–November 1976 at the invitation of the Labour Party and in the same year addressed a delegation of United States senators. In January 1978, he was a member of a delegation of Soviet Parliamentarians to Washington and attended the first meeting of the WPC Presidential Committee to be held in the US, which prepared the way for the creation of the WPC-affiliated 'US Peace Council' in November 1979. He also made a special visit to Italy to promote Soviet opposition to NATO's modernisation proposals, and in December 1980 he and Zagladin were in France, where they criticised the French Government's programme to develop the 'neutron bomb'. In October 1979, Zagladin attended the Anti-NATO Conference, sponsored by the ICESC, a subsidiary of the WPC, at de Haan in Belgium; afterwards he led a Soviet delegation into the Second Chamber of the Dutch Parliament to lobby against the proposals to modernise NATO's INF. The senior staff of *Pravda* also work closely with the ID; indeed its chief editor, V. G. Afanasiev, who is a member of the CPSU Central Committee, has been a regular participant at meetings of the WPC, of which his paper's political observer, G. A. Zhukov, is on the Presidential Committee.

Another time-honoured Soviet practice has been to employ, in a similar capacity, well-known Soviet writers, intellectuals and journalists as 'peace emissaries' to support and advance the work of front organisations. In 1948, Alexander Fadeyev, the novelist, gave the keynote speech at the launching of the World Congress of Intellectuals for Peace at Wroclaw and, in the 1950s, Ilya Ehrenburg was a regular speaker at peace conferences. More recently Anatoly Karpov, the Soviet international chess champion, became chairman of the Soviet Peace Fund, the source of financial backing for many international front organisation events. Today the role of such Soviet travellers has been refined. Apart from specific campaign issues – whether it be the 'neutron bomb' or cruise missiles – Soviet peace emissaries always stress that *détente* must continue. They may imply that there are hawks and doves even inside the Kremlin and that Western concessions must be made on substantive issues, so that the hawks may be defeated in the interests of peace. The work of such visiting Soviet emissaries, like the activities of the Soviet journalist Victor Louis and others, is less propaganda for public consumption than high-level disinformation intended to influence Western élites.

7 Campaigns Against NATO

Many of the front organisations' long-standing techniques have been deployed in their current anti-NATO modernisation and anti-nuclear weapons campaigns. But the methods employed have become more sophisticated to appeal as widely as possible to Western public opinion, with the obvious intention of exploiting the genuine element of pacifism, distrust of all things nuclear and impatience at the lack of progress over arms control which inspire the anti-nuclear movements outside their immediate control. Continuous repetition of the argument that NATO's nuclear modernisation would create a new and dangerous phase of the arms race has caused many people not normally sympathetic to echo the Soviet claims. The greatest advantage derived by the Soviet Union from its activities has been to force NATO governments on to the defensive with public opinion in their own countries. So the justification for NATO's collective response to what was originally a Soviet nuclear build-up – the deployment of the SS-20s – has had to be provided against a background of opposition often ranging from scepticism to outright hostility. This chapter describes the activities of the international front organisations in the United States and in the United Kingdom, and ends with a general review of the involvement of these organisations in the anti-nuclear campaign in Europe in recent years.

THE UNITED STATES

The front organisations now operating in the US, under the guidance of the WPC in the current peace and disarmament campaigns first attracted public attention between 1966 and 1975 in the anti-Vietnam war movement. The National Mobilisation

Committee to End the War in Vietnam and its successors, the New Mobilisation Committee (New Mobe) and the People's Coalition for Peace and Justice, worked closely with American WPC officials, many of them Communists, who coordinated their activities in key cities and who travelled abroad to take part in WPC meetings. One such key city was Chicago, whose Peace Council comprised about 30 organisations, Communist and non-Communist. This council was run by a small group of six people, many of whom were to reappear in connection with other front activities: Sidney Lens, already an experienced activist; Dorothy Hayes, representing the WILPF, under strong Communist influence; Ben Friedlander, representing SANE (the National Committee for a Sane Nuclear Policy); and Eva Friedlander, representing the Chicago affiliate of Women Strike for Peace (WSP), the US affiliate of the WIDF, who coordinated American deserters from Vietnam in Sweden; Jack Spiegel and Sylvia Kushner. Five of the six were members of the Communist Party of the USA (CPUSA); Lens had been associated with a dissident Trotskyist group known as the Revolutionary Workers League.

Strong Communist influence was shown in the composition of the US delegation to the WPC's World Assembly of Peace in East Berlin in 1969. It included members of the Clergy and Laity Concerned (CALC) which had co-sponsored an anti-Vietnam war demonstration at the White House in 1967; other WSP and WILPF members; various quasi-religious groups including the Methodist Federation for Social Action, one of the CPUSA's oldest fronts; a substantial number of veteran Communists, including two US members of the WPC presidential Committee, Herbert Aptheker and Dr Carlton Goodlett; Barbara Bick of WSP, and Stanley Faulkner for the National Lawyers Guild, the US affiliate of the IADL. In May 1969, the Stockholm Conference on Vietnam Emergency Action emerged as one of the WPC's main instruments, and the 31 members of its International Liaison Committee, apart from the WPC President Romesh Chandra and Alexander Berkov of the Soviet Peace Committee, included Irving Sarnoff and Ronald Young, both officially representing the US New Mobilisation Committee (whose 'Fall Offensive' culminated in three days of riots in Washington in November 1969).

Another example of WPC influence over the anti-Vietnam war

movement in the US was in New Mobe's West Coast newsletter, February 1970, which referred to a meeting in Vancouver to discuss international cooperation to end the war in Vietnam. The Vancouver meeting had been initiated by Carlton Goodlett and Irving Sarnoff at a WPC meeting in Africa the previous month at which Romesh Chandra was present.[1]

After the victories of the North Vietnamese, Pathet Lao and Khmer Rouge, the WPC's New Stockholm Appeal in 1975 concentrated on 'a great new world-wide offensive against the arms race', harnessing the organisations built during the anti-Vietnam war agitation, to the new campaign. In September 1975, an eight-member WPC delegation, headed by Romesh Chandra and including the British MP, James Lamond, toured New York, Washington and eight other cities. The WPC's *Peace Courier* reported in November that in Washington the delegation had met some twenty members of the House of Representatives and the Senate. Accompanying the delegation on its tour were Karen Talbot, the WPC's chief representative at the United Nations in New York, Sylvia Kushner and Carlton Goodlett. That the WPC was also aiming at US religious leaders was shown by their contacts with Presbyterian, Lutheran and Methodist clergymen.

Thereafter the revived pro-Soviet 'peace movement' appeared to make little headway in the US until a meeting of the WPC Bureau, the first to be held on US soil, was convened in January 1978 in Washington. It was held in conjunction with a public conference entitled 'Dialogue on Disarmament and *Détente*', and immediately after the arrival on 22 January of Boris Ponomarev, head of the International Department of the CPSU, who on that occasion had gone to Washington as leader of a delegation of the Supreme Soviet. It was intended to bring pressure on Congress to stop development of the 'neutron bomb'. As Karen Talbot said, 'this is a very crucial moment in the Strategic Arms Limitation Talks. The neutron bomb is in limbo and the US participants in the meeting will raise the question of how to build stronger opposition to this and other weapons of mass destruction'. The *ad hoc* national committee set up for the WPC meeting included the late Abraham Feinglass, a vice-president of the WPC Praesidium and a CPUSA member, and Katherine Camp, international president of the WILPF.

The wide interest in the work of the WPC Bureau was indicated by the participation in the sessions and in special meetings inside the Congress itself of Bureau members with Representative John Conyers (since 1959 a member of the National Lawyers Guild). In June 1978 the WPC organised a meeting of parliamentarians in New York, ostensibly in support of the first UN Special Session on Disarmament. Its objective was met when the parliamentarians duly declared 'that the production of the neutron bomb accelerates, in a tragic fashion, the arms race . . . this meeting appeals to parliamentarians and all other elected representatives of the people to reject the fabrication and deployment of the neutron bomb'.[2]

Further signs of WPC influence in United States 'peace' campaigns were provided by the appearance of three WPC activists – Werner Rümpel, of the East German Peace Council, Nico Schouten, the Communist leader of the Dutch 'Initiative Group to Stop the Neutron Bomb' and Terry Provance, head of the American Friends Service Committee (AFSC) Disarmament Programme – at a demonstration in Washington sponsored by Mobilisation for Survival (MFS) in October 1979. MFS had made its first appearance in April 1977 at a conference in Philadelphia 'to work with non-governmental organisations to create the maximum impact on the UN Special Session on Disarmament in May 1978'. It had rekindled past ties by rallying many of the anti-Vietnam War front organisations and their principal activists, notably Provance, who had already demonstrated his skill as a 'peace fighter': he had headed the 'National Peace Campaign – Stop the B-1 Bomber' in 1973 and had been a member of the US delegation to the WPC's World Conference to End the Arms Race in Helsinki in September 1976.[3] At the demonstration in October 1979 there were ritual denunciations of US and NATO plans to deploy cruise and Pershing II missiles, and some 500 demonstrators marched to the Department of Energy. Measured against the size of similar demonstrations in Europe, such protests in the US were pretty ineffective.

In fact, although planned at a Chicago meeting in 1978, it was not until November 1979 that a new US Peace Council was formally established at an inaugural conference in Philadelphia, again attended by a WPC delegation led by Romesh Chandra. In a retrospective article in August 1980, S. A. Karaganov, writing in *USA: Economics, Politics, Ideology* (a magazine published by Arbatov's Institute of the US and Canada in Moscow), commented that 'the convention in Chicago set extremely broad objectives for the council and its constituent organisations. They included resisting the plans of NATO and the Pentagon to begin a new round in the race for strategic weapons and further struggle for the ratification of SALT II. A resolution on the Middle East condemned the Camp David agreements ... and the decisions of the convention appealed for recognition of the Socialist Republic of Vietnam and the People's Republic of Kampuchea, and for the lifting of the embargo on trade with Cuba. In connection with these and many other issues, the Peace Council and many of its coordinated organisations are carrying out energetic explanatory work through the mass media and their activists all speaking at various gatherings and organising demonstrations and protest rallies'.

In an article in the *World Marxist Review*, published in Prague in November 1982 and entitled 'Anti-Nuclear-War Protest in North America; the Spectre of the Soviet Threat is Receding', Bruce Kimmel of the CPUSA wrote that 'the founding in 1979 of the US Peace Council, affiliated with the WPC, was an historically significant event. The growth of the USPC in so short a time to over 40 local chapters testifies to the fact that people are ready for action to maintain and consolidate peace. ... What adds significance to the Council's activity is the example it sets for other peace organisations on how to overcome anti-Soviet prejudice and fear'.

At its inaugural conference, the new Peace Council passed a resolution 'requiring a shut down of nuclear plants and of nuclear arms production'.[4] It elected as its Executive Director Michael Myerson, formerly secretary of the Peace Commission of the New York State Communist Party (in the 1960s he had been the first US citizen to visit North Vietnam).

In March 1981, the first national conference of the American Nuclear Freeze Campaign was held at Georgetown University in Washington DC. According to *The Mobilizer*, a 'peace movement' newspaper, the organisers comprised some 300 predominantly white middle-class people from 33 of the American States, the UK and the USSR. Among the Soviet guests were Yuri Kapralov, a KGB officer serving as counsellor at the Soviet Embassy since 1978, who took an active part in the discussions.[5] But by this time, the national coordination of the freeze movement was passing into the hands of people with a different outlook and motives; the origins and development of this movement are examined in detail in Chapter 11.

On the same day, 20 March, as the conferences began in Georgetown University, another organisation entitled International Physicians for the Prevention of Nuclear War was also holding its first annual conference in Virginia. The head of the Soviet delegation, which included Brezhnev's personal physician, Evgeny Chazov, was Georgi Arbatov, who concluded with a summary of the arguments for preventing the deployment of new 'destabilising' weapons such as cruise and MX missiles, without mentioning the new generations of Soviet missiles, nuclear submarines or the Soviet Backfire bomber.[6] After the Georgetown and Virginia conferences, the US Peace Council arranged for another WPC delegation, headed by Romesh Chandra, to visit Washington where they met, among others, some of the same Congressmen who had greeted the earlier delegation in 1978.

With the revival of the freeze campaign in 1981, Mobilisation for Survival sponsored a Nuclear Weapons Facilities Task Forces Conference, attended by representatives of some 46 'peace' and disarmament organisations. This was held in October 1981 at Nyack, New York, at the headquarters of the Fellowship of Reconciliation (FOR). As co-convenor of the MFS International Task Force and the American coordinator of the Amsterdam based anti-nuclear World Information Service on Energy (WISE), Terry Provance also addressed, with Nino Pasti of Generals for Peace and Disarmament, an anti-NATO demonstration of some 15 000 people in Bonn in April 1981. This showed the close collaboration between the MFS and the pro-Communist and Anti-NATO 'peace movement' in the Federal Republic. Apart from the German Communist Party (DKP), the rally's sponsors included the German Peace Union, the German Peace Society, the League of Anti-Fascists and Democratic Initiative for Women.

Participants in the Nyack Conference in October 1981 were told that the months ahead would be 'a key time to organise local public meetings and/or demonstrations demanding the suspension of all US plans to deploy cruise and Pershing II missiles'. The agenda called for support for a nuclear freeze, solidarity with the European peace movements, 'creative dramatic actions' against large corporations and attempts to attract more followers by blaming social ills on the 'military budget'. Two weeks later, Romesh Chandra again flew to New York to attend a meeting of the US Peace Council at which one Congressman spoke about the need to recruit blacks and other minorities into the disarmament movement and another Representative, John Conyers, emphasised the importance of transferring funds from the defence budget to welfare programmes.[7]

On the same day as the US Peace Council met in November 1981, some 500 people took part in a conference on 'The Arms Race and the US', organised by the Riverside Church in New York, attended by Yuri Kapralov.[8] Apart from the usual anti-Vietnam War activists, the speakers were drawn from the Washington Institute for Policy Studies and included Admiral Gene Le Rocque, the director of the Center for Defense Information. The main themes were *détente* and cooperation with the Soviet Union; some members of the audience held up placards painted with the 'Ban the Bomb' insignia of the British CND.

Mobilisation for Survival held its fifth national conference at the University of Wisconsin in Milwaukee in December 1981 at which the members of more than twenty peace and disarmament groups participated. While the main focus was on the forthcoming United Nations Special Session on Disarmament in June 1982, the business of the Conference also included the practical planning of 1982 demonstrations against the Strategic Air Command headquarters in Omaha; the Whiteman Air Force Base in Missouri which contains Minuteman missiles; the Bendix nuclear weapons facility in Kansas City; Honywell's Minnesota facilities and the submarine communications system project in Michigan and Wisconsin.[9] At the end of January 1982, the Campaign for the Special Session on Disarmament (CSSD) convened a meeting in New York of 300 disarmament activists representing 90 groups to plan for two weeks of disarmament activities terminating on June 12 with a peace march and rally. At this meeting, the CSSD was renamed and reorganised into the 12 June Disarmament Coalition (J-12DC) whose members, apart from the CPUSA, included twelve other peace groups. In support of the J-12DC, the AFSC and CALC co-sponsored a tour of 39 American cities between 20 March and 4 April 1982 by leading representatives of the peace movements in Italy, the Federal Republic, Netherlands, Denmark and the United Kingdom.[10]

The US Peace Council, in a letter from Michael Myerson dated 1 March 1982, urged its members to support the activities around the UN Special Session on Disarmament and to make mobilisation for 12 June 1982 its first priority for the next 100 days. Members were ordered to join the local 'June 12th coalitions'; to reserve buses for New York for that weekend; to involve local trade unions, community organisations, churches, local affiliates of national organisations in support of 12 June; and persuade local unions, city councils and other bodies to pass resolutions in support of the UN Special Session and the 12 June demonstrations.[11] Finally, emissaries from 13 international fronts, including Romesh Chandra, arrived in New York to join nearly one million Americans who took part in the nuclear freeze rally on 12 June 1982. There were also large demonstrations in Los Angeles, San Francisco, Denver and other cities. The size and success of the demonstration in New York cannot be attributed exclusively to any one of these organisations, all of which were involved, and were helped by a number of fringe groups unconnected with the issues of 'peace and disarmament'.

Besides the Russians who attended the various meetings mentioned above, there was a continuous attempt by Soviet agents to influence various elements of the United States peace movement. By 1982 more than twenty such agents were identified as being engaged in this activity. These included three KGB officers accredited to the United Nations: Sergei Paramonov, Vladimir Shustov and Sergei Divilkovsky, all of whom had visited Riverside and other churches and meetings of peace organisations. Earlier KGB contacts with the US Peace Council included Andrei Kokoshin and Nikolai Mostovets, the head of the North American section of the International Department of the CPSU.[12]

THE UNITED KINGDOM

British Communists and their sympathisers have for many years made extensive use of front organisations to extend their influence. They have been widely involved in the Soviet-controlled organisations established during and immediately after the Second World War, and have fully exploited them in their domestic political campaigning, with varying degrees of success.

In a country where Communism has for long had little direct appeal, successful front organisations offer Communists a means of countering their weakness and of disseminating their propaganda. Such bodies can expect to reach an audience beyond the limited range of the CPGB, whose policies had often been seen to follow too slavishly the Moscow line, for example over the changes in Soviet policy at the start of the Second World War (see Chapter 3). A typical, but significant, post-war example of this attitude was in the reaction of Harry Pollitt, then Secretary-General of the CPGB, to the American (Baruch) Plan for international control and development of atomic energy put forward in 1946. This is recorded in a recent book by the American author Michael Straight. In Straight's view, if the Russians rejected this 'constructive and generous offer', an arms race would follow that could end in a third world war. Pollitt's reaction was: 'This atomic bomb of yours has altered the balance of forces, and revived the old dream of destroying the Soviet Union. But the Soviet Union will have the bomb before long, so it's a short-term war or none at all, I take the long view.' In other words, as Straight comments, the CPGB had no mind of its own and would bring no pressure to bear on the Kremlin; it would insist that the US share its technology with the Russians, not as a step towards international control but in order that the Russians could produce their own bomb; only then, in Pollitt's view, would 'the balance of forces' be restored and the world be safe again.[13]

Since the 1920s the front organisations in Britain have sought to exploit the socialist leanings of some sections of the intelligentsia: the involvement of writers, artists, scientists and others has been a key objective. They have also tried to cultivate support among Labour supporters and inside the trade union movement, whose leaders exercise real influence on the left of the political debate. In recent years, front organisations have played some part in developing understanding between Communists and sections of the Labour left, thereby carrying Communist influence into the Labour Party. Behind such slogans as 'ban the bomb', the 'promotion of world peace', 'opposition to racialism' and the 'advancement of international fraternity', front organisations not directly connected with the CPGB but echoing the Soviet line enable the Party to distance itself from any unwelcome pro-Soviet stance: more important, from Moscow's viewpoint, when the CPGB, which since 1968 has been increasingly aligned with Euro Communism, is less than enthusiastic about some aspect of Soviet policy, the front organisations at least are able to echo Moscow loud and clear.

The operations of British front organisations were severely circumscribed between 1933 and 1972, the years in which the Labour Party formally proscribed many of the leading international Communist bodies, domestic friendship societies and other such organisations, membership of which it deemed to be incompatible with that of the Labour Party. Both before and after the Second World War many Labour and trade union leaders, such as Clement Attlee and Hugh Gaitskell, Arthur Deakin and Will Lawther, spoke out against Communism in uncompromising terms; the TUC itself, which in 1945 had taken a leading part in the formation of the WFTU, withdrew from it in 1949. Nevertheless, despite such numerous obstacles as the damaging effects of divisions among Communists and the creation of rival Marxist organisations, British supporters of the WPC, the WFTU, the WFDY and similar bodies succeeded in keeping their cause afloat.

By the 1970s a changing political climate led to a partial revival in their fortunes. The Labour Party National Executive Committee, which had enforced the proscribed list, began to incline further to the left and to include some individuals sympathetic to Soviet policies. It also found difficulty in monitoring the proliferation of new Marxist groups, mainly Trotskyist, that emerged in the 1960s. After the proscribed list had been discontinued in 1972, bodies previously thought dormant, even dead, began to renew their activities with the encouragement of some Labour politicians. Thus, by the 1980s nearly all the major international front organisations again enjoyed some support in Britain, although many sections of the left remained strongly suspicious of organisations so long identified as Soviet creatures.

Since its inception in 1949, the WPC has had the support of some British affiliated organisation. About 40 British intellectuals attended the original conference in Wroclaw, Poland, in 1948 from which the WPC emerged.[14] They were organised in the British Cultural Committee for Peace, renamed in 1949 the British Peace Committee (BPC) which remained the British section of the WPC until 1973. Throughout its existence as a WPC affiliate, the BPC was proscribed by the Labour Party, together with other organisations connected with the WPC, including the now defunct Authors' World Peace Appeal, Musicians' Organisation for Peace, Artists for Peace and Science for Peace, and regional groups for Wales and Yorkshire. Two other bodies proscribed during that period which are both still active were the Medical Association for the Prevention of War and Teachers for Peace.[15]

In 1973 a World Congress of Peace Forces in Moscow was attended by a British contingent including many Communists. This led to the formation of a new body: the All-Britain Peace Liaison Group (ABPLG), which was soon to replace the BPC. In January 1980 the ABPLG held a major conference in London: the 155 delegates included members of the Labour Party, the Communist party, the New Communist Party (a pro-Soviet group, about five hundred strong, which had broken away from the CPGB in 1978) and of trade unions and pressure groups active in the 'peace movement'. Speakers included James Lamond MP, Alf Lomas, a Labour member of the European Parliament, and the then Yorkshire miners' leader, Arthur Scargill.[16] One absentee from the conference, Romesh Chandra, the president of the World Peace Council, was refused admission to the United Kingdom. In his unavoidable absence, the conference resolved to form a new organisation which was later launched in April 1980 as the British Peace Assembly (BPA), with the support of, among others, the Fire Brigades Union, the train drivers' union (ASLEF) and such front organisations as the National Assembly of Women, the British-Soviet Friendship Society and the British Vietnam Association. The BPA President is James Lamond MP (who is also a WPC vice-president) and the Assembly is now the WPC's official British affiliate. BPA vice-presidents include a WPC Presidential Committee Member, Gordon Schaffer, and Alf Lomas, former chairman of the ABPLG. In 1982 the BPA chairman was James Layzell, its vice-chairman Harry Francis, its secretary, Jean Pavett, and its assistant secretary Florence Croasdell, all WPC members. The BPA is 'pledged to promote and support initiatives from the World Peace Council and other international bodies with similar aims'.[17] In June 1980 James Lamond also became chairman of a group of about 20 left wing Labour MPs called Parliamentarians for Peace.[18] He visited Belfast shortly afterwards to encourage the extension of WPC activities to Northern Ireland.[19] He also visited the USSR as the guest of the Soviet Peace Committee at about that time.

Among the other international front organisations, the WFTU has had only qualified success in establishing itself in Britain. In general contacts between British unions and WFTU have been conducted through individual trade unionists, who have pressed unsuccessfully for the TUC's affiliation to be switched back to WFTU. The periodical *World Trade Union Movement* is prepared in Prague in a number of languages including English. The London office of WFTU publications was closed down in 1978, although in practice WFTU is not without local representation.

There have however been increasing contacts in the past decade between the TUC and the official trade union organisations of eastern Europe, as well as repeated attempts by interested parties to bring WFTU and the ICFTU more closely together. In 1978, 24 British trade unionists from 12 different unions attended the 9th World Trade Union Congress in Prague as observers; in 1982, 33 British trade unionists, led by Alex Kitson of the Transport and General Workers' Union, attended the Tenth World Trade Union Congress in Havana in a similar capacity.

The WFDY enjoys rather more support in Britain. Like WFTU, it was founded at a conference in London in 1945 and likewise soon fell under Communist control. For many years its appeal was largely confined to Communists. By 1973, however, at the Tenth World Youth Festival in East Berlin, jointly organised by the WFDY and the International Union of Students (IUS), British participation extended beyond the Young Communist League to include Labour Party members, Young Liberals, and members of the Student Christian Movement and the United Nations Youth Association. At the Eleventh World Youth Festival in Havana in 1978, the British delegation was over 200 strong and embraced a number of non-political youth bodies.

But not even British Communist support for WFDY has been unqualified. At the 11th WFDY Assembly in Prague in June 1982 it was the British Young Communist League which not only went on record as openly opposing the introduction of martial law in Poland and the Soviet invasion of Afghanistan, but also criticised WFDY's handling of the issue of peace. 'While we welcome the positive contribution which the socialist countries have made to the reduction of tensions in the past, and we share the view that US imperialism and its most dedicated allies are primarily responsible for present tensions in the world, we do not accept that these powers are the exclusive source of world tensions. The Young Communist League is deeply concerned by aspects of the external policy of China, especially the unprovoked attack on Vietnam, but we are opposed to the expression of a collective condemnation of the external policy of China, by a gathering of this kind'.[20]

Among the smaller international front organisations, one which is mainly based in London is the World Federation of Scientific Workers (WFSW). Its president for many years, the late Dr Eric Burhop, was awarded the Lenin Peace Prize in 1946. It was founded at a conference in London organised by the British Association of Scientific Workers, to which he belonged, shortly after the Second World War. Its present president is French, Jean-Marie Legay; its Secretary-General is British, Dr John Dutton.

By the early 1950s a network of 'friendship societies' had also come into being to further relations between Britain and the Communist countries of eastern Europe. Each was largely dependent on the appropriate embassy in London: almost all were proscribed by the Labour Party until 1972. These bodies tend to concentrate on social and cultural activities of a highly political character, with tours arranged for dancers and musicians from abroad and talks on life in Communist countries by London-based diplomats and other spokesmen for Communist governments.

The largest of these bodies is the British–Soviet Friendship Society (BSFS). Although the present organisation was formed in 1946, its antecedents go back to the Friends of the Soviet Union originally established in 1927. The BSFS chairman is the former Labour MP, William Wilson; its treasurer is James Lamond MP, and other officers include Allan Roberts, MP for Bootle, one of the Labour MPs who visited Afghanistan in 1980 as the guest of the Babrak Karmal regime. The existence of these self-styled friendship societies in various countries enables the Soviet Union and its East European allies to cultivate friends and sympathisers locally without directly involving local Communist parties; similar societies exist to promote close ties with other Communist regimes elsewhere (for example, in Britain the British Vietnam Association and the newer Friends of Afghanistan).

As a political party, the CPGB has had a disastrous record. Its 1983 membership of 15 691,[21] in reality supposed to be even smaller, is the lowest since before the Second World War. It has failed to win any parliamentary seats since 1950. But of all the extreme left-wing groups in Britain its influence in the trade union movement remains easily highest – in 1982 there were three open

Communist Party members on the TUC General Council, though the figure fell to one in 1983 – and it enjoys a common outlook on key issues, especially defence and disarmament, with some sections of the Labour Left.

The CPGB seeks to maintain its influence inside the trade union movement by promoting *ad hoc* pressure groups. Some of these are fronts in the true sense and are kept on a fairly tight rein, such as the Labour Research Department, founded in 1924, and the Liaison Committee for the Defence of Trade Unions founded in 1966. Others reflect the broader 'united front' tactic which the CPGB first adopted with various refinements in the 1930s and again in the post-war era. The Party's present strategy is to develop what it calls a 'broad democratic alliance' to bring together Communists, Labour left-wingers, sympathetic trade unionists, youth generally and members of the ethnic minorities, the 'peace movement', the environmental lobby, the feminist movement and others more usually associated with the so-called 'New Left'. In this enterprise Communists compete for influence with the Labour left itself, the Trotskyists and many independent radical groups.

Similarly, Communist sympathisers have gained strong influence inside a number of pressure groups such as the Anti-Apartheid movement, the Chile Solidarity Campaign, the National Union of Students, and Liberation (formerly the Movement for Colonial Freedom). The 'Peace Movement', notably the Campaign for Nuclear Disarmament (CND), has been a particular target for CPGB efforts (see Chapters 8 and 9).

The CPGB's Trotskyist competitors sustain their own front organisations. Some may enjoy Libyan funding; Libyan exiles maintain that President Gadaffi has contributed considerable sums to the Trotskyists who run the Workers Revolutionary Party (WRP), the largest Trotskyist group with a reputed membership of about 3000, and its publication *News Line*, although the WRP denies these reports.[22] The Socialist Workers Party, formerly known as the International Socialists, was instrumental some years ago in founding the Right to Work Campaign and the Anti-Nazi League and runs the Rank and File Movement inside some fifteen trade unions. Perhaps the best known Trotskyist group is the Militant Tendency, with over 2000 supporters inside the Labour Party. This has past links with a secretive Trotskyist group formerly called the Revolutionary Socialist League (RSL), which infiltrated the Labour Party in the mid-1950s by use of the Trotskyist tactic of 'entryism'. In 1964 the RSL as such was buried, and the *Militant* newspaper launched as the dissolved League's principal outlet.[23] The paper's directors were expelled from the Labour Party in 1983.

This kaleidoscope of competing Marxist groups has made life more testing for the established front organisations. Through the support they have received from some members of Parliament and leading trade unionists, as well as from members of the Communist Party, these organisations have exerted considerable influence on the left of British politics. But their Soviet bias no longer has any mesmeric appeal for the younger generation, while their methods have been imitated by their rivals. The political field on the far left has seldom been so crowded with so many overlapping and often competing organisations.

WESTERN EUROPE

Besides the United Kingdom, front organisations have also been very active in other countries of Western Europe. In recent years they have especially concentrated on the anti-nuclear weapons campaign. In several of these countries the Communist party has played a more active role in politics than in either the United Kingdom or the United States. It has therefore been more openly concerned with the development of the indigenous 'peace movements' than in these two countries. The non-Communist leaders of these movements have not always welcomed Communist involvement, which they have seen as liable to prejudice their prospects for securing broad national support. For this reason, some have made efforts to emphasise the differences in their approach from that of the Communists.

A brief account of the development of the campaigns by the front organisations against the 'neutron bomb' and NATO's plans to deploy Pershing IIs and cruise missiles in Western Europe is given below.

These campaigns have unfolded in successive phases. The campaign against ERW (the 'neutron bomb') began in the summer of 1977. The ERW is a highly accurate anti-tank weapon which was intended to enhance the credibility of the Western deterrent against the overwhelming superiority in tanks possessed by the Warsaw Pact forces in central Europe. Its special characteristic is to minimise collateral damage; this was reckoned to increase its credibility in the eyes of potential enemies and thus to improve the deterrent's effectiveness. From the start, however, Moscow Radio's internal and external services presented the proposed weapon as a horrific new means of mass destruction. From 25 July to 7 August 1977 in particular, that theme was given extensive propaganda coverage. In those two weeks, about 13 per cent of all Soviet broadcast items were devoted to labelling the deployment of the 'neutron bomb' as a threat to peace. The inhumanity of a weapon 'which killed people and left property intact', was emphasised: NATO was accused of producing a bomb to be used against human beings, not tanks. The political message was a warning that deployment of the weapon would endanger *détente*, the arms control negotiations and above all peace itself, as the increased danger of full-scale nuclear war would oblige the Warsaw Pact to equip itself with even more lethal weapons. From mid-1977 to 1978, *Pravda* carried a regular column on its foreign page entitled 'No to the Neutron Bomb' (a phrase soon picked up by Western campaigners) which contained extracts from speeches, protest actions and foreign press articles remonstrating against the new weapon, many of them in fact originating from the front organisations. These in turn were reproduced in the Soviet *New Times* and *Moscow News*. Between 1978 and 1981 this particular campaign largely lapsed. The column reappeared in *Pravda* on 7 February 1981, shortly after hints that the Reagan administration was considering reactivating the ERW programme (and similar comments also appeared at this time in the East German *Neues Deutschland*.)

During the campaign's first phase, the principal front organisations dutifully followed the Soviet lead. There were parallel statements from the WIDF in East Berlin on 19 July 1977, from the WFTU in Prague on 20 July and from the WPC in Helsinki which, on 27 July, called for a 'week of action devoted to protests against the neutron bomb' to be held from 6 to 13 August. National 'peace committees' dutifully repeated the Soviet arguments in their conference and resolutions. In addition, the WPC subsidiary ICESC held a colloquium on the 'neutron bomb' in October organised by the Belgian Canon Raymond Goor, a regular participant at WPC meetings.

The campaign was however not confined to Europe; strenuous

efforts were made to mobilise opposition to the 'neutron bomb' on a world-wide basis. The campaign reached India early in 1978, where it was predictably led by the All-Indian Peace and Solidarity Organisation and the Indian Society for Cultural Relations with the USSR. In Mexico, from 1 to 4 February 1978, the WPC and the Mexican Peace Movement jointly campaigned against the weapon at the Second Latin American and Caribbean Conference for Peace, Sovereignty and Economic Independence, and their call carried the message to all affiliated organisations south of the Rio Grande. In Japan, a protest march against the weapon was held in Tokyo on 24 April 1978.

After the announcement from Washington in September 1977 that the US would not produce the weapon before agreement had been reached on its deployment with its Western European allies, the second main phase of the campaign opened in January 1978 with Brezhnev's letter to the heads of Western governments warning them that the deployment of this device would gravely endanger *détente*. Many Western parliamentarians and trade union leaders received similar letters from members of the Supreme Soviet and from Soviet trade union officials. From 27 February to 2 March 1978, the Special Non-Governmental Organisations (NGOs) Committee on Disarmament, which is under strong Soviet and WPC influence, organised a seminar in Geneva on the 'neutron bomb'. President Carter in April 1978 'deferred' the production of these weapons. The Russians and their allies regarded this as a significant victory and it gave added impetus to the campaign which began shortly afterwards against the modernisation of NATO's INF.

At this point, in the second half of 1978, the WPC and its subsidiaries mounted a wide range of meetings. After a year's experiment and experience, a new style of campaigning had emerged, by a progression starting in Moscow Radio's external services, with the message subsequently relayed overseas by the front organisations and followed by authoritative Soviet statements. After the announcement by the Reagan Administration on 9 August 1981 that it was authorising the assembly of the ERW, the propaganda cycle began again, stressing the fact that the US decision had been taken without consulting its leading Western European allies, and arguing that the weapon would increase the probability of nuclear confrontation and would make Western Europe, rather than the US, bear the brunt of nuclear destruction.

Campaigns Against NATO

The campaign against the projected deployment of NATO's INF effectively began early in 1979. It included many of the arguments already developed against neutron weapons. But since deployment of cruise and Pershing II missiles was not due to start until late 1983, the Soviet propaganda apparatus had more than four years in which to mobilise Western opinion against weapons which were still not in place. This gave the Russians a propaganda advantage: they were able from the start to represent NATO's plans as deliberate escalation of the arms race and to play down the SS-20 deployments, which had begun two years earlier, as normal replacements for the previous generation of intermediate range systems.

Thus in a powerful speech on 6 October 1979 in East Berlin, Brezhnev took as his theme that 'the implementation of these schemes [for NATO modernisation] would essentially change the strategic situation in the continent'. He offered to reduce the Soviet intermediate range nuclear systems in western Russia on condition that the NATO plans were scrapped. In the following week over 20% of Moscow Radio's output was devoted to launching the anti-INF campaign, and it was maintained at a level of about 12–14% until the end of the year.[24] On 11 December 1979, the eve of the NATO Council's decision to proceed with preparations for NATO's INF deployment, a meeting of eight front organisations in East Berlin, headed by the WPC, the WFTU and the WFDY issued a statement urging the NATO countries 'to reject the proposals of the Pentagon, calculated to lead to a fresh round of the arms race'. From 26 to 28 May 1980, the WPC-inspired ILF of Peace Forces held a meeting in Vienna against NATO's INF modernisation. By early 1980 the campaign had been well and truly launched and its running was being made by, and could safely be left to, the indigenous 'peace movements' in the West. The WPC was therefore able to transfer its efforts to the Third World, and at a WPC Presidential Bureau meeting in Madagascar in January 1981, over a hundred affiliated organisations supported the statement that 'through NATO's nuclear weapons, the countries of the Mediterranean, the Middle East, the Gulf and the entire world' were at risk.[25] In Geneva on 5 February 1981, Romesh Chandra, the WPC President, proclaimed February 1981 a 'Month of Action' against NATO's new nuclear weapons.

At the WPC's World Parliament of Peoples for Peace in Sofia in

September 1980, a round table meeting of trade unionists revived a proposal, first suggested by WFTU in 1978, for a trade unionists' meeting on the social and economic consequences of disarmament. In the event over 200 participants from 62 countries, including representatives not only of WFTU but of the World Confederation of Labour (WCL), the International Confederation of Arab Trade Unions (ICATU) and of some unions affiliated to the ICFTU as well, attended the conference eventually held in Paris in December 1981. Similar trade unions meetings were held in the margin of the WPC's 'World Assembly for Peace and Life, against Nuclear War' in Prague in June 1983. About 500 people from 82 countries participated in a meeting of trade unionists which discussed the social and economic effects of the arms race. Their conclusions were, not surprisingly, highly critical of the 'NATO reactionary forces'. This meeting was held on the initiative of a WFTU subsidiary, the International Trade Union Committee for Peace and Disarmament (also known as the Dublin Committee). These meetings in Sofia, Prague and elsewhere, have been intended to line up the world's trade unionists behind Soviet disarmament slogans – opposition to NATO's new weapons, support for 'nuclear free zones' and a 'nuclear freeze'.[26]

All these campaigns by the front organisations have taken place within the context of a continuous barrage of Soviet propaganda, statements by political and military leaders, government declarations, articles in the Soviet press for overseas consumption and radio broadcasts, aimed at discrediting and disrupting the NATO plans for INF deployments. These attacks took on an increasingly threatening tone in 1983, as the deadline for deployment approached and the Russians achieved no success, either in the INF negotiations in Geneva or through their propaganda efforts, in securing the abandonment of NATO's plans. These Soviet efforts set the tone for the activities of the front organisations from the time of the NATO Double-Track decision in December 1979 until the Soviet withdrawal from the negotiations in November 1983.

Part III
Critics: Peace Movements in the West

8 Origin of the Peace Movement in the United Kingdom, 1930–62

Although there have always been those, especially among church members, who have espoused pacifist ideals, an overt British 'peace movement', intent on mobilising the public against war and all things military, only emerged in this century, gathering strength in the early 1930s. Signs of widespread interest in pacifism then began to appear in the literature of the day and in public and parliamentary debate.

A spate of 'trench memoirs', dating from the late 1920s, was published during 1931 and 1932. Many of them have since become classics: among them, Richard Aldington's *Death of a Hero*, Robert Graves's *Goodbye to All That*, and Siegfried Sassoon's *Memoirs of an Infantry Officer*. Their themes were similar, displaying disgust at the bloodshed of the First World War and emphasising the waste of war in general. The politicians were blamed for having deceived the soldiers into thinking that they were fighting for a better world which, in the event, had failed to materialise.

Possibly of even greater impact was the debate on the air peril to come, with subsequent public alarm about the prospects of an aerial 'knock-out blow'. Initially, statements about the danger of air attack emanated from a small group within the RAF which, led by the late Lord Trenchard, envisaged a future European war as being won by strategic bombing alone. This group saw increased expenditure on creating a strategic bombing capability as a way of establishing the RAF as an independent service. Such prominent strategists as General J. F. C. Fuller enlarged on the terrors of air attack: 'London for several days will be one vast raving Bedlam, the hospitals will be stormed, traffic will cease, the homeless will shriek for help, the city will be pandemonium. What of the Government of Westminster? It will be swept away in an avalanche of terror. Then will the enemy dictate his terms . . .'.[1]

These predictions, reinforced by memories of the limited destruction wrought by German Zeppelin and twin-engined bomber raids during the First World War, stirred the imagination. Curiously, concern about the air peril in no way reflected developments in the international arena. Until 1933, only the French Air Force could have endangered Britain and war with France was, to say the least, extremely unlikely. The existence of an effective Lutfwaffe was not to become common knowledge until March 1935.

Thus, in the early 1930s, discussions on the 'knock-out blow' avoided nominating any possible enemy. Nevertheless, there was an underlying sense of threat, illustrated by Beverley Nichols' words in *Cry Havoc!*, published in 1933: 'All the world knows that its neighbours are arming. You have only to go to any cinema, and see the weekly newsreel, to get enough evidence to convince the most optimistic pacifist. Every other picture shows an army on the march. The faces are the same, and they are all marching to the same destination – Death – for the same reason – Nothing. Only the flags are different.'

In the 1920s, the majority of British people put their faith in negotiated disarmament. Public pressure had however at first been muted, partly because most people were simply relieved that the war was over, and partly because there was a general assumption that German disarmament would be followed by Allied disarmament, as stated in the League of Nations Covenant. Successive British governments had inspired hope for a lasting peace in Europe in the 1920s by their involvement in disarmament negotiations and the Ten Year Rule.* By the end of the decade, however, the failure of the negotiations to achieve significant results (with the one solitary exception of the 1925 Protocol banning the use of chemical and bacteriological weapons) served to push the issue to the forefront of politics. As Samuel Hoare, a former Foreign Secretary, remarked in his memoirs, 'the combination of all these forces, moral, political and religious, created so strong a volume of opinion in favour of disarmament that no government, right, left or centre, could resist it'.

* The Ten Year Rule, adopted in 1919 and later extended, based defence expenditure on the assumption that there would be no war for ten years.

Attention was focused on the World Disarmament Conference at Geneva, which began in 1932. The Cabinet was in truth virtually unanimous in its endorsement of the popular view. Throughout his political career, the Prime Minister, Ramsay MacDonald, remained faithful to the conviction he had expressed as Labour's leader during the 1923 election campaign: 'We have to abandon absolutely every vestige of trust in military equipment.' He involved himself continuously in the affairs of the Conference, putting forward his own proposals and urging agreement. Likewise, Stanley Baldwin, the senior Conservative in the National Government, had not concealed his own anxieties when he commented in 1932 that 'no power on earth can protect the man in the street from being bombed. Whatever people may tell him, the bomber will always get through'.

In the event, the conference, on which so many hopes were pinned, failed. British attempts at compromise, which at the time seemed realistic and found wide support, conflicted with the French obsession with national security. Hopes for agreement were raised when Britain and France agreed on a proposal in October 1933 but on 14 October, Hitler gave notice of Germany's withdrawal from the conference and her intended withdrawal from the League of Nations. German rearmament was accelerated, with little effort at concealment. By 1934 it was generally recognised that the search for agreed multilateral disarmament had failed. Although efforts to achieve some kind of air force disarmament agreement continued until 1939, the World Disarmament Conference collapsed in June 1934.

The progressive failure of the National Government to secure results at Geneva was matched by a new phase in the development of the 'peace movement'. Up to that time, there was no effective national campaign body to represent the anti-war mood, still less the pacifist standpoint. The 'No More War Movement', successor to Fenner Brockway's No Conscription Fellowship of 1914 had never really got underway; it had only 3000 members in 1931, and increased its membership by a mere 500 between 1933 and 1937, when it amalgamated with the Peace Pledge Union. The combined membership of all the peace groups did not exceed 25 000 in 1932.

The League of Nations Union (LNU), founded in November 1918 to mobilise support for the League, was a more successful body, despite the fact that the League's aims actually represented, through its commitment to collective security, a solution which involved real risk of war.² The LNU had recruited members through a vast range of activities, from summer schools to films and publications, including its monthly journal *Headway*. Its individual membership increased from 3000 in 1918 to 406 000 in 1931. In addition, the Union had more than 3000 corporate members by 1930, including Church congregations, professional and community service groups, trades unions and cooperative societies, bringing hundreds of thousands more into the fold.³ The thrust of its campaign was opposition to war; detailed discussion of League sanctions was avoided. Lord Robert Cecil, the LNU's chairman, told the House of Commons in July 1919 that there could be 'no attempt to rely upon force to carry out a decision of the Council or the Assembly of the League. That is almost impracticable as things stand now. What we rely upon is public opinion . . . and if we are wrong about that, the whole thing is wrong'. In his view, collective security provided Britain with the conditions for disarmament.

The LNU, however, operated under constraints which were to hamper its influence. Its difficulties lay in its diverse membership which included Liberals (from whom most of its leaders came), Conservatives, pacifists, and some left-wing radicals. They were, as A. J. P. Taylor describes them, 'for the most part moderate men, respectable, high minded; men of the Establishment, not dissenters'.⁴ While there was constant pressure from LNU Branches for more radical policies, the leadership was not in a position even if it had so wished to dicate to the government. It became particularly obvious during the 1932 Manchurian crisis that, unlike a 'stop the war' movement, the LNU was not a single-issue pressure group; in times of crisis it felt inhibited from saying anything which might alienate the sympathies of the government and compromise its future influence. Efforts to preserve unity amongst its members, who disagreed on almost everything except the importance of the League, and at the same time to retain the ear of those in power, forced it to maintain a safe but delicate balancing act which neither pleased its members, nor impressed outsiders.

The National Government, however, did not regard the LNU as genuinely representative of British public opinion on international issues. In this they were justified since the membership figures were aggregated to include all those who had ever joined, rather than current subscription-payers, and membership turned over very rapidly. When the LNU celebrated topping 1 000 000 in March 1933, its actual subscribers numbered less than 400 000 and their number was already in decline.[5] Although half the members of Parliament were LNU members, membership in itself did not involve acceptance of any specific commitments. From their involvement in LNU activities many MPs derived the impression that the membership was apathetic and the leadership divided. A jaundiced view of the LNU was to persist throughout the 1930s: another former Foreign Secretary Austen Chamberlain, who had served on its Executive Committee, commented that it was composed of 'some of the worst cranks I have ever known and, led by Cecil, they are ready to proclaim the proper solution to every problem and dictate indifferently to His Majesty's Government or to the League on how it should be handled'.[6] Although the pacifists were in fact in the minority, the organisation was often dismissed as pacifist.

Most people joined the LNU to demonstrate their desire for disarmament. In contrast to his ambivalence over sanctions, Lord Robert Cecil had shown himself prepared to stand out against the Government on this issue, resigning from the Cabinet in 1927 over the Conservative Government's 'soft-pedalling' at the Geneva Naval Disarmament Conference. After the German withdrawal from the World Disarmament Conference, however, there was very little for the LNU to do. With the disarmament door apparently closing, some 'peace groups' began to look for alternative means to promote their message.

Such pacifists as the Rev Donald (now Lord) Soper, basing their ideas on Gandhi's doctrine of 'non-violence', tried to organise a 'Peace Army' during the Manchurian crisis to interpose itself between the combatants. In 1933 the non-pacifist National Peace Council became a focus for pacifists by publishing, from April onwards, a monthly paper called *Peace*; in the summer of 1933, a few Methodist pacifists, led by Henry Carter, formed the Methodist Peace Fellowship. Notoriety was won for the cause when, in February 1933, a leading pacifist, C. E. M. Joad successfully persuaded the Oxford Union to pass the motion that 'This country will in no circumstances fight for its King and Country.' In fact the debate was ignored outside Oxford until a few days later when an anonymous letter in the *Daily Telegraph*, in fact written by a senior member of its staff, called in provocative terms for the debate to be reopened.[7]

Nevertheless, from then on, as international hostilities became more frequent and the LNU began to demand firm collective action under the League, its membership slowly declined. By 1938, membership had fallen to around 260 000. Indeed, it was partly to attract new members and dispel its pacifist image that the LNU, in 1934 and 1935, organised its famous Peace Ballot as a national referendum on the League and disarmament. This was enormously popular, attracting more than $11\frac{1}{2}$ million replies. The results published in June 1935 gave the strong impression that the whole country was behind collective security and negotiated disarmament: pacifists came out of the Ballot very badly.

Over $10\frac{1}{2}$ million respondents supported Britain's continuing membership of the League of Nations, with less than 360 000 against. Nearly $10\frac{1}{2}$ million, in answer to three questions, 'Are you in favour of an all-round reduction in armaments by international agreement?', 'Are you in favour of an all-round abolition of national military and naval aircraft by international agreement?', and 'Should the private manufacture and sale of arms be prohibited by international agreement?', voted yes, with less than 870 000, 1 700 000 and 750 000 against in each case. The final question was divided into two: 'Do you consider that, if a nation insists on attacking another, the other nations should combine to stop it by: (a) economic and non-military measures? (b) if necessary, by military measures? More than 10 million gave positive answers to (a) with only 600 000 against; and more than 6 750 000 voted also for joining, if necessary, in military sanctions against an aggressor; those answering 'no' to (b) were less than 2 600 000.[8] Provided by the LNU with an alternative answer to question five, 'I accept the Christian pacifist answer', pacifists secured only 14 121 votes in answer to question 5a, and only 17 482 votes for 5b, fewer than either the doubtfuls or abstentions.

Although superficially conclusive, however, the Ballot was an unreliable measure of public opinion in Britain. Given the way the first four questions were framed the results were predictable. The final question was more revealing, though even this avoided placing the respondents in a position where they had to choose specific military involvement. Nor did the Ballot offer the voter the opportunity of expressing his views on whether Britain should rearm if others continued to rearm. Moreover, the propaganda leaflet accompanying the questions actively encouraged positive votes by merely saying: 'In this ballot you are asked to vote only on peace or war – whether you approve of the League of Nations, or not'.[9] Thus, the Ballot tended to confirm the impression that collective security was an alternative to war, a policy which would eliminate the need for large national armies. The Government was dubious about the results. Neville Chamberlain accused Cecil of fraud, and Eden believed that it promoted an unrealistic view of collective security as a kind of abstract principle; he argued that the separation of economic and military sanctions in question 5, implied that economic sanctions could be applied without the risk of war. Churchill was later to put another gloss on these findings. There were those at the time who argued that, had Ministers wished to exploit the answers to the last two questions in the Ballot (which became the last two clauses of the Peace Pledge) by, say, closing the Suez Canal against Italy in 1935 or by using military sanctions under the Covenant of the League to defend Abyssinia or in response to Hilter's reoccupation of the Rhineland in 1936, they could have done so with a clear conscience. As Churchill was to write; 'It [the Peace Ballot] was regarded in many quarters as a part of the pacific campaign. On the contrary, Clause 5 (on sanctions) affirmed a positive and courageous policy which could, at this time, have been followed with an overwhelming measure of national support'.[10]

It was not to be. Moreover, while the Ballot succeeded in capturing the public's imagination, it served to convince yet more people that even economic sanctions under the League were unacceptable as 'coercive instruments' and they therefore withdrew from the LNU. In July 1935, Canon Dick Sheppard formed the Sheppard Peace Movement, the precursor of the pacifist Peace Pledge Union (PPU), established early in 1936, which drew together most of the leading pacifists of the time: sponsors included the Labour peer, the first Lord Ponsonby of Shulbrede, Vera Brittain, Bertrand Russell, Aldous Huxley, Osbert Sitwell and the present Lord Soper.

The leaders of the PPU were less clearly part of the political establishment. Nor were its members part of a 'youth culture', as members of protest movements often are today; they were often inspired by strong religious feelings, usually non-conformist. Joad believed that the 'ordinary pacifist was a non-smoking, non-drinking vegetarian'.[11] They lobbied against rearmament, spreading their message through the weekly *Peace News* and through local groups. An early activist Laurie Hislam, later a member of the Committee of 100, panicked a crowd in Downing Street on the eve of war by lobbing tennis balls, which were mistaken for hand grenades, into its midst as a means of demonstrating the horror of war. The PPU's strategy created a force of opinion which no government could ignore. As Canon Sheppard said in July 1935 in the Albert Hall, 'send me a million men like you and then any government must look out'.

Unlike previous pacifist organisations, the PPU attracted sympathisers who were not committed pacifists, those 'with only slight political knowledge but with a recent realisation of the fearful imminence of war, who are fascinated by the direct simplicity of the crusade'.[12] in 1936, in the aftermath of the Abyssinian crisis, PPU membership was growing at the rate of 4500 per week, and reached 118 000 by the end of the year. Although growth faltered after that, a new surge after war had started achieved a membership total of 136 000 in April 1940, the largest figure ever reached by a British pacifist organisation. Even at its peak, however, it represented only a third of contemporary LNU membership in what was for the latter, a period of sharp decline. Moreover, the PPU experienced its fair share of defections to the LNU. Whilst some LNU members took fright at the risks inherent in collective security and turned to pacifism as a safer means of preserving peace, there were as many pacifists who came to doubt the practicality of pacifism as a means of preventing war.

The PPU leadership was predominantly Christian; the bulk of its members was not, being inspired by purely humanitarian motives. Denis Hayes, himself a conscientious objector and historian of the movement during the period 1939–45, emphasised that 'the typical PPU objector was broadly humanitarian, broadly moral, broadly ethical' – rather than strictly religious or political.[13] Indeed the influence of humanitarian pacifists within the PPU was a factor contributing to the growth of explicitly Christian pacifist societies just before the war: the Anglican Pacifist Fellowship, founded in 1937, attracted 1500 members by 1939 and the Methodist Peace Fellowship 3500. The Fellowship of Reconciliation, a First World War Christian pacifist society whose fortunes had been low until the mid-1930s reached nearly 10 000 in 1939, and continued to grow until the end of the war, when its membership stood at over 13 000.

In addition to pacifists, there was another small group which seemed almost indistinguishable from the pacifist camp, namely 'war resisters', extremists in the Labour movement who advocated the unity of the international working class in opposing capitalist war. Among their leaders were three 'Red Clydesiders', Campbell, Stephen and McGovern, who tried through the Independent Labour Party, to commit the Labour movement in 1932 to unilateral disarmament. They were supported by pacifists in the Labour Party: Lord Ponsonby believed the move would cause an immense stir abroad and 'that other nations would immediately follow'.

In August 1932 pro-Communists formed the British Anti-War Movement, also advocating 'war resistance' and campaigning against the Disarmament Conference, which they dismissed as a cover for the rearmament of Germany. Its leaders rejected the League because its ultimate sanction relied on force, and feared, not a fascist war against Britain, but a fascist takeover from within. It was widely believed at the time that the Anti-War Movement was a Communist front organisation. Although it claimed to function on behalf of all pacifists, its leaders successfully avoided the issue of whether they would condone war against fascism. Moreover, it had been founded in the wake of the World Anti-War Congress held in Amsterdam in 1932, which, despite the exclusion of Soviet representatives by the Netherlands government, had been both Communist-dominated and contemptuous of pacifism.[14] Its operations coincided closely with Soviet policies. The Labour Party proscribed it as a Communist front organisation after only a year's existence. In 1934, when the Soviet Union joined the League, it was re-named the British Movement Against War and Fascism but, once the Communists began to prosecute the Popular Front by working through local peace councils in 1936, it was allowed to lapse. It is of interest that before the Comintern's switch in 1934, the Communist Party viewed the League of Nations as the 'League of Brigands'; after the Soviet Union joined the League, it regarded it as an alliance of peace loving powers.

The appeal of 'war resistance' had a brief impact on the Labour Party. The newly formed Socialist League, which contained many

Anti-War Movement members, began in 1933 to try to commit Labour to 'war resistance'. At the Labour Party Conference in Hastings in 1933, Charles Trevelyan, supported by Percy Collick and Philip Noel-Baker, put forward a motion requiring the executive to conduct anti-war propaganda and 'to work within the Labour and Socialist International for an uncompromising attitude against war preparations', including a general strike. The motion drew support from the pacifists within the Labour Party who, at that time, included George Lansbury, its leader. He declared: 'I would close every recruiting station, disband the Army and dismiss the Air Force. I would abolish the whole dreadful equipment of war and say to the world "Do your worst!" '

In 1933 a 'war resistance' motion was passed, largely as a result of the vagaries of the Party's voting system. From 1934, however, the tide of 'war resistance' began to ebb. The resounding conclusion of the 1934 Conference was that 'this country might have to use military and naval forces in support of the League' and it is the duty of the Party 'unflinchingly to support our Government in all the risks and consequences of fulfilling its duty to take part in collective action'.[15] Similarly the trade union leadership, dismayed by Hitler's destruction of the German labour movement and sceptical of spontaneous working class action against fascism, totally committed the TUC to collective security and the League at its annual Conference in Southport in June 1934. 'War resistance' never regained its foothold in the Labour Party, although Socialist Leaguers continued their agitation and youth branches, in particular, continued to find the arguments attractive.

With its renewed commitment to the League the Labour Party stood firmly for 'peace'. In by-elections between 1933 and 1935, Labour Parliamentary candidates described themselves as 'peace men' and, conversely, branded the Government as 'war mongers'. They captured votes which, had they been cast at a General Election, would have threatened the National Government's majority. Baldwin was to tell the Commons in November 1936, when he tried as Prime Minister to justify the failure to rearm sooner, 'in 1933 the Disarmament Conference was sitting at Geneva and there was probably a stronger pacifist feeling running through this country than at any time since the war. ... My position as the leader of a great party was not altogether a comfortable one. . . . Supposing I had gone to the country and said that Germany was rearming and that we must rearm, does anybody think that this pacific democracy would have rallied to that cry at that moment? I cannot think of anything that would have made the loss of the election from my point of view more certain'.

The main emphasis in the Labour platform at the time of the Fulham East by-election in October 1933 was on the broad issue of war versus peace although, as *The Times* pointed out on 27 October, the victorious Labour candidate, John Wilmot, 'was unable to suggest anything more, except in the vaguest platitudes, which the government might have done or could do now to secure world peace; and his pronouncements in favour of international cooperation, were an echo of what the Prime Minister and Mr Baldwin have recently said'. After his election, however, Wilmot said that 'British people demand . . . that the British government shall give a lead to the whole world by initiating immediately a policy of general disarmament.' To this, Lansbury added that all nations should 'disarm to the level of Germany as a preliminary to total disarmament'.[16]

It was clear that neither the Labour Party nor the general public understood the military implications of collective security in 1933. Most people were probably similarly uninformed at the time of the Peace Ballot. By the time of the General Election in 1935 the situation had again changed; Hitler was in power in Germany and Mussolini had invaded Abyssinia. The Labour Party's annual conference in October had shown that support for pacifism was on the wane. Lansbury resigned the leadership following the defeat of his pacifist motion rejecting collective action against Italy, and Ernest Bevin was warmly applauded when he said: 'I hope that conference will not be influenced by either sentiment or personal attachments. . . . It is placing the Executive and the Movement in an absolutely wrong position to be hawking your conscience around from body to body asking to be told what to do with it.' Nevertheless the Labour Party, under Attlee's leadership, fought the General Election on an anti-rearmament platform, which they succeeded in combining with the support for the League and collective security. Though they recovered some ground in comparison with 1931, they still faced a Government with an overwhelming majority. There was strong support for Baldwin's policy that peace through collective security, based on the League, required a deliberate programme of rearmament.

Within a month of the Election the government's standing suffered badly from the disastrous episode of the Hoare-Laval agreement, the basis of which was appeasement of Mussolini. Hoare was constrained to resign and Baldwin to apologise to the House of Commons. Although the government's majority was impregnable, the mistrust which this affair engendered was a major factor in delaying the Labour Party's acceptance of the need for rearmament, which the logic of their collective security policy dictated. The atrocities committed by Franco's supporters in the Spanish Civil War were to play a large part in the Parliamentary Party's conversion in 1937. The small number of pacifists remaining in the Party found it difficult to ignore what was being done to Socialists. Fenner Brockway commented: 'It is not the amount of violence which determines good or evil results, but the ideas, the sense of human values, and above all the social forces behind its use. With this realisation, although my nature revolted against the killing of human beings just as did the nature of those Catalonian peasants, the fundamental basis of my old philosophy disappeared'.[17] Thus the Labour Party's passionate call for arms for Spain was in sharp contrast to the government's policy of non-intervention and the international action taken to enforce it. This policy was attacked as amounting to appeasement of the dictators.

The Parliamentary Labour Party's argument for not voting in favour of the defence estimates had been that it represented a way of registering their condemnation of the Government's past and present handling of foreign policy, not a vote against defence. Dalton, playing on the contradiction between Labour's call for arms for Spain but no arms for Britain, managed to persuade the Parliamentary Party that they could not continue to deny the country the means to defend itself on the basis of a 'Parliamentary quibble'. When the vote on the Service estimates came up in July, 1937, the Labour Party abstained from voting, thus making their protest against Government policy clear. Only six Labour MP's actually voted against, together with four members of the Independent Labour Party and the single Communist.

The failure of the government to act when Hitler remilitarised the Rhineland in March 1936 was consistent with the prevailing state of public opinion. For all the brave talk by the Labour Party

– and particularly by a Labour left-wing increasingly in sympathy with the Communists – about the need to stand up to the dictators, neither the party nor the country as a whole was in the mood for any policy which carried with it the risk of war. Moreover there was at that time a widespread feeling of guilt about the Versailles Treaty. Lord Lothian's remark that 'the Germans were only going into their own back-garden' was symptomatic.[18] The government were also conscious of the unreadiness of the armed forces and of the need for time to carry out their plans for rearmament. Chamberlain, who became Prime Minister in May 1937, pursued an active policy of appeasement, involving direct negotiation with the dictators outside the framework of the League, which lasted through the series of meetings with Hitler in 1938 until after Hitler's invasion of Czechoslovakia in March 1939. This policy had the support of influential sections of the press: *The Times, Daily Express, Daily Mail* and *Observer*. This was in no way the result of pressure from a coordinated 'peace movement'. Backed by an ample parliamentary majority, with only relatively few dissenters, Chamberlain was determined to conduct a foreign policy which, though it may have been disastrous, he himself believed in firmly, and which at the time undoubtedly reflected the aspirations of the British public, ill-informed as they were about the real issues despite the warnings of Churchill and others. In the debates on the Munich Agreement in October 1938, Chamberlain reiterated his belief that his action had avoided war and he had been right to take it; his purpose was 'to work for the pacification of Europe' even though 'the path which leads to appeasement is long and bristles with obstacles'. He was enthusiastically applauded.

The irony is that although he accused those who favoured sanctions of being pacifist, Chamberlain's policy was closest to the pacifist line. Most pacifists were careful to dissociate themselves from appeasement, which Peace News called a 'mere "bargaining chip" or bartering of advantages for the sake of easing the politicians' paths', viewing Chamberlain's policy as a deal with Germany based on mutual interest. But they could not easily draw a distinction between their policy and that of the Government. In the Lords, Ponsonby, who had supported non-intervention in Spain, insisted that 'there was nothing on our side to be ashamed of' in the Munich settlement. The first issue of the *Christian Pacifist* argued that 'the policy of appeasement, though the word has recently been given a new and less favourable content by its opponents, is one which in itself deserves our healthy support. It is an honest attempt to settle grievances instead of quarrelling and finally fighting about them'.

After Hitler's occupation of Czechoslovakia most former 'appeasers' were finally disillusioned. This produced a further irony. The pacifists' remaining allies in the dwindling appeasement lobby increasingly consisted of those close to fascism. Oswald Mosley was playing the 'peace card' and it was perhaps inevitable that allegations began to be made after 1939 that the PPU was pro-Nazi. Pacifists, offended by such accusations, were not blameless: for instance, in May 1939, the PPU Peace Service Handbook incuded the pro-Nazi organisation The Link in its list of societies working for international reconciliation. Some articles in *Peace News* even attacked the Jews, which led George Orwell to comment in 1941 that 'after Dick Sheppard's death British pacifism seems to have suffered a moral collapse . . . many of the surviving pacifists now spin a line of talk indistinguishable from the Blackshirts . . . and the actual membership of the PPU and the British Union overlap to some extent'.[19]

Although after 1937 the Labour leaders were often critical of what they viewed, with reason, as lack of energy in the rearmament programme, there still remained some significant ambiguities in their thinking about what was needed for adequate defence. Thus in April 1939 they strongly opposed the introduction of national service. But when war came, only a handful of Labour members of Parliament joined Lansbury in demanding the continuation of efforts to preserve peace. Subsequently a group of 22 Labour MPs also met to try to promote peace negotiations and more than 70 constituency parties came out in favour of a truce, although after France fell little more was heard from them. However the Communists who had reversed their policy, after the Nazi Soviet Pact (see Chapter 3), remained a potentially dangerous force for creating unrest in industry, although the People's Convention, a Communist-sponsored attempt in January 1941 to mobilise public opinion against the government's conduct of the war, attracted little support.[20] The few remaining pacifists were generally tolerated during the 'phoney war' of the winter of 1939, but by the summer of 1940 there was a reaction and many private employers and more than 100 local authorities dismissed their pacifist employees. Government policy however was to recognise genuine 'conscientious objection'. Most conscientious objectors contributed in some form or other to the war effort and a special non-combatant corps, set up in the army in 1940, reached a membership of 7000. Only about three out of every hundred objectors went to gaol. Often however the arguments advanced by the relatively few conscientious objectors in wartime seemed remote from the widespread revulsion against war in the early 1930s. Nevertheless there were some who remained constant to their original principles throughout the war, such as Donald Soper and Bishop Barnes of Birmingham; many others, among them Russell and Joad, decided that Nazism had to be resisted by force.

The peace movement in the 1930s comprised a number of groups which rarely, if ever, managed to unite on a common policy or to form an effective lobby against the government. By the end of the war there was a completely new issue which henceforth was to dominate virtually all its thinking and activities: nuclear weapons. But it was not until 1958 that the movement again gained a following, this time under the flag of a major new organisation, the Campaign for Nuclear Disarmament (CND) which suddenly erupted on to the public stage early in that year and quickly attracted widespread support.

Since 1945 defence and nuclear issues had aroused little public attention. This was partly due to lack of information about the effects of nuclear weapons and about British involvement in their manufacture and deployment, and partly to the concentration on other issues such as the Cold War and post-war reconstruction. The Government's alarm about the possibility of the Americans using the atomic bomb in the Korean War and the international debates about control of nuclear weapons were not much discussed outside fairly narrow circles. Beyond this many people still remembered with relief that the American bombs on Japan in August 1945 had been instrumental in bringing the Second World War to an end. Early in the Cold War, Bertrand Russell, later to become president of CND, was among those who advocated threats to use atomic weapons on the Soviet Union. The prevailing mood was undoubtedly one of extreme hostility to Stalin's policies and those who appeared sympathetic to the Soviet Union were liable to be labelled as Communists or fellow-travellers. The first British atomic test in 1952 aroused little opposition. Nevertheless, the peace movement was regrouping. In 1949, the PPU established a Non-Violence Commission to discuss the possibility of 'direct action' to force the withdrawal of American forces from Britain, stop the manufacture of atomic weapons in Britain, seek the withdrawal of Britain from NATO and disband her armed forces. In 1950, the most active British 'peace' group at the time, the British Peace Committee, a communist front organisation proscribed by the Labour Party in June 1950 (see Chapter 7), claimed more than a million British signatures to the Stockholm Peace Appeal demanding the 'unconditional prohibition of the atomic weapon' under strict international control. (Harry Pollitt had again changed his mind.) When, in April 1954, Britain was developing her own hydrogen bomb, a broader Hydrogen Bomb National Campaign was set up and soon claimed a comparable number of signatures to a petition calling for disarmament and the strengthening of the United Nations but stopped short of demanding the abolition of nuclear weapons.

Among the leaders of the new peace movement were some who had maintained their pacifist convictions throughout the Second World War and others whose beliefs resulted from the bombing of Hiroshima in 1945. Canon John Collins, for example, already increasingly concerned as an RAF chaplain about the ethics of saturation bombing, claimed that 'the horrifying news of the dropping of the atom bomb on Hiroshima, at first almost numbing by reason of its terrible significance, stirred me to such moral indignation that I soon realised that my old attitudes towards war could no longer stand, and that I must do everything possible by way of protest'.[21]

By 1957, concern was growing about the hazards of nuclear tests. In February, in an effort to coordinate the 100 local protest groups around the country, the National Committee for the Abolition of Nuclear Weapon Tests (NCANWT) was formed, later to be merged with CND. In April an Emergency Committee for Direct Action Against Nuclear War (DAC) was established under the chairmanship of Michael Randle, a pacifist, with as its immediate target the coordination of non-violent protest against the Christmas Island test of the British H-bomb due to take place in May. Although the Labour Party in 1955 had endorsed the government's decision to manufacture the H-bomb and generally supported the Conservative defence policy, the peace groups expected to be able to secure Labour's backing for their policies.

But though some thirty Labour MPs joined a Labour H-Bomb Campaign which attracted some support from local parties and trades unions, their efforts were not at that time successful. At the Labour Party Conference at Brighton in September 1957, a resolution committing the Party to refusing to test, manufacture or use nuclear weapons was defeated by 5 836 000 votes to 781 000. Aneurin Bevan, then shadow Foreign Secretary, defended the British Bomb, urging delegates not to send a British Foreign Secretary 'naked into the international conference chamber'.

Meanwhile the Defence White Paper of April 1957 had linked the ending of National Service and a reduction in the size of the armed forces with the adoption of a strategy based on nuclear deterrence. The new policies were well received; the ending of National Service was a popular move as well as being justifiable on economic grounds, and reliance on nuclear weapons, as a means of compensating for shortage of conventional weapon-power, was generally regarded as realistic. Many pacifists were also initially in favour of the policy, viewing the reduction of forces as a small step towards an unarmed world.

By the end of 1957, however, opposition to the strategy of 'massive retaliation', was becoming more vocal. Plans for stationing Thor missiles in England aroused fears that this would increase the likelihood of nuclear attack, although American nuclear bombers had been based in the UK since 1948. An article by J. B. Priestley in the *New Statesman* in November gave those already active in 'peace work' the idea of starting a mass movement against nuclear weapons themselves, not just against tests. At a meeting convened at Canon Collins' house on 16 January 1958, gathering together such NCANWT representatives as Peggy Duff and various individuals, including J. B. Priestley, Rose Macaulay, Sir Julian Huxley and Michael Foot, the Campaign for Nuclear Disarmament was born, with Bertrand Russell as president and Peggy Duff as organising secretary. When the Campaign was publicly launched at a mass meeting on 17 February, Collins was nominated CND's chairman.

The support for CND's inaugural meeting was unexpected. Westminster Central Hall was filled with 5000 people, and four other halls were required to accommodate the overflow. Most originators of the campaign, by now constituting the executive, went to the meeting only with the idea of gaining support for a campaign to force governments to negotiate general nuclear disarmament. Priestley and A. J. P. Taylor, however, with their demands for unilateral disarmament, received the strongest applause and in the end, at St Pancras Town Hall the following day, the revised policy statement drawn up outlining CND aims, reflected the demands of the more radical element:

We shall seek to persuade the British people that Britain must:
(a) Renounce unconditionally the use or production of nuclear weapons and refuse to allow their use by others in her defence.
(b) Use her utmost endeavour to bring about negotiations at all levels for agreement to end the armaments race and to lead to a general disarmament convention.
(c) Not proceed with the agreement for the establishment of missile bases on her territory.
(d) Refuse to provide nuclear weapons for any other country.

Further elaboration of this policy came at the 1960 CND Annual Conference which called also for British withdrawal from any alliance based on the use of nuclear weapons, which in practice meant NATO, and at the 1961 Conference, when CND adopted the concept of positive neutralism. Although the precise formula for this has varied over the years, the commitment to non-alignment and against nuclear alliances has remained CND policy ever since.

Apart from a wide range of publications, including the monthly paper *Sanity*, CND gained its publicity from marches, especially the Easter weekend marches between Aldermaston, the location of the Atomic Weapons Research Establishment, and Trafalgar Square. The first Aldermaston March was in fact, conceived and run by the DAC; and since the CND Executive was wary of the DAC, it offered moral support but it was not closely involved. In 1959 however, DAC being reluctant to repeat the exercise, CND, encouraged by the peaceful character of the 1958 march and the support it had received – between 5000 and 10 000 joined in during the last mile – took over the organisation, attracting to the rally in Trafalgar Square about 20 000 people.[22] Figures continued to increase until 1962 when Peace News estimated that 150 000 people attended the final rally in Hyde Park.

As CND regarded itself as a spontaneous movement rather

than an organised pressure group, there was no formal individual membership until 1966. The much publicised marches were therefore the barometer by which people judged CND's growth. Geoffrey Hawkins has described the marchers as coming from 'the morally aware middle class. Their frustration with politics is an intellectual reaction, the reaction of those who are used to believing that they can somehow influence what governments and oppositions do through the existing democratic machinery.... It is those who are relatively prosperous, and who have been betrayed by those in whom they had some faith. ... The great majority of the population perhaps never expects anything from politics, from that section of society that they always refer to as "them" '.[23] Peter Worsley, formerly a CND National Council member, gives a more sympathetic but not dissimilar account: 'most of them were liberal-minded Labour voters who had, however, never been involved in politics before, even though they regarded themselves as "political" ... CND was a movement of young people.... There was an overall distinctive style, the new public face of a distinctive political culture.... Above all, it was *public*: people who would have previously been horrified even to think of walking in the gutter.... It involved a departure from conventional norms of respectable behaviour ... involving a degree of readiness to risk being labelled as "nutty" or stupid, even ostracised by the neighbours if need be'.[24]

Many well-known personalities – actors, writers, artists and scientists – marched and contributed their talents to CND* but it was easier to identify groups amongst the thousands marching, than individuals. Distinguished by their banners, these included not only CND regional organisations, amounting to more than 450 by 1960, but also churches, trade unions, Constituency Labour Parties, smaller peace organisations, youth movements, university groups and, after 1960 when the Soviet Union and the CPGB changed their tactics towards unilateral disarmament, many Communist organisations. Pacifists and non-pacifists bodies were brought together around one cause. The cohesion of these groups, however, proved transitory. Collins had argued for a 'short sharp campaign', appealing to the youthful majority, and

---

* It was just prior to the first Aldermaston March that the designer and CND member, Gerald Holtom, produced the CND symbol which is still adorning its badges, banners and leaflets today. The broken cross inside the circle portrayed firstly, the semaphore for the initials N D, and secondly, the death of man, the circle the unborn child.

along with most of the Executive, believed that 'if CND were to be at all successful, it would need to take into consideration political expediencies, and to gear itself to the realities of parliamentary democracy'.²⁵ Thus, CND's first aim was to win a majority for CND within the Labour party, and secondly to persuade the British people of their case in order to elect a Labour Party committed to unilateral disarmament. This was not a recipe for cross-party unity in support of a common non-partisan cause.

The more militant DAC, committed to 'non-violent direct action', co-existed uneasily with CND, although the latter was never reconciled to the methods adopted by the Committee which virtually invited arrest. By 1960, Russell had reached the conclusion that a more active campaign of civil disobedience was required. In October he resigned from the presidency of the CND and, with such prominent supporters as John Braine, John Osborne, Augustus John and Arnold Wesker, formed the Committee of 100 for the purpose of organising 'civil disobedience' on a massive scale. This led to frequent confrontations and arrests at demonstrations over the next two years, which attracted much publicity and some admiration, especially from younger supporters of CND. But the illegality was contrary to CND's policy and the vast majority of CND's supporters wanted a campaign which would promote its aims by legal and democratic means. The split between Collins and his Executive on the one hand and Russell and the Committee of 100 on the other in turn created tension within the CND which opened the way for infiltration by other extremists, such as Anarchists and Trotskyists, who saw their opportunity to foment disorder.

CND's attempts to attract the Labour Party's interest at first failed completely. In the late 1950s, the Labour Party had been sympathetic to NCANWT and any other group urging multilateral disarmament. But when NCANWT merged with CND and the latter adopted unilateralism, Labour's interest faded. CND also lost the support of the United Nations Association (successor to the LNU with a large membership, amounting to nearly 60 000 in 1957). Until mid-1960, the Communist-controlled British Peace Committee (BPC) had more influence at trade union and party conferences. The situation changed when the Paris 'summit meeting', the first four power summit with the Russians since 1955, collapsed in May 1960, before it had even begun work and the Russians withdrew from the Ten Power Disarmament

Committee. CND's demands for unilateralism became much more appealing. In addition, the cancellation of the 'Blue Streak' missile at about the same time by the Conservative Government was seen by many, especially in the Labour Party, as a clear indication that the cost of an independent British deterrent was beyond Britain's capacity. For the Labour leadership this seemed to provide the basis for compromise with those in the Party opposed in principle to nuclear weapons. So the Party's new official policy was to support Britain's membership of NATO but to rely in future on the United States for the provision of nuclear weapons to meet Alliance needs.

However, unilateralism was fast gaining ground in the Unions. By the time of the 1960 CND Easter march, the Union of Shop, Distributive and Allied Workers (USDAW), the first big union to hold its annual conference, had voted in favour of unilateral disarmament. Several other unions followed suit, and a resolution in the same sense was passed at the Trades Union Congress in September. At the Labour Party's 59th annual conference at Scarborough in October a 'multilateralist' resolution embodying the Party's new policy was narrowly defeated. In its place, a 'unilateralist' resolution, introduced by the Transport and General Workers' Union and demanding 'a complete rejection of any defence policy based on the threat of the use of strategic nuclear weapons' as well as the permanent cessation of manufacture and testing of such weapons and their removal from the United Kingdom, was passed. This was to prove – until 1980 – the high point of CND's influence in the Labour Party. But it was not reflected in the voting of the Parliamentary Labour Party, where there was a hard-core of only about 50 unilateralists, and several MPs sponsored by Trades Unions which had supported the unilateralist resolution at the Party conference continued to support the Party leadership. Moreover the leadership, led by Hugh Gaitskell, succeeded in reversing the 1960 unilateralist decision at the subsequent Blackpool conference in 1961.

Opinion polls at this time indicated that CND's objectives commended themselves to between one-fifth and one-third of the population. The Committee of 100 did a great deal to discredit CND as a whole in the eyes of the public. One poll conducted in the autumn of 1961 recorded that 60% of those interviewed disapproved of the type of activity undertaken, particularly by the Committee.[26] As Collins explained 'because the public was not able to distinguish between CND and the Committee of 100, it enabled our opponents to write off CND as irresponsible'.[27]

CND had succeeded in drawing together diverse peace organisations where others in the past had failed. It helped focus public attention on the issue of nuclear weapons, encouraging debate and making many converts. Nevertheless, despite its efforts, a week before the 1964 General Election, 55% thought that it was 'very important' that Britain keep the 'independent nuclear deterrent', 17% – fairly important, and 4% – don't know. By the end of 1964, it was clear that it had failed to influence the policies of those then in power and that, though vocal, its aim of unilateral disarmament remained a minority view. Troubled by internal conflicts, it was widely regarded with scepticism. That groundswell of public opposition to 'The Bomb' which it had sought to create never fully materialised. The developments in the early 1960s which led to this decline are considered in Chapter 9.

9 The Peace Movement in the United Kingdom, 1963–83

The peace movement in the United Kingdom went into decline between the early 1960s and 1980. Two events marked the start of the decline. First, CND lost the broad support of the Labour Party. The unilateralist policy adopted by Labour's annual conference in 1960 was reversed when Hugh Gaitskell's pledge, as party leader, to "fight, fight and fight again" against unilateralism prevailed at the 1961 conference. Between 1964 and 1979, during two periods in office covering a total of 11 years, successive Labour Governments maintained support for the British nuclear deterrent and for the policy of multilateral negotiations as the only acceptable basis for disarmament. Although unilateralist resolutions were passed at the party's annual conferences in 1972 and 1973 they had little effect on party policy, failing to attain the two-thirds vote necesary to secure policy changes. It was not until 1980 that the Labour Party conference once again voted to put its weight behind a policy of British unilateral disarmament and not until 1982 that the two-thirds barrier was again breached.

The second event was the conclusion of the Partial Test Ban Treaty in 1963. Coming soon after the shock of the Cuban crisis – itself a setback to unilateralists – this was the first significant multilateral agreement relating to nuclear arms control. Although limited in scope (its prohibitions did not extend to underground nuclear explosions), it was rightly hailed as a major breakthrough. It was followed by ten years of negotiations aimed at controlling the deployment and spread of nuclear weapons to which both Labour and Conservative Governments contributed. Among the multilateral agreements concluded in this period, to all of which the United States, Soviet Union and United Kingdom are parties, were the Outer Space Treaty of 1967 and the Sea Bed

Treaty of 1971, prohibiting the deployment of nuclear weapons in these two environments; the Non-Proliferation Treaty of 1968, in which the undertaking of the non-nuclear signatories not to acquire nuclear weapons was balanced by the commitment of those already possessing them to 'pursue negotiations in good faith on effective measures relating to cessation of the nuclear arms race' (over 120 nations have so far signed this Treaty); and the Biological Weapons Convention of 1972. The period culminated with the bilateral US-Soviet SALT-1 agreements in 1972, comprising the Anti-Ballistic Missile Treaty (limiting deployment of ABMs in both countries) and the Interim Agreement placing ceilings on the land-based and submarine-based strategic ballistic missiles of both countries. Limited though these were they represented, and were seen as, a major first step in the process of restraining the nuclear armouries of the two superpowers.

It was against this background that in the 1960s support for the CND, which had grown into a major popular movement since 1958, began to wane. The celebrities, the distinguished figures in literature and the arts who had been active in the early years, gradually withdrew. The moral fervour, which had given CND the aspect of a crusade, and which had proved such a powerful attraction to young (and not so young) idealists throughout the country, died down. As noted in Chapter 8 many were alienated by the increased emphasis on direct action and, by implication, illegal 'civil disobedience', favoured by the breakaway Committee of 100, as opposed to the policy of peaceful demonstration which had marked CND's start. The numbers participating in the Aldermaston Marches, which had proved such an enormously popular annual event in the early years, fell away until the marches ceased to attract notice. The CND hard liners dissipated their efforts in fields of action, such as the protest against American policy in Vietnam, which were not seen as being directly related to the original and single unifying objective of nuclear disarmament. The smaller groups virtually faded away. The movement had to face the fact that, in the words of one of its members, 'unilateral nuclear disarmament did not have majority public suport'; it had, in short, 'failed to win the support of ordinary people'.[1]

One factor contributing to CND's decline in the 'lean period' between 1964 and 1980 has been identified as 'the attentions of the Communist Party, especially when they began to make it a serious target as their main peace front after 1963'[2]. During this period Communist party members and other extreme left-wingers acquired increasing ascendancy over the organisation. John Cox, a leading Communist, was chairman from 1971 to 1977. When he took over, the general secretary was a former Communist who had resigned from the Party in 1957 because of the events in Hungary. By the time Cox gave up the chairmanship, the general secretary was a Communist who held the post until succeeded by Monsignor Bruce Kent in 1979. At various times in recent years Communists (among others) have also filled the posts of vice-chairman, national organiser and press officer. The CPGB's national congress in November 1981 resolved that the Communist Party had made a substantial contribution and many of its members had for years played active roles in the organisations of the 'broad movement for peace'. CND with its mass campaigning base was especially important. The subsequent biennial Party Congress in 1983 at which delegates voted to campaign against cruise and Trident Missiles while supporting moves for a nuclear 'freeze' received extensive publicity because of the attendance of Bruce Kent. He told the delegates that he was proud to have been invited, and delighted to be able to attend: 'My appearance here is something that I owe you and we owe you for what has been happening over the past few years.' He expressed thanks to the few groups which had contributed to keeping the peace movement in being 'in the lean years', naming the Society of Friends in the religious world and the Communist Party in the political world. He went on: 'We owe a debt of gratitude to the *Morning Star* newspaper, which has given steady, honest and generous coverage of the whole disarmament case. I do not believe we are so very far apart on many of the major issues. We are partners in the cause for peace in this world. The nation should be indebted to the *Morning Star*, not just CND.'[3]

There was no surprise at Communist support, or indeed at Communist attempts at exploitation of CND, since Moscow's decision in 1960 to support CND for tactical reasons. Not only did the activities of CND suit the objectives of the Soviet 'peace campaign' (the purpose of which was to reinforce Soviet Government policies), which found natural allies in the CPGB, but such support was also wholly consistent with the CPGB's general policy orientation. This was set out in 1980 by Tony Chater, a former chairman of the CPGB, who was a member of the

Presidential Committee of the WPC from 1969 to 1975 and has been editor of the *Morning Star* since 1974. After emphasising that peaceful co-existence created the best conditions for the transition from capitalism to socialism and that the fight for peace was central to this process, Chater concluded that 'the threat to peace does not come from the Soviet Union. It comes from the dominant section of monopoly capitalism – the military industrial complex'.[4]

Despite subsequent differences between Chater's hard-line views and those of the majority in the CPGB executive this still provides the ideological background to Communist involvement in CND and similar groups. But although Trotskyists as well as Communists exert a disproportionate influence on some local and specialist groups (Trotskyist influence in Youth CND and Labour CND was a source of major concern to the national leadership in 1983), the greatly increased size of CND since 1980 and its loosely coordinated structure make this difficult to sustain at the centre. Moreover, communist efforts to secure positions of influence in recent years have not gone without criticism within the organisation. John Cox not only failed to be re-elected as chairman in November 1981, but was criticised at the time for lack of frankness about his party membership. The position, as regards the central direction of the CND, was correctly stated by one prominent Communist Jon Bloomfield, who wrote in 1982: 'Communists who hold positions in the CND are elected to them like anyone else'.[5] That there are perhaps as many as a dozen members and former members of the Communist Party on the 110-member National Council (see below), and that several of these serve on the Executive Committee, are not in doubt; nor is Bruce Kent's claim that in strict numerical terms CND has more Quakers than Communist Party members among its supporters.

Not surprisingly the Soviet Peace Committee has welcomed contacts with CND. In 1982 the Committee for the first time sent an official observer to CND's annual conference, in the person of one of its vice-Chairmen, Vikenti Matveev, a writer on international affairs for *Izvestiya*.[6] (They did so again in 1983). This followed a series of visits to the Soviet Union organised by the CND earlier in the year. In January, Fenner, now Lord, Brockway led a mixed party of CND and Quaker groups, which was officially sponsored by the Soviet Peace Committee; at their final meeting, General Tatarnikov, the Soviet representative, made it clear that he was only prepared to sign a joint declaration on condition that no reference was made to the idea of unilateral cuts in nuclear forces, which had originated from the Generals for Peace and Disarmament and which, at a previous meeting, he had appeared to approve. In May, the chairman of the Soviet Peace Committee, G. A. Zhukov, met a CND Delegation led by the chairperson, Joan Ruddock; and in October, the Soviet Peace Committee received the CND General Secretary, Bruce Kent. On 18 July 1983 in an interview with *Pravda*'s London correspondent Maslennikov, Bruce Kent was reported by Moscow radio to have said that with the deployment of nuclear missiles in Britain, 'the nuclear arms race on the continent of Europe will enter a new and even more dangerous phase. That is why we take a positive view of the Soviet initiatives which are directed towards not having the new models of US nuclear missiles deployed on our continent'.

During the past four years some of the statements made by CND's leaders, and some of CND's activities, have displayed a one-sidedness bordering on naïveté. The Russians and their sympathisers within CND have made every effort to exploit this tendency. In 1983, in Britain as in West Germany (see Chapter 10), they overestimated the extent to which they could rely on the pressures generated by the peace movements to achieve their objectives. Moreover, whatever ambitions they may have had – and may still harbour – they have not succeeded in converting CND at national level into a Communist front organisation.

CND's revival may be said to date from the beginning of 1980. It had begun to show signs of renewed life when in January 1978 it adopted a policy resolution, which called for a series of nuclear disarmament measures to be adopted internationally and for specific unilateral steps to be taken by the British Government as the basis for unofficial British lobbying at the 1978 United Nations Special Session on Disarmament. CND's activities at this session were subsumed within the general coordinating role played by the much older National Peace Council on behalf of a wide range of British non-governmental organisations. In the same year, a petition was launched against the proposal to deploy Enhanced Radiation Weapons in Europe, which attracted considerable support; the sponsors claimed to have attracted a quarter of a million signatures. But CND's national membership in January 1980 was still no more than 3000. Its return to prominence was largely due to four events, two positive and two negative. The first positive event was the NATO Double-Track decision of 12 December 1979. The second was the British decision to adopt, on purchase from the United States, the Trident Missile as the successor to Polaris in the 1990s; although this was not formally announced until July 1980, Government policy for the future of the British nuclear deterrent had been foreshadowed in Parliament in January. The main thrust of all CND's subsequent campaigning has been to secure the cancellation of Trident and of the basing of cruise missiles in the United Kingdom. The two negative developments, which undoubtedly influenced many people who joined CND at that time and since, were American in origin. One was the failure of the United States Congress to ratify the SALT II Agreement, signed by Presidents Carter and Brezhnev in July 1979; the other was the dismissive attitude adopted by President Reagan and his advisers during the 1980 US Presidential election campaign and in the early months of his Administration both to SALT II and to the idea of arms control negotiations generally. This initial impression died hard, with the result that many people still remain unconvinced of the genuineness of the US Administration's arms control policies.

These factors, positive and negative, were the principal contributors to CND's revival, but they were not the only ones. Many people who had welcomed the arms control agreements in the 1960s and early 1970s felt frustrated at the lack of further progress. No new agreement on limiting nuclear weapons had entered into force since SALT I in 1972; the slow pace of what were seen as highly technical debates, whose complexities were difficult for any but the expert to understand and whose practical results were conspicuous only by their absence, induced scepticism, if not despair, at the prospects for future multilateral negotiations. The theory of deterrence and the need to modernise NATO's nuclear arsenal in order to maintain its credibility were either imperfectly understood or questioned. Little sustained effort was made by NATO or its member Governments to explain these matters in terms which the public could understand and accept. They failed not only to put across clearly the Alliance's policies but also to publicise the amount of effort which, despite the disappointing outcome, was being made to negotiate worthwhile agreements with the Soviet Union. Meanwhile the Soviet Union was doing its best to fill this gap by presenting, in disingenuous terms, its own interpretation of NATO's policies and of its own efforts to achieve disarmament. A new British generation had grown up, too young to have taken part in the earlier campaign of 1958–62 and with no memory of the origins of collective Western defence. Some ill-advisedly insensitive words in the West were contrasted with some deceptively soft words from the East; fear of nuclear war was fanned by doubts about the ability of deterrence to prevent it and a belief that the West was actually planning to fight it. Irrational and ill-formed though these reactions might be, they nevertheless formed a powerful stimulus to CND's popular resurgence.

It was this tide, and this mood, that E. P. Thompson, a Marxist who left the CPGB over Hungary in 1956 and who admits that his CND membership had 'lapsed', caught with his essay *Protest and Survive*, published in 1980.[8] The title was a parody of *Protect and Survive*, the Home Office pamphlet on civil defence plans, which CND opposes as wholly ineffective. Shorn of hyperbole, Thompson's thesis was that, although deterrence may have 'worked' in inhibiting major 'conventional' war in Europe for over thirty years, supporters of this concept have both ignored the 'unthinkable' consequences which would result from its failure and accepted, without considering the implications, American decisions aimed at ensuring that any resultant 'limited' war would be confined to Europe. He regarded deterrence as a 'degenerative state' which results in an accumulation of repressed violence and is driven by an 'inter-operative and reciprocal logic which threatens all impartially'. Arguing from a 'general and sustained historical process' rather than from specific episodes, he reached the view that 'a general nuclear war is not only possible but probable, and that its probability is increasing'. He did not spare the Russians: the SS-20 is 'a foul, unnecessary and threatening weapon' and the Soviet state was the 'most dangerous in relation to its own people and to the people of its client states'. But his main criticism was reserved for NATO, regarded as a creature of the United States. The latter in his view seemed 'to be the more dangerous and provocative in its general military and diplomatic strategies, which press around the Soviet Union with menacing bases'. Thompson advocated a programme of protest as 'the only realistic form of civil defence'. Its main aim would be the creation of a European zone free of nuclear weapons and bases from, in the first place, the Atlantic to the Urals to be achieved through pressure brought by each national peace movement on its

Government. In the West such action would be favoured by the Soviet Government and in the East would 'for a time be contained'; but success in the West would in due course produce in the East 'those conditions of relaxation of tension which will weaken the rationale and legitimacy of repressive state measures and will allow the pressures for democracy and *détente* to assert themselves'. As for Britain, 'we must detach ourselves from the nuclear strategies of NATO', give up our 'independent' deterrent, close all nuclear bases and refuse to accept American cruise missiles. While his essay may be criticised as one-sided and unrealistic, his interpretation of NATO policies as ill-informed and his view of the United States as coloured by prejudice, of all the documents to emerge from the peace movement since 1980 this was the most successful in articulating the feelings of a broad spectrum of many who were concerned about current East–West relations. As a result Thompson became the chief evangelist for the new campaign for European Nuclear Disarmament (END).

CND estimated its national membership by the end of 1980 as 9000[9], 20 000 a year later and 50 000 in 1982.[10] By December 1983 it claimed over 80 000 individual members. The constitution lays down rules for establishment of regional organisations and specialist sections. Between annual conferences, the CND is governed by a national council, consisting of five representatives from each of the 16 regions, one from each of seven specialist sections and 23 members directly elected by the conference. The council meets every two months and appoints a small executive committee to deal with daily business. In addition to the specialist groups, by 1982 there were said to be 950 local groups comprising an affiliated total of some 250 000 members.[11] Such support was demonstrated by the Trafalgar Square rally on 26 October 1980, which 100 000 people attended and the rally in London a year later, on 24 October 1981, which attracted about 150 000 people. This event, in common with those in subsequent autumns, coincided with a series of demonstrations in Western Europe during 'International Disarmament Week', when large marches were held in Bonn, Brussels, Amsterdam, Rome, Madrid and Paris. A similar rally was held in Hyde Park in June 1983, for which CND claimed an even larger attendance, and a march in London on 22 October 1983 (the date chosen for demonstrations all over Western Europe).

CND's aim, as set out in the 1980 constitution, is 'the unilateral abandonment by Britain of nuclear weapons, nuclear bases and nuclear alliances as a pre-requisite for a British foreign policy which has the world-wide abolition of nuclear, chemical and biological weapons leading to general and complete disarmament as its prime objective'. Unilateral British disarmament is thus intended as the first step. In its '30 Questions and Answers' in 1983, CND claimed that the distinction between unilateralism and multilateralism was false, used by those who wished to divide the peace movement, and that it supported all 'genuine disarmament processes' by whatever means: but the distinction was reasserted by the insistance that 'every country can and should take its own disarmament steps, here and now, without waiting for agreement by anyone else'. This policy was reflected in resolutions adopted by an overwhelming majority of the 1300 delegates at the annual conference in Sheffield in November 1982. The conference also decided, by only 680 to 642, to give greater priority to the demand for British withdrawal from NATO, ignoring Thompson's advice that 'we cannot allow our enemies to paint us into a corner. The slogan "NATO out of Britain, Britain out of NATO" is a good one, but it must be taken with a nuclear free zone in Europe, and the break-up of both blocs', NATO and the Warsaw pact.[12] British unilateralism was again the basis of the main policy decisions at the annual conference in December 1983, attended by 2000 people. Top priority was given to the cancellation of the Trident and cruise missile programmes; and the conference, with an even-handedness which was criticized by communist and other far left participants, declared (this time by a large majority) its belief that 'British withdrawal from NATO would be a positive step in the unravelling of both NATO and the Warsaw Pact', and resolved to step up its campaign to this end. In a further gesture of even-handedness, an emergency resolution condemning the deployment of cruise missiles and calling for an intensification of the campaign for their removal, also deplored the Soviet decisions to end the INF talks and to deploy new weapons in Europe since the latter 'will inevitably result in another round of weapon deployments by the USA and NATO'.

Although facing some calls to revive illegal civil disobedience, the 1982 annual conference decided that the campaign should be conducted by 'non-violent direct action' linked with offers to win greater support from the Labour movement. The 1983 conference reaffirmed its commitment to 'peaceful activities' only, and threatened withdrawal of membership from anyone advocating the use of violence. The policy was put to the test soon after the 1982 conference when, on 12 December, 30 000 women unilateral disarmers, including visiting groups from West Germany and Denmark and representatives from other countries, surrounded the base at Greenham Common in Berkshire, where preparations were being made for cruise missile deployment, with no major incident occurring. Thereafter there was a succession of demonstrations during the first half of 1983, the largest being those at Greenham Common, Burghfield and in Glasgow. As usual the focus was on unilateral British action; Bruce Kent was however reported as saying that 'no proposal which allows for the introduction into Europe of any first-use missiles like cruise or first-strike weapons like Pershing II will be acceptable to the Soviets. Nevertheless the Soviet should begin now to withdraw a substantial proportion of their SS-20s, irrespective of the so-called zero talks in Geneva. Such a withdrawal would give evidence of their good faith'.[13] To sustain their claim to even-handedness CND leaders have made public reference to the campaign's opposition to the Soviet SS-20 and its condemnation of the invasion of Afghanistan and of suppression of human rights in Poland, and attributed shared responsibility for the arms race to both major military blocs. There is no reason to doubt that these views are genuinely held by those who thus express them. But they have not succeeded in counteracting the impression, strongly reinforced by the predominant emphasis at demonstrations and meetings around the country and in much of their writing, that CND's criticisms are directed almost exclusively at the United States and NATO.

CND's relations with the Labour movement have always been close, and were further strengthened when the Labour Party, by two-thirds majority at its 1982 annual conference, adopted unilateralism as its official policy for the ensuing General Election. CND's own leaflet for the June 1983 election was carefully neutral, emphasizing that 'survival' was the key issue and urging voters to 'find out your candidate's stand in the nuclear election' before deciding how to vote. CND's chairperson, Joan Ruddock, was less equivocal, declaring that 'given the Conservative Government's record we have to create a position where people who support our stance cannot vote Conservative'.[14] But the election results showed that (as in 1962) unilateralism had 'failed to win the support of ordinary people'. This view was supported by an opinion poll in October, which showed 77% in favour of Britain maintaining or improving its nuclear weapons and 73% for Britain's continued membership of NATO, and no majority against either Trident or cruise missiles.[15] Nevertheless CND claimed a 60% increase in membership in the year ending December 1983, and its annual conference resolved to seek close association and joint action with both the TUC and the Labour Party.

The General Election results however led to some heart-searching within CND. The National Council decided in July to reduce its emphasis on unilateral disarmament and to make a 'freeze' on nuclear weapons one of the key themes for the 22 October demonstration. In Bruce Kent's words: 'we are doing our best to broaden our base to involve people who are concerned about the freeze. There are a lot of people who may not have got into the present arguments about cruise, Trident and SS-20s, but who see urgent need to stop the escalation of nuclear weapons at all levels. CND should be reaching out to people who may not agree with us from A to Z but do agree from A to K'.[16] Many CND groups gave their support to a major advertising campaign in favour of the freeze concept, which included the placing of full-page advertisements by the Nuclear Weapons Freeze Advertising Campaign in the national press, for example, in *The Times* of 28 September. The proponents of the freeze claimed that their proposal was based on the freeze movement in the United States (see Chapter 11). Their advertisement contained much tendentious reasoning about the fallacy of deterrence and the development of the arms race and some questionable assertions about the advantages of a freeze. The case was supported by none of the rigorous examination of the problems, including the need to avoid undermining deterrence, which has characterised the freeze movement in the United States; its unilateralist purpose was revealed in the final section which gave the implications for Britain as being the cancellation of Trident and of cruise missile basing. The freeze failed to attract support to, or within the CND. At the 1983 annual conference, it was recognised that a 'unilateral freeze' would conflict with the American concept and a 'multilateral freeze' would weaken CND's unilateralist policies. So the freeze was dropped from CND's national campaign agenda.[17]

Since 1980 the peace movement has received growing support

from the 'nuclear-free zone' movement sponsored by certain left-wing local authorities. This began when Manchester City Council on 5 November 1980 passed a resolution calling on the government not to manufacture or position any nuclear weapon within the city boundaries. This resolution was communicated to all local authorities throughout the country. The idea of declaring 'nuclear-free zones' as a form of anti-nuclear protest caught on. Its attraction as a symbol of protest obscured the fact that the adoption of 'nuclear free' status could not be expected to provide any exemption from nuclear attack or its effects. By May 1982, about 170 Council, Borough and District authorities had passed similar resolutions; these were mainly in the North of England and West of Scotland, but included the GLC and all eight county Councils in Wales, enabling supporters of the movement to claim that, in February 1982, Wales had become the first nuclear-free country in Europe, if not in the world. The movement spread to Western Europe and, in April 1983, a conference of 200 mayors representing nuclear-free boroughs in the five NATO countries due to receive cruise missiles met in Brussels. They issued an appeal to colleagues in both Western and Eastern Europe to declare their boroughs nuclear-free as a step towards a nuclear-free Europe. However, at the subsequent press conference no one could say whether there was any chance that mayors in eastern Europe would be free to respond to the appeal. In the United Kingdom the efforts of the 'nuclear-free' councils, strongly supported by CND, were instrumental in securing the cancellation of the government's civil defence exercise, 'Hard Rock', planned for the autumn of 1982. This was regarded by CND as a major achievement in view of their opposition to any form of civil defence planning. It resulted however in the strengthening of the government's powers to require local authorities to make plans for civil defence.

Church members of all denominations have played a prominent role in the peace movement. Bruce Kent claimed in July 1983 that 23% of the CND membership were 'practising Christians'.[18] A leading member of Christian CND, Canon Paul Oestreicher, who takes his stand on the principle that 'nuclear war could never fulfil the conditions of a just war' as defined by traditional Christian doctrine, has insisted that 'on no major Christian occasion should the Church be allowed to forget that a failure to support the struggle against a nuclear holocaust would be a betrayal of the Gospel'.[19] Canon Oestreicher, an Anglican priest, was a member of the Church of England Working Party which, under the chairmanship of the Bishop of Salisbury, published a report, *The Church and the Bomb*, in 1982. This important document concluded that 'the nuclear element in deterrence is no longer a reliable or morally acceptable approach to the future of the world'. The report's practical prescription was to opt for a strategy of unilateral measures 'in the hope of getting multilateral reductions moving'. It suggested that, because of the excessive number of nuclear weapons in existence, for the United Kingdom to adopt a unilateral policy within NATO might 'actually increase security and at the same time create an initiative which might well lead to positive moves from others'. The report therefore recommended not only that greater efforts should be made to achieve multilateral disarmament but also that the United Kingdom should embark on a phased programme of unilateral renunciation of all existing or projected nuclear weapons and removal of nuclear bases from Britain. This programme should, if possible, be negotiated with other members of NATO; but, whatever the outcome, the authors of the report claimed to see no moral objection to Britain's continued membership of the Alliance and acceptance of the protection provided by American and NATO nuclear deterrence.[20] At the end of the debate on the report on 10 February 1983, the General Synod of the Church of England rejected unilateralist policies by a large majority but called upon all countries 'publicly to forswear the first use of nuclear weapons in any form'.[21] When the general synod next met on 8 November, a motion to debate the issue of cruise missiles was rejected by majority vote.

Of quite a different order is the Greenham Common Peace Camp. This was started by 40 women members of a group called Women for Life on Earth who marched the 125 miles from Cardiff to Newbury in August 1981. On arrival, they chained themselves to the fence by the main gate of the Greenham Common RAF base, the larger of the two sites for cruise missiles in the UK and one to receive its first missiles in December 1983. The women set up camp outside the main gate and, with many changes in the original personnel, have ever since sustained their physical protest against cruise missiles and the 'arms race'. They have no formal organisation and no designated leader, although Helen John has frequently spoken on their behalf. Their method is physical obstruction, including breaking into the base and impeding its normal functioning, and many of the women have been fined or imprisoned on conviction for criminal offences. They place great emphasis on the importance of an exclusively women's protest against policies decided mainly by men. They have achieved much notoriety and engendered widespread criticism for their activities and the conditions in which they live. Since they rely, for promotion of their cause, on publicity for their chosen method of protest rather than on reasoned argument, they have not been deterred by these vicissitudes which have indeed attracted sympathy, from women in particular, both in Britain and in other countries, who look on Greenham as a symbol of female protest in a male-dominated world. Three of their members visited Moscow in May 1983 with the hope of meeting women 'peace campaigners'. They were received by the official Soviet Peace Committee, but evidently had some success in making informal contacts with ordinary Russians under the watchful gaze of the KGB.[22] The women even took a member of the unofficial Group for Establishing Trust, Olga Medvedkova, (see Chapter 12) to their meeting with the Soviet Peace Committee. It was doubtless this move, possibly reinforced by the contents of their notes which were seized when they left Moscow, that led the Soviet authorities to cancel at the last minute in September 1983 a second and larger visit, during which the women had again hoped to 'chat informally to people at random'.[23] This caused a group of the women on 25 January 1984 to stage a sit-in at the Soviet Embassy in London in support of their demand for visas and the release of Medvedkova, which ended when they were removed by the police at the request of the Embassy.[24]

CAMPAIGN FOR EUROPEAN NUCLEAR DISARMAMENT

Despite such international links, the main outlook and activities of the British groups so far described have been largely domestic. One of the most important initiatives in 1980 was the launching of the campaign for European Nuclear Disarmament (END) by the Bertrand Russell Peace Foundation in association with CND and other peace organisations. The European Appeal, originally drafted by E. P. Thompson but much revised in consultation with supporters in other European countries, was published in London on 28 April 1980. It does not apportion guilt between East and West for the existing dangerous situation in Europe since 'guilt lies squarely on both parties'. It calls for joint European action, East and West, to 'free the entire territory of Europe, from Poland to Portugal, from nuclear weapons, air and submarine bases' and urges the United States and Soviet Union 'to withdraw all nuclear weapons from European territory'. (No doubt in the hope of attracting Soviet support, European Russia was omitted from Thompson's proposal for a nuclear-free zone from the Atlantic to the Urals.) As a basis for progress towards its objective, the Appeal stresses the need 'to act as if a united, neutral and pacific Europe already exists'. It attracted many distinguished sponsors and widespread support in Western and 'neutral' Europe. END, which describes itself as 'an idea, a strategy, a political orientation within the peace movement', originally had no individual membership; since July 1983 its constitution provides for a small coordinating committee elected by 'END supporters' who have registered written support for its aims. The organisation sees its purpose as being to facilitate 'the process of consultation between the European peace movements' and to promote 'the European dimension in the British peace movement and abroad'.

Central to END's purpose is the encouragement of every kind of exchange between East and West in Europe. But Thompson wrote in 1981 that: 'to allow the Western Peace Movement to drift into collusion with the strategy of the World Peace Council – that is, in effect, to become a movement opposing NATO militarism *only* – is a recipe for our own containment and ultimate defeat', and added that the 'state-sponsored Peace Committees have never throughout their whole 30-year existence fluttered an eyelash in protest against any action of Soviet militarism'.[25]

Discussion of this problem took place at a conference in London in May 1982 when Zhores Medvedev, the exiled Soviet dissident, maintained that in the Soviet Union there were no independent movements; the so-called 'peace organisations' which protested against the 'arms race' never criticised the Soviet Government. Thompson added that peace organisations in the Soviet Union, unlike those in Hungary, had never published any END statement critical of Soviet policy; he suggested that the minimal requirement for any future cooperation with official Soviet (and other East European) organisations should be Soviet agreement to disseminate such material. Representatives of these organisations were not officially invited to the END sponsored European Disarmament Conference in Brussels in July 1982.

This position led logically to the rejection by END of the attempt by the Soviet Peace Committee to co-sponsor the Second END Convention held in West Berlin in May 1983. The Committee had threatened that, if it were not invited as co-sponsor, it would use its influence 'with the real anti-war movement' to ensure that the conference failed. This view was put forcefully to Bruce Kent and others during their visit to Moscow in October 1982 when END was criticised for supporting the right of citizens in Eastern Europe to organise independently and to criticise the military policies of their own governments as well as those of the West. Kent's view was that 'END's policy of linking disarmament and human rights is correct, but we must avoid giving the impression that things in the West are fine and all the problems are on the other side'. (As CND's '30 Questions and Answers' put it, 'before we get too self-righteous about our freedoms, it is well to remember that in many parts of the Western military bloc – from South Korea to Turkey – no "independent" peace movements could possibly exist'.) Although he warned against causing the Soviet Peace Committee 'to feel that it was becoming isolated', he supported the END decision to limit the organising committee for the Second Convention to groups which had endorsed the 'European Appeal'. Ken Coates, the director of the Bertrand Russell Peace Foundation, summed up the general British (and Western) view when he said that 'the independent peace movement has a right to meet itself on its own terms without having them dictated to us'.

This stand provoked a lengthy letter from G. A. Zhukov, the president of the Soviet Peace Committee, to some 1500 prominent 'peace activists' in Western Europe. The tone of this letter, despatched in December 1982, plainly revealed Soviet disenchantment with the END and the Russell Foundation. Zhukov asserted that the outcome of the 1982 Brussels Convention 'was not to rally but to disunite the anti-war movements'; 'the real mass peace movements of the Socialist countries' were not invited to take part but instead the attempt was made to substitute people who were active 'not in the struggle for *détente* and disarmament but in undermining the socialist system', who had left their countries and had 'nothing in common with the struggle for peace'. He complained of discrimination against Soviet public organisations which supported the peace policy of the Soviet Government and its stand 'for the elimination of all nuclear weapons from the whole European continent' on grounds that these organisations were 'official' and 'dependent'. He claimed that talks with the committee responsible for organising the Berlin Convention had revealed that its purpose was 'to distract the attention of the peace-loving public away from the main source of deadly peril', the plans to deploy new US nuclear missiles in Western Europe, and that the attempt of the organisers to apportion 'equal responsibility' to East and West was aimed at 'the disorientation, demobilisation and undermining of the anti-war movement'. He strongly criticised the organisers for their alleged 'selective approach in choosing the would-be participants' because they feared 'the appearance of real opponents' and therefore preferred 'to engage in anti-socialist propaganda in the absence of plenipotentiaries of public opinion in the Soviet Union and other Socialist countries'. Declaring that 'all this will contribute to fomenting a "Cold War" among the participants in the anti-war movement in Europe', he roundly concluded that the Soviet Peace Committee would 'not be a party to this wrecking undertaking'.

END's Coordinating Committee replied vigorously in an open letter published in the *New Statesman* in January 1983. The depth of their disagreement with the Soviet authorities and their rejection of the 'wholesale condemnation of non-aligned forces in the Western peace movement', was made clear. END strongly objected to Zhukov's demand that 'the Western peace movement must applaud without reserve all Soviet policies', and called upon his help in securing publication in *Pravda* of the text of the END Appeal 'which opposed NATO modernisation and called on the Soviet Union to halt at once its deployment of SS-20s'. They rejected as 'wholly unrealistic' Zhukov's demand that issues other than the NATO missiles should be kept off the agenda of the peace movements, and pointed out that Western activists who were concerned about offences against human rights in Latin America, South Africa and Turkey were equally concerned about the Warsaw Pact intervention in Czechoslovakia in 1968, about 'events' in Poland and about civil rights in the Soviet Union and Eastern Europe. After criticising Soviet official harassment of the

Moscow Group for Establishing Trust, the authors concluded 'we read your letter with astonishment'.[26]

An equally robust letter published on behalf of the Russell Foundation in END Bulletin 12 (1983) stressed the movement's firm commitment to non-alignment and ended by saying that 'your letter does your Committee a disservice by offering such unsubtle attempts to represent us simply as *agents provocateurs* in the service of the Western Powers'.

This correspondence led to a detailed analysis by Thompson in the *Guardian* in February 1983, in which he argued *inter alia* that 'the deterrent remains immensely serviceable to the Soviet rulers in freezing the *status quo* in Europe and in holding together their increasingly restive client states. At any time from 1980 to 1982 they could have halted the build up of the SS-20s'. After declaring that the aim of Soviet diplomacy, with the aid of the Western peace movement, is to reverse the post-war balance of power and to uncouple Europe from US strategies, Thompson concluded that the intended result is to enable the Soviet Union to 'preside benevolently over the wreckage of NATO'.[27]

The Soviet attack continued in 1983. In a lengthy official propaganda booklet issued in response to the American Defense Department's study of *Soviet Military Power* (1983), the Western peace movements were sharply criticised for suggesting that blame for the arms race attached equally to Governments of the East as well as the West and for 'meddling' in the internal affairs of socialist states. Asserting that the Soviet peace programme is supported by the whole population, the booklet concluded that 'the overwhelming majority of Soviet people cannot agree with the idea that the battle for peace should always and everywhere have an anti-Government thrust'.[28] The role expected of Communists in the West was made clear by Vadim Zagladin, deputy head of the CPSU's International Department, in *Pravda* on 23 July. He described their duty as being to mobilise the peace movements for the struggle against imperialism and warned against 'the ideological and propaganda manoeuvres of the class enemy' which have 'succeeded in persuading a certain segment of the masses that not only imperialism but also socialism is responsible for the current growth of tension', views which in some countries have even 'penetrated Communist ranks'.

The Second END Convention duly took place in West Berlin, from 9–14 May 1983, with 3000 people from 25 countries taking part but no representatives of the Soviet or East European Peace Committees. Messages of support were received from unofficial groups in the Communist countries and a secret meeting was held in East Berlin with unofficial East German peace campaigners who were prevented from attending the Convention. The main emphasis was on measures to prevent the deployment of Pershing II and Cruise missiles in Europe and on the demand for a European nuclear free zone, and the hope was expressed that representatives from the East European countries would attend the Third Convention in Perugia, Italy, in July 1984. Against this background, it is not surprising that Thompson voted against the controversial decision of the CND National Council to send observers to the Conference organised by the WPC World Assembly for Peace and Life in Prague in June 1983. But he was in a minority and, though he himself refused an invitation to attend, CND sent two official observers.

The official proceedings of the Prague Assembly (see Chapter 5) and the treatment of the East European unofficial peace movements, in Prague and elsewhere (see Chapter 12), fully justified Thompson's position. In July 1984, the unofficial representatives from Eastern Europe were again prevented by their governments from attending the END Convention. But, surprisingly, in view of the tough line they had adopted in 1983, the official Soviet Peace Committee and its counterparts in Bulgaria, Hungary, Poland and Rumania, not only accepted invitations but also sent delegations to the Perugia Convention. It is not clear what they expected to gain from this; no doubt they found some sympathisers among the West European representatives, but by all accounts they were subjected to some sharp questioning about their governments' policies. Their answers are likely to have satisfied most of the Western Europeans present.[29]

10 Peace Movements in Western Europe

Though British in origin, the scope of END's European Appeal is pan-European and it has from the start been supported by peace movements throughout Western Europe. This chapter examines recent development of the indigenous peace movements in Western European countries. It does not cover all countries and it has not been possible to refer to all the many hundreds of groups involved in the West European peace movements. Nevertheless some general points can be made.

The first is the very different origins and motives of the individual national peace movements. The United Kingdom, for instance, has had its own nuclear weapons programme for 35 years and American nuclear weapons have been based on its territory since 1948; but it has a long tradition of anti-war protest, going back many years before Hiroshima. In Germany the anti-militarism of the early years after the Second World War, a reaction against the Nazi period, has resurfaced in the anti-nuclear weapons movement in a country whose fears are now not so much for a revival of its own past as for the prospect of becoming the battlefield of Europe. In France, national defence is an issue on which parties from virtually all points in the political compass unite and the *force de frappe* is supported equally by the Communists and the Gaullists; moreover France did not participate in NATO's 1979 Double-Track decision (although President Mitterrand, unlike his predecessor, supports it) and is not therefore faced with the practical political problem of having to accept the basing of American missiles on French territory. Anti-nuclearism in the Netherlands finds strong support in the churches; in Scandinavia it derives from a mixture of moral attitudes and respect for the Nordic balance. In Italy, the peace movement has been weak partly for the pragmatic reason that Comiso, in Sicily (the Italian base for GLCM), is a long way from

Rome and partly because the Communist party, under its Eurocommunist leadership, does not oppose NATO and does not wish to destabilise the Government. In Greece the reverse applies; the Government claims to embody the peace movement and is concerned to avoid being outflanked on the left.

The second point is the wide spread of membership. While the peace movements in most countries may be predominantly left-wing in their political orientation, they are not exclusively so. Their membership in fact covers the whole political spectrum, from right to left; and all denominations of the Christian church. Many of the individual peace groups are 'single-issue' bodies, which exist solely, or primarily, to participate in the campaign against nuclear weapons and are mostly, for that reason, of recent formation. Groups often cater for a particular profession, political party or religious denomination. One of the remarkable features of the major demonstrations throughout Western Europe in the second half of October 1983 – for which the organisers claimed more than 3 million participants – was the enormous diversity of views represented under the slogan of 'peace'.

Thirdly, while there are policies on which the national movements may be divided, they are all united in their opposition to the deployment of cruise and Pershing II missiles in Europe. They disagree over their attitude towards NATO; the German Greens want to withdraw, the Dutch IKV favour continued membership, and the British peace movement tends to be equivocal. But they all support the idea of a nuclear-free Europe, as outlined in the European Appeal and in END's aims (see Chapter 9).

Finally, the relationship between the indigenous peace movements on the one hand, and the international front organisations and the domestic Communist parties on the other, between the critics and the adversaries, differs from country to country. In the case of the United Kingdom, it is normally possible to make the distinction although there are many ways in which the two intermingle and overlap, and CND has sometimes appeared cavalier – some would say naïve – in its attitude towards the risks involved. In the Netherlands and Germany, the development and activities of the indigenous peace movements have at times seemed more closely associated with Communist-controlled organisations. When considering the movements in these and other Western European countries, it is therefore sometimes difficult to distinguish clearly between adversaries and critics. Nevertheless the genuinely indigenous peace movements have more recently come to recognise the dangers of too close cooperation with NATO's adversaries, and have taken steps to separate their own policies and actions from those of organisations whose aims and affiliations they do not share. The balance is however a delicate one. All the West European critics have strongly resented efforts by the Russians to dictate their policies and lay down with whom they should or should not meet. The Zhukov letter and the Soviet attitude to the 1983 END Convention in Berlin (see Chapter 9) highlighted the true nature of the Soviet efforts.

THE NETHERLANDS

In the Netherlands, the campaign against nuclear weapons originated from two main sources, the Churches and the Communist Party (CPN). For reasons connected with the recent history of the party and its relations with the Soviet Union, the CPN was slow to get off the mark in the early 1970s. But by the end of 1977 it was playing an active part, and had re-established close links with the CPSU and the WPC. Opposition by the Churches to NATO's nuclear modernisation plans was also developing in the 1970s within existing religious groups. Their role was crucial in securing mass support for the peace movement.

The two most important religious groups were the Interchurch Peace Council (IKV) and the Dutch branch of the Roman Catholic organisation, *Pax Christi*, which was influential with some sections of the Christian Democratic Party (CDA). IKV, by the mid-1970s, was a nation-wide organisation with more than 300 groups close to the grass roots of Dutch religious sentiment. This powerful religious body, capable of acting right across the political and social spectrum, was already in existence in the Netherlands before Moscow's campaign against the 'neutron bomb' began. It did not – and does not – demand Netherlands withdrawal from NATO; its object is the removal of all nuclear weapons from Dutch territory as a first step towards the goal of general and complete disarmament on the world-wide scale. This was the basis of the Campaign which IKV launched in 1977 under the leadership of Mient Jan Faber. Since its inception IKV has grown steadily in authority, both within its own country and among other comparable bodies in Western Europe. It was on the IKV's initiative that the Netherlands Congress against Nuclear Armaments was established in April 1978 as a roof organisation for all 'peace' bodies in the Netherlands irrespective of political or religious affiliation. Since 1982 IKV has taken on responsibility for running the International Peace Coordination Centre, which provides facilities for the exchange of information, ideas and plans between the Western peace movements. Its contacts with the Communist sponsored organisations in the Netherlands are described below. But it was, in December 1982, expressly cleared by the Netherlands Government of any suspicion of subversive intentions, and there have been reports that periodic consultations take place between Dutch Ministers and the Secretary-General (Faber) and other leading members of the Council.

For many years before 1977, the CPN had been isolated from the rest of the world Communist movement. The Secretary-General, Paul de Groot, had quarrelled with Moscow in 1956 over 'destalinisation' and his subsequent relations with the Soviet Union were cool. To maintain his position within the CPN – where he had a significant following – de Groot, a Stalinist, banned connections with other Communist parties which had criticised Stalin. CPN members were forbidden to make contact with Soviet bloc embassies, and Dutch front organisations were isolated from their pro-Moscow counterparts in other countries. However, after the CPN's poor showing in the Dutch general election of 1977, an internal power struggle developed between de Groot's supporters and opponents. He retired from politics in August of that year and, his opponents triumphant, the CPN immediately restored relations with the Soviet and other Eastern European embassies in the Netherlands. The key task of maintaining relations with foreign Communist parties was in the hands of Joop Wolff, the member of the new Politburo responsible for the CPN's foreign relations and defence questions and, since 1977, a member of the Dutch parliament. As an official of the WFDY, Wolff had been in close contact with Alexander Shelepin (Vice-Chairman of WFDY, 1953–58, and KGB Chairman, 1958–61). His links with the CPSU were reinforced when, during the 1950s, he served as the Moscow correspondent of the Dutch Party newspaper, *de Waarheid*. The fact that Moscow's campaign against the 'neutron bomb' began just before de Groot's fall explains why the CPN was not immediately able to respond to the WPC's 'Week of Action' against nuclear modernisation from 6–13 August 1977. But by then the new CPN leadership was again ready to fall in with Moscow's wishes and eager to redeem its reputation by vigorous campaigning. Because of the CPN's historic association with the German section of the Comintern, it was natural for it to re-establish close relations with the CPSU and the East German Socialist Unity party (SED) after years of isolation.

Shortly after the CPN was purged of de Groot's influence, a 'spontaneous initiative' for a 'broad anti-neutron bomb movement' was launched on 19 August 1977, involving 131 people who had rallied under the slogan 'Stop the Neutron Bomb'. The secretary of this new Initiative Group was Nico Schouten, a member of the CPN's Amsterdam district committee, although at the time the Group denied that it had links with the CPN. Although this denial became increasingly suspect over the next two years, it was only in December 1979, when the Group had scored a major success with its campaigning, that a Dutch Communist MP, M. Bakker, revealed publicly that it had been organised by the CPN.[1] It was then estimated that of the 131 original signatories of the appeal, about 45% were either Communists or Communist sympathisers.[2]

A month after the Appeal was launched over 100 more clergymen and theologians came out in support, many of whom were not regarded as left-wing, let alone Communists.[3] Instrumental in this development were several members of the left-wing movement 'Christians for Socialism' (CVS) who were among the original signatories. On 29 September, the Initiative Group launched a 'People's Petition' against Enhanced Radiation Weapons for which by March 1978 they claimed to have obtained a million signatures. Several hundred groups were formed and meetings were held on both local and national levels, which brought people with widely differing motives into the campaign. A critical role was played in the People's Petition by the CVS, who claimed to have promoted cooperation between the IKV and the Initiative group. Apart from giving high priority to participation in the 'peace movement', one of their declared objectives was to turn the IKV into an extra-parliamentary political group, and they planned to establish links between it and the Christian Peace

Conference, the international front organisation based in Prague (see Chapter 4).

Many of the clergy who had joined the Appeal in September 1977 had close links with leading members of the CDA, the major party in the coalition government and the one to which the then Prime Minister, Andries Van Agt, belonged, and used their influence in favour of the adoption of an anti-nuclear policy. Eventually, on 3 February 1978, the CDA executive committee came out in opposition to deployment of the 'neutron bomb'. This followed the letter sent by Brezhnev in January 1978 to the heads of all Western governments warning them that the production and deployment of this device would generally endanger *détente*, and was claimed as a major success by the Initiative Group.

Meanwhile the CPN was engaged in efforts to restore its links with the CPSU and a high level exchange of visits between the two parties took place to this end. During a visit to Moscow in October 1977, on the sixtieth anniversary of the 1917 revolution, the CPN president, H. Hoekstra, had talks with Mikhail Suslov, who was in overall charge of the front organisations, and Vadim Zagladin, the first deputy head of the ID (see Chapter 6). On 5 November 1977, *Pravda* played up a speech by Hoekstra in which he emphasised the CPN's role in the anti-neutron bomb agitation. But, presumably in the hope of playing down the CPN's role for home consumption, no mention was made of this in the Dutch Party newspaper, *de Waarheid*. After Hoekstra's visit, an official of the CPSU's ID Oleg Kharkhardin, who was also a vice-chairman of the Soviet Peace Committee, visited Amsterdam in December 1977; he was followed by D. N. Mochalin, head of the German section of the ID, who met senior CPN officials in January 1978. Another visitor to Amsterdam, in December 1977, was the president of the World Peace Council, Romesh Chandra. Since the WPC was coordinating the campaign against the 'neutron bomb' under the direction of the ID, there was little doubt that the visits by these three officials were connected with the preparations for the 'International Forum against the Neutron Bomb' which took place in Amsterdam from 18 to 20 March 1978 under the sponsorship of the Initiative Group. Later, Nico Schouten was to admit that the Group had 'to a limited extent cooperated with the WPC'.[4] This forum represented the climax of the Dutch campaign against the neutron bomb. 1500 representatives from East and West Europe gathered to hear 70 speakers from 27 countries. A mass demonstration took place on 19 March in support of the 'Amsterdam Appeal to the peoples and governments of the world' not to accept the weapon on their territories.

The CPN's efforts paid off. After President Carter announced his decision to defer production of the neutron weapon, on 7 April 1978, *Tass* immediately claimed that it reflected the enormous pressure from the international protest movement against the 'bomb', in which the Netherlands 'plays such a big role'. The Central Committee of the CPN declared at its session of 8–9 April 1978 that the mass action against the weapon had shown that 'it is possible to act upon the contradictions in NATO'.[5]

The success of the campaign encouraged the CPN to think that Dutch public opinion could be harnessed to a more direct attack on NATO's nuclear modernisation programme. Writing in the CPN monthly, *Politiek en Cultuur*, in April–May 1978, H. Akkermans considered that public opinion could bring the Netherlands into line with Norway and Denmark by supporting a ban on the storage of NATO nuclear weapons on its territory. The Initiative Group followed this by asserting in its 5th *N-Bulletin* (May 1978) that the agitation against the 'neutron bomb' had been the catalyst which showed that a campaign could be launched against any nuclear weapons on Dutch soil. Little doubt remained about the Initiative Group's close Communist connections when it sent an official delegation to Moscow on 24 May to thank the Soviet Peace Committee for its assistance in organising the Amsterdam Forum in March. According to Dutch press reports, the delegation accepted the offer of the Soviet Peace Committee to pay its air fares to New York to attend the First UN Special Session on Disarmament in June.

After the success of the March Forum and despite the American decision in April, the Initiative Group was determined not to lose momentum. The Group organised an 'International Symposium Against the Neutron Bomb' on 16 December 1978 in Amsterdam. Nico Schouten in his opening address argued that the threat of the 'neutron bomb' had actually increased since Washington had taken the decision in September to produce the 'basic components' of the weapon. Amongst the participants was Italian Nino Pasti, later one of the Generals for Peace, who had shortly before in the columns of the Moscow Weekly, *New Times*, echoed the arguments advanced by Akkermans in *Politiek en Cultuur* for rejecting the storage of nuclear weapons on Dutch soil.

But by this time the Initiative Group had a new target, the proposals being discussed in NATO for modernising its theatre nuclear forces. In September therefore the group changed its name to the 'Joint Committee: Stop the Neutron Bomb, Stop the Nuclear Arms Race', as being a more appropriate title for an organisation now also committed to opposing NATO's new proposals. In this broadened effort the WPC played its familiar coordinating role and the East German SED was also active. In February 1979, an extraordinary session of the WPC was held in East Berlin under the leadership of Werner Rümpel, Secretary-General of the East Germany Peace Committee, who had helped to organise the Forum in Amsterdam in 1978. During March 1979, Rümpel paid several visits to the Netherlands for consultations with the CPN, which in its turn, later sent a delegation to East Germany. One result was the announcement by the Joint Committee in June 1979 that an international *Estafette* (Relay Race) would be held to further the campaign. Under the slogan 'Stop the Neutron Bomb, Stop the Mass Destruction Weapons', the *Estafette* planned to visit all the countries in East and West Europe which had signed the Final Act of the Conference on Security and Cooperation in Europe (CSCE) at Helsinki in 1975. It was not particularly successful as a political event, but it received much publicity, notably when the Dutch delegation, including three members of the CPN, was presented to the Pope through the intervention of one of his former teachers who was Vice-President of the Polish Peace Committee.

As the critical NATO Council decision approached in late 1979, the CPN and the WPC stepped up their activities. An offshoot of the WPC, the Brussels-based ICESC held a major 'International Forum' on 26–8 October 1979 at De Haan, near Ostend, which concentrated on opposition to NATO's plans. It was attended by Vadim Zagladin, who, two days later, led a seven-man Soviet delegation into the Second Chamber of the Dutch Parliament to lobby its Permanent Committee for Foreign Affairs against NATO's proposed new missiles. This was unprecedented in a NATO country. The campaign in the Netherlands against NATO's modernisation proposals reached a high point with a massive torchlight procession in Amsterdam on 15

November 1979, organised by the Joint Committee. The main speaker once again was Nico Schouten.

The Netherlands Government made their acceptance of the NATO Double-Track decision in December 1979 subject to the reservation that they would postpone a decision on whether to accept deployment of the new missiles for two years, pending progress of arms control talks between the Russians and Americans. This followed the recommendation of Premier Van Agt's CDA in November. After the Double-Track decision the Joint Committee continued to organise meetings and demonstrations against deployment. In November 1980, for example, another International Forum was held under its auspices in Amsterdam at which those attending, all from European countries, were invited to consider what could be done to stop the arms race and how to promote peace and security and improve the international climate. The forum was addressed by representatives of 'peace movements', Communists and others, in NATO countries as well as by delegates from several East European 'peace committees', but the United States and the Soviet Union were not invited. The idea of a 'European nuclear free zone' received much support.

Increasingly the churches and the Communist Party found common cause in the anti-nuclear campaign. Their different motives and ultimate objectives were initially blurred in their united opposition, first to the neutron bomb and later to the deployment of cruise missiles in the Netherlands following NATO's Double-Track decision. In an article in the *Haagse Post* (15 December 1979), the Secretary-General of the IKV (Faber) claimed that the anti-neutron bomb movement had mobilised many churchgoers who did not usually take an active part in politics or demonstrations. In the same issue, Nico Schouten stated that his members had helped to set up IKV branches: in his opinion, Communists who were also Christians had played a useful role in the IKV. By this time the Dutch Labour Party was firmly opposed to cruise missiles and was pressing for the abandonment of all the country's nuclear commitments. The CDA were divided, but an important section was against accepting cruise missiles.

Virtually the last occasion for cooperation between the Joint Committee and the IKV was at the large demonstration in Amsterdam on 21 November 1981, called specifically to protest against the introduction of the new nuclear missiles in NATO countries. An estimated 400 000 people took part. This was just three days after President Reagan made public his offer to the Soviet Union of the so-called 'zero option'. By then however the IKV were becoming concerned about their association with the Communist line, and especially after the declaration of Martial Law in Poland in December, 1981, they began to distance themselves from a position which so clearly followed Moscow's policy. They did not therefore play a prominent part in the further consultative meeting organised by the Joint Committee in February, 1982, also in Amsterdam, of 'leading members of peace and disarmament movements from 21 European countries, the USA and West Berlin which in the past year have carried out the most impressive mass activities'.[6] The East German Peace Council was represented by Gunter Drefahl and Werner Rümpel, both members of the Presidential Committee of the WPC. Shortly after this, in May 1982, Wim Bartels, the IKV's international secretary, walked out of a religious conference in Moscow when its organisers refused to let him address the main forum of the meeting, insisting that he could only speak in the closed sessions of small working groups. As the only representative present of the West European peace movements, Bartels had agreed to attend the conference, organised by the Russian Orthodox Patriarch Pimen of Moscow (a member of the WPC), on the express condition that he could openly explain the ideals and aims of the peace movements in Western Europe.[7]

The Dutch authorities were also concerned about the extent of Soviet involvement in the activities of the peace movement. On 13 November 1982, *de Telegraaf* made known the existence of an official study of Soviet influence on the nuclear arms debate produced by the Dutch Security Service for the Minister of Interior. This identified Anatoli Popov, a former Press Attaché expelled from the Soviet Embassy in The Hague in 1961 and now a member of the ID, as having been a member of the Soviet delegation which visited the Netherlands in 1980 at the invitation of the Joint Committee. In January 1982, Popov had returned as head of the Soviet delegation which helped to organise, with Joop Wolff, the Communist MP, and the Joint Committee, the February Consultative meeting. In his statement to the Dutch Parliament on 16 December 1982, however, the Minister of Interior was careful not to charge the IKV with subversive activities. Since its deliberate effort to dissociate itself from

Communist influences, the IKV has gained in stature and acceptability in the Netherlands as the principal representative of Dutch anti-nuclear opinion.

By 1983, not only was the IKV concerned to dissociate itself from the Communists but all was not well between the CPN and Moscow. During 1982 the line taken by the Dutch party and by the Joint Committee, which it controlled, was increasingly at odds with that laid down by Soviet Peace Committee, especially over their attitude towards END. The Zhukov letter of December 1982 was as much addressed to the Dutch peace movement as to their British counterparts. Nico Schouten's reply made it clear that he found unacceptable the Soviet Committee's attempt to suppress views with which they did not agree. This was why the Russians turned to the Netherlands Committee for European Security and Cooperation, a subsidiary of the front organisation of the same name, to organise Dutch representation at the Prague Assembly in June 1983 rather than the CPN and Joint Committee; the IKV, like the British CND, sent observers. Later in the year the IKV and Joint Committee again joined forces in the massive demonstration in The Hague on 29 October; if the attendance claimed – 550 000 – is correct, this represented some 4% of the country's population, a remarkable achievement for the organisers.

The decision on whether or not to accept the Dutch quota of 48 cruise missiles was twice postponed to await progress in the arms control negotiations. Successive government crises in May 1981 and May 1982 complicated the issue; but in June 1984, the government decided to postpone deployment from 1986 to 1988 and make the numbers deployed conditional on no further Soviet deployment of SS-20s and progress in the INF negotiations.

WEST GERMANY

The point of departure for the current campaign against nuclear weapons in the Federal Republic was the NATO Double-Track decision of December 1979. Earlier campaigns – such as the opposition to the rearmament of Germany in the early 1950s and against the siting of American nuclear weapons on Federal territory a few years later – had taken place in a political climate in which the need for German participation in Western defence was accepted by the vast majority in all three main political parties.

Both the 'People's Enquiry against Remilitarisation' (1951/52) and the 'People's Enquiry on Atomic Weapons' (1958) were failures. The Communists did not succeed at that period in using these movements as vehicles for their efforts to create alliances serving the interests of Soviet foreign policy. The discussion within NATO about possible American production of ERW and their deployment in Germany led to protests, and, conscious of the extreme sensitivity of this issue, the Government adopted a conditional position, insisting that, if the United States decided to produce them, they should be introduced into the MBFR negotiations in Vienna. This proposal was rejected by the Russians and, faced with European unwillingness to share responsibility for the decision, President Carter suspended it in April 1978. The focus of the anti-nuclear campaign thereafter shifted to the plans for modernising NATO's INF.

Since 1980, opposition to nuclear weapons, and in particular to the deployment of Pershing II and cruise missiles in the Federal Republic, has attracted support from the churches, environmental groups and since late 1983 among members of the Social Democratic Party (SPD). The campaign, from 1980 onwards, was fuelled by concern about the dangers of a nuclear confrontation between the superpowers in Central Europe in which Germany would be the main victim; fears that the proposed new missile deployments represented an added threat to peace; anti-militarist objections to the Bundeswehr and NATO by a section of German youth; and doubts about the direction of American policies on *détente* and arms control under both President Carter and President Reagan.

From the start, the German Communist Party (DKP) made every effort to exploit these factors. It played the major part in the preparations which led to the launching of the Krefeld Appeal in November 1980. This took place at a weekend rally in Krefeld on 15 and 16 November, which, although attended by little more than 1000 people, attracted wide publicity and subsequent support. The initiative for the gathering came from, among others, General Gert Bastian, subsequently a leading member of Generals for Peace and Disarmament, Petra Kelly, of the newly formed Green Party, and Pastor Martin Niemöller. The rally was organised by the German Peace Union (DFU), which, founded in 1960, was a forerunner of the present DKP before the latter was legalised. The ex-Communist Klaus Rainer Röhl, until 1973 the publisher of the periodical *Konkret* which for years was secretly funded by the East German SED, has revealed that he, his former wife Ulrike Meinhof and others founded the DFU with money 'straight from East Germany'.[8] The DFU has close links with the DKP, through its secretary-general, Heinz Dreibrodt, and the chairman of its Finance Committee, Georg Hausladen, both Communists, and is represented on the WPC. The organising committee for the rally was largely composed of DKP members, and the principal speakers were Peter Tümmers, a member of the DKP's Executive Committee, and Martha Buschmann, a member of the DKP Praesidium. The Appeal amounted, in simple terms, to a demand for rejection of the proposed increase in NATO nuclear armaments in Central Europe, and the organisers announced their aim of collecting a million signatures in support of it. So successful were their efforts that two million signatures were claimed within one year.

Even during the preparatory stages of the Appeal, the SPD National Executive expressed its opposition to this initiative. Former Federal Minister Erhard Eppler, representing the left-wing of the SPD, advised against signing a petition which had been initiated by Communists. The Federal Executive Committee of the Confederation of Trade Unions (DGB) gave a firm warning against participation. Its chairman, Heinz Oskar Vetter, declared that 'If you are going to talk about Pershings you must also talk about SS-20s.' Notwithstanding this, the local branch of the Education and Science Union as well as the Union's Executive Committee, the Trade, Banks and Insurance Unions, and the Industrial Printing and Paper Union supported the Krefeld Appeal.

This led to efforts by the SPD to provide an alternative focus, independent of Communist influence. In May 1981 left-wing SPD politicians and members of the Federal parliament organised a meeting at Bielefeld to launch the Bielefeld Appeal which opposed the deployment of new missiles and called for a reduction in the defence budget and the convocation of a European disarmament conference. This initiative did not, however, long maintain its separate identity. Cooperation quietly developed between the participants in the two Appeals, which were soon afterwards amalgamated. Then in a further attempt to keep the SPD apart from the DKP, in August 1981 the chief executive of Recklinghausen, Rudolf Pezely (SPD), and the mayor of Datteln, Horst

Niggemeier (SPD), founded the 'Citizens for Peace in Freedom'. In their declaration of principles, they stated: 'We want the Federal Republic of Germany to remain in future, as now, a free and independent state. . . . Our Federal Army, together with the NATO Alliance, guarantees us peace.' For this reason, the Datteln Petition, which they sponsored was 'for disarmament, but not unilaterally by us'. This new group was supported among others by Kurt Biedenkopf (CDU), and the SPD Minister of Justice of North Rhine-Westphalia, Inge Donnepp. By December 1981, almost all the mayors of the towns in the Ruhr had signed the Datteln Petition.

Nevertheless, in a climate of opinion in which nuclear weapons and the arms race were increasingly regarded as the main threats to peace it was the Communist Krefeld Appeal which continued to attract the greater response. Most of those who supported it were unaware that this Appeal was due to a Communist initiative and that the campaign's progress was in large measure due to the fact that the DKP was responsible for its organisation and publicity. Moreover some organisations of the Evangelical Church which joined the Peace Movement failed to dissociate themselves unambiguously from policies and activities which were subject to strong Communist influence or to perceive the risks of continuing association with international front organisations.

The 1981 Bonn rally was a case in point. In October 1981 about a quarter of a million people took part in this mass rally which was addressed by, among others, Pastor Heinrich Albertz, formerly mayor of Berlin, the writer Heinrich Böll, winner of the Nobel Prize for Literature in 1972, and, as principal speaker, Erhard Eppler, a member of the SPD executive committee. This rally was a triumph of organisation. The demonstrators, from all over Germany and beyond, travelled by coach to the outskirts of Bonn and marched in well-disciplined silence, to the main assembly point. The rally was ostensibly organised by two Evangelical Church organisations, the Action Group for Peace and Reconciliation (ASF) and the Action Group Service for Peace (AGDF). As both had numerous international contacts, there was a significant foreign involvement in the rally: for example, the Dutch IKV organised a march to Bonn by about 4000 Dutch demonstrators. But the ASF and the AGDF had contacts with international front organisations as well. They had both been represented at the

WPC's World Congress of Peace Forces held in Moscow in 1973 after which was established the West German Committee for Peace, Disarmament and Cooperation (KFAZ), closely linked to the WPC and the DKP. An ASF delegate also attended the WPC's World Parliament of Peoples for Peace in Sofia in September 1980 (see Chapter 5). Furthermore, the ASF had been a corporate member of the West Berlin Preparatory Committee for the WFDY-IUS tenth World Youth Festival in East Berlin in 1973 and its secretary, the Rev Volkmar Deile, was a member of the Regional Committee in the Federal Republic of the CPC based in Prague. Communists had also taken part in events during a Week of Peace which the ASF had organised from 16–22 November 1980 and in its assessment of this event the AGDF noted in February 1981 that, in certain areas, cooperation with the Communists had 'worked'. As a result of these associations Communist influence on the slogans and speeches at the Bonn rally was strong and led the Office for the Defence of the Constitution (the BFV) to report to the Federal Ministry of the Interior that 'following the demonstration, it is the DKP above all which can take the credit for achieving a positive result in the campaign objectives which it was set by the Communist Party of the Soviet Union, namely to block NATO rearmament'. But for all this, neither the ASF nor the AGDF, on the basis of their membership and their policies, can be described as a Communist front organisation.

On 21 November 1981, the Krefeld Appeal movement held its first anniversary rally in Dortmund. On that occasion, Communist control was even more evident than at the foundation meeting in 1980. The speakers included Martha Buschmann, from the DKP, Werner Stürman, chairman of the Communist youth organisation Young Socialist German Workers (SDAJ), and Klaus Mannhardt, a WPC member and chairman of the German Peace Society – Union of Opponents of Military Service (DFG-VK) which was under strong Communist influence. Buschmann spoke of 'our good neighbours in the East' and announced that 'no one is threatening us from that quarter. The Soviet Union wants peace; it needs it'. Mannhardt explained that the attitude of the authorities had made it clear that this would not happen voluntarily: it would be essential to compel a change of course and make the implementation of NATO's Double-Track policy politically impossible.

15 000 people participated in the Dortmund anniversary rally, compared with only one thousand at the foundation meeting in Krefeld. After Dortmund, hundreds of volunteers from five pro-communist organisations (German Peace Union, the DFG-VK, the Committee for Peace, Disarmament and Cooperation, the Association of the Victims of the Nazi Regime – League of Anti-Fascists, and Democratic Initiative for Women), as well as from dozens of smaller groups, supported the campaign and collected signatures in supermarkets, cinemas, office blocks and factories. A third forum in support of the Krefeld Appeal was held in Bonn-Bad Godesberg on 17 September 1983. This meeting was supported not only by the initiators of the Appeal but also by SPD members and several organisations associated with the DKP. The forum maintained that opposition to the stationing of intermediate range American missiles on Federal German territory was increasingly a 'civic duty'. It was claimed that there were 5 million signatures in support of the Appeal.

Despite all their efforts and the major role they play, the influence of the DKP in the German peace movement as a whole should not be overestimated. The movement is large – estimates vary from more than 2000 separate groups down to 300 – because it has met with a strong response from many levels and sections of the population. This has come, especially, from the left-wing of the SPD, including a number of parliamentarians, from students and from some trade unions. But it is the Green Party which has made the greatest impact on the peace movement. This party was formally established on 13 January 1980. In origin it was an amalgamation of mainly conservative environmentalists and left wing radicals, many of whom were members of the Communist party. Although the new party decided by majority vote, after a long and bitter debate at its foundation conference at Karlsruhe, that members of other parties could not be members of the Greens, the new party's orientation moved rapidly to the left. In June 1980, the party split as a result of the adoption of left-wing policies and the defeat of the Conservative candidate for the chairmanship. Since then, the party has been dominated by the radicals; it has based its defence policy on the immediate dissolution of NATO and the Warsaw Pact, rejection of the NATO Double-Track decision, unilateral German disarmament, withdrawal of all foreign forces from Germany and the creation of a European nuclear-free zone. It has also called for the dismantling of Soviet intermediate range missiles and condemned Soviet policies in Afghanistan and Poland. Increasingly the Greens felt their association with the Communist party in the peace movement a political and electoral liability and took steps to emphasise their differences, especially in their attitude towards the policies of the Soviet Union, which the DKP was not prepared to criticise.

Open signs of a rift came at an organisational meeting on 5 April 1982 in Bonn to plan a major demonstration against President Reagan's visit to attend the NATO summit on 10 June. The Greens, who openly acknowledged their former cooperation with the DKP, complained that the DKP were attempting to monopolise public sentiment against nuclear weapons. The meeting passed a resolution describing the goal of the NATO summit as 'support of the Reagan Administration's attempt to achieve world-wide hegemony'. It rejected separate resolutions calling on the peace movement to use only non-violent methods in demonstrations, condemning Soviet interference in Poland and Soviet intervention in Afghanistan, and expressing support for the Polish Solidarity movement. By a large majority, it adopted a motion condemning US action in Central America, the Middle East and southern Africa, but said it would welcome political solutions in Poland and Afghanistan, involving the lifting of martial law and the withdrawal of Soviet troops.[9]

Ulrich Tost, a member of the Green Party's Federal Council, said: 'The Communists dominated the meeting completely. It took place under seemingly democratic rules but that was a joke. We could barely get a word in.' Petra Kelly, another Council member, referred to a large group at the meeting which was there 'only to help a certain bloc.... This peace movement has shown itself incapable of discussion'. If the movement was split, she said, it would be the fault of the DKP. When asked why her party had been unable to combat the Communists at the meeting, she replied, 'it is not our style to work in this centralised fashion'. She added that the objective of the Green Party was 'a non-aligned peace movement that called for a Europe without nuclear weapons and the dissolution of the power blocs, East and West'.

Despite complaints from representatives of the Green Party that the DKP was manipulating the arrangements, a demonstration involving between 200 000 and 300 000 people duly took place on the occasion of President Reagan's visit to Bonn on 10 June 1982. By comparison with the rally in October 1981, there were conspicuous absentees, namely the ASF and the Dutch IKV: an IKV spokesman expressed the fear that anti-nuclear protest was being diverted into a new German patriotism, exemplified by the banners called for German reunification. The ASF Secretary, the Rev Volkmar Deile, made the more telling criticism that the plans for the demonstration failed to mention the deployment of the SS-20s and concentrated exclusively on NATO's intention to instal cruise and Pershing II missiles.[10]

As expected, the slogans were predominantly anti-American. There was only a mild attempt to balance them by reference to the armaments build up in the East, echoing the East German theme of 'swords into ploughshares' (see Chapter 12). A related march of 40 000 in West Berlin sponsored by a mixture of church groups, young socialists, supporters of the city's Alternative List (which is linked with the Green party) and others to coincide with the Bonn demonstration, passed off without incident. But on 11 June, another demonstration by 2–3000 people, who defied a police ban on such activities in the centre of West Berlin, led to street battles. On 12 December, the third anniversary of the Double-Track decision, thousands of supporters of the peace movement, with the participation of the Green Party, took part in anti-NATO demonstrations in Munich, Dortmund, Hamburg and Frankfurt, as in other major cities in Western Europe.

The Soviet authorities placed strong hopes on the emergence from the March 1983 Federal elections of a majority hostile to the basing of cruise and Pershing II missiles in the Federal Republic. During the election campaign they made strenuous propaganda efforts, including the threat of dire – but unspecified – consequences which would follow deployment, to influence the results and displayed considerable confidence in the prospects for success. They were however disappointed; the election confirmed the CDU/FDP Coalition in office with a clear majority. It did however introduce a new element into the Parliamentary scene; the Green Party won 5.6% of the votes and thus secured for the first time representation in the Bundestag, with 27 seats. Besides Petra Kelly, the Green Deputies included General Gert Bastian, who was a leading participant in the major demonstration against the deployment of Pershing II missiles which took place in April 1983. (Bastian also, with Petra Kelly, took part in the unofficial meeting in East Berlin in June with East German unofficial peace campaigners who were not allowed by their government to attend the second END convention in West Berlin, which was strongly supported by the Green party.) After the election in March, Chancellor Kohl lost no time in making plain his support for the full implementation of both tracks of the NATO decision of December 1979, and has been constant in maintaining his support for deployment of the new missiles in the absence of an arms control agreement. Meanwhile, since the election, the SPD in opposition has moved rapidly towards a policy of rejecting the 1979 decision, which, when in government, they had done so much to promote. The vote in the Bundestag on 22 November 1983 on the basing of the Pershing II and cruise missiles in Germany was 286 in favour (CDU and FDP), 226 against (SPD and Green Party) and one FDP abstention. This brought to an end the consensus on defence policy which had lasted since 1960.[11] The Russians withdrew from the INF talks in Geneva on the following day.

Despite sporadic outbursts of violence at demonstrations and meetings, the German peace movement as a whole has declared its opposition to violent action to promote its policies and objectives. In this respect, the resolution against violence which was rejected at the April 1982 meeting in Bonn was not typical. The conduct of the debate at the biennial Kirchentag of the Protestant Church in Hanover in June 1983, hard-hitting and passionate though it was, was more in keeping with the policy of the movement. In a statement issued to the press immediately after the Kirchentag, on 14 June, a number of peace groups, including the ASF, the Women's Peace Foundation (AFF), the Union of German Students' Organisations (VDS) and the DFG-VK, reaffirmed the determination of the peace movement to remain non-violent in its actions, although accepting the need to resort to civil disobedience. This image was somewhat tarnished a week later when about 20 000 members of the peace movement greeted US Vice-President Bush at Krefeld in what the police described as 'one of the most violent anti-American demonstrations for many years'. It was claimed however that the violence was caused by a hard core of militants who had arrived from other towns and mingled with the would-be peaceful protestors.[12]

The biggest event yet was the anti-nuclear action week from 15 to 22 October 1983. A coordinating committee headed by Josef Leinen, the Social Democrat who runs the Association of Citizens Initiative Groups, one of the principal organisations in the anti-nuclear movement, was set up in Bonn. This committee, established several months in advance, comprised representatives of 26 'peace' organisations and 'interest' groups, only two of which were avowedly Communist. The aim was to promote demonstrations all over the country throughout the week as a massive protest against INF deployment and nuclear weapons generally. As a feat of organisation the week was an undoubted success. Official estimates put the total number of demonstrators on 22 October at 500 000; the organisers claimed 1.3 million. Pledges of non-violence had been given in advance and, apart from one incident in Hamburg, they were fulfilled. But some of the strains within the movement were revealed. Former Chancellor Willi Brandt, who played a major role in swinging the SPD from being pro-deployment when in office to an anti-deployment policy in opposition (shortly after to be confirmed at a special party conference), was the principal speaker at a rally of some 200 000 in Bonn. While opposing cruise and Pershing missiles, he urged support for NATO and the continuation of disarmament negotiations. He was publicly attacked by Petra Kelly, leader of the Greens, for not calling for the abolition of all nuclear weapons and for German withdrawl from NATO.

Following the Bundestag Vote in November, the deployment of the first Pershing IIs went ahead at Mutlangen, near Stuttgart in December. The numbers involved in protests on that occasion were insignificant in comparison with the turn out on 22 October. By the end of the year, the unity of purpose which had brought such diverse elements together had largely evaporated. The Green Party remains as a political rallying point for non-violent protest, though there is little support for its demand for withdrawal from NATO and its future parliamentary prospects are uncertain, as a result of increasing internal tensions which led, in February 1984, to the resignation of General Bastian. His resignation followed ominous signs of a revival of communist influence on the 'peace' policies of the Green Party.

SCANDINAVIA

Norway and Denmark, though fully supporting NATO's deterrent strategy, decided in 1957 not to permit the stationing of nuclear weapons on their territories in peacetime. Finland is precluded from doing so by her Treaty with the Soviet Union; and the question of providing bases for nuclear weapons has never arisen for neutral Sweden. With the aims of weakening Norway's and Denmark's links with NATO, the Russians mooted the idea of a 'Nordic Nuclear Free Zone' in the late 1950s. The proposal was taken up by President Kekkonen of Finland, who, during his long period in office, was its principal advocate, with Soviet encouragement. He got little response from the other Nordic countries. But the idea was readily available for exploitation both by international front organisations and by the Soviet Government when the time was ripe.

Kekkonen relaunched his proposal in May 1978, to prevent the dangers to Nordic countries arising from the prospective employment of cruise missiles. But it was not until two years later that the proposal was more widely taken up. By then two issues were engaging the neutralists and those who were concerned about nuclear weapons. One was the NATO Double-Track decision of December 1979 which was supported by both Norway and Denmark but which aroused deep misgivings in those countries. The second was the agreement negotiated between the United States and Norway to provide for the prepositioning in Norway of equipment (not including nuclear weapons) needed by American reinforcements in the event of war. It was asserted that this would make Norway vulnerable to nuclear attack; parallel negotiations with Denmark never got under way because of the Government's fear of political repercussions. In 1980, opposition to these two developments led to strong support in Norway, especially within the ruling Labour Party, for a Nordic Nuclear-Free Zone, which was subsequently included among the Party's aims in its 1981 election platform. In Denmark support was much less evident, despite the unpopularity of the NATO decision. In Sweden the idea was put forward that, for a start, the zone might be confined to Sweden and Finland.[13]

Although there had been earlier indications that the Russians would not agree to the inclusion of any part of their territory in the zone, the Norwegian view was that at least part of the Kola Peninsula must be covered. They obtained no satisfaction on this point, until, on 26 June 1981, Brezhnev replied in an interview with *Suomen Sosialidemokraatti*, the daily paper of the Finnish Social Democratic Party, to a set of prepared questions submitted to him several months earlier. He said: 'We regard with understanding the striving of peoples in various parts of the world to set up non-nuclear zones in order to strengthen their security . . . the Soviet Union has already stated its positive attitude to the specific proposal to set up a non-nuclear zone in Northern Europe . . . and is prepared to assume an obligation not to use nuclear weapons against the Northern European countries which will . . . renounce the production and acquisition of nuclear weapons and their deployment on their territories. This guarantee of the Soviet Union could be formalised either by a multilateral agreement or by bilateral agreements with each of the countries participating in the zone. . . . It stands to reason that the importance of establishing such a zone for the participants in it would be greater if similar guarantees were given to them also by the NATO nuclear powers.'

To this guarantee was added, for the first time, the offer to consider 'other measures applying to the Soviet territory adjacent to the Nordic nuclear free zone'. This interview was reported prominently in the Soviet press. The offer of 'measures' in Soviet territory encouraged the Scandinavian supporters of the proposal, which was clearly the Soviet intention, and the Russians made efforts to keep the issue alive. It was discussed at a meeting which the Swedish Under-Secretary of State for Foreign Affairs had with the Soviet Deputy Foreign Minister in September 1981, and Moscow Radio, in a broadcast in Swedish on 11 September, made sure that this was known throughout Scandinavia. But despite persistent official requests for clarification, the Soviet authorities have never been willing to explain just what were the measures Brezhnev had in mind.

Meanwhile the anti-nuclear campaign was under way. A large Nordic Peace Conference was held in Aalborg (Denmark) on 23 and 24 May 1981 in which prominant speakers from all Scandinavian countries took part. General Gert Bastian gave the introductory address, and urged the abandonment of NATO's plans; he supported the demand for a 'nuclear-free Northern Europe' as an important first step towards a nuclear-free Europe, with a 'nuclear-free world' as 'the ultimate aim if we are to survive'. The leading Danish sponsor of this conference, at which the Soviet Peace Committee and the WPC were represented, was the *Samarbejdskomiteen for Fred og Sikkerhed* (Cooperation Committee for Peace and Security) which had campaigned against the neutron bomb in 1977. A Danish Social Democratic parliamentarian, Lasse Budtz, who resigned from the Committee in 1978, has described it as 'a Communist front organisation that is clearly directed against only one of the super powers', and called the WPC the Committee's 'international umbrella organisation'.[14] The Committee was founded in 1974 by 31 Danes who had participated in the World Conference of Peace Forces in Moscow in 1973. Its main foreign contacts, apart from the WPC itself, are two WPC subsidiaries, the ILF of Peace Forces in Helsinki and the ICESC in Brussels. Several Danish trades unions are associated with its activities as well as the Danish Committee for the Workers Conference in the Baltic area, Norway and Iceland.

On 21 June 1981, a first Nordic Women's 'Peace March' was organised from Copenhagen to Paris to publicise the concept of a Nordic Nuclear Free Zone as part of a nuclear-free Europe. The initiative for the March came from the local branch of 'Women for Peace', an international movement founded in Switzerland in 1976. Though the organisers were not connected with the WPC and other front organisations, some front organisation officials, including Freda Brown, Australian president of the WIDF, took part in the March, which was addressed in Paris by General Nino Pasti, head of the Italian affiliate of the WPC. On their arrival in Paris on 'Hiroshima Day' (6 August) the members received a warm message of support from Brezhnev which was broadcast on Moscow Radio. Representatives of 'Women for Peace', among them the organisers of the 1981 March, attended an International Conference against the Arms Race and for Disarmament in Europe held in Stockholm in June 1982 under the auspices of the Swedish Peace Committee (*Svenska Fredskomitten*), an affiliate of the WPC. In the following month 300 women set out on a second Nordic Women's Peace March, this time from Stockholm to Minsk, via Leningrad and Moscow. The slogans for this March, supposedly unexceptionable, were: 'No to nuclear weapons in East and West', 'No to nuclear weapons in the world', and 'Yes to disarmament and peace'. Although the participants had few illusions about the efforts the Soviet authorities would make to try to manipulate the March, they considered the publicity which they expected to secure within the Soviet Union would be worthwhile. But they were disappointed. Much of their journey was spent in a special 'peace train' arranged by the Soviet Peace Committee and they were compelled to take part in a time-consuming programme of sight-seeing. Their opportunities for marching and for rallies were severely restricted and all their speeches and contacts were closely controlled and supervised. Their activities were given little publicity and reports were regularly distorted so as to give them an anti-Western slant and to omit any criticisms of Soviet policies. Finally, the Soviet Peace Committee attempted to link the Nordic Women's March with a Soviet-sponsored March from Moscow to Vienna which followed immediately afterwards. Most of the Nordic marchers returned to Stockholm sadly disillusioned by their experience.

Four months after the 1981 Women's 'Peace March', Moscow Radio broadcast a propaganda attack on alleged NATO pressures to induce Scandinavian countries to accept nuclear weapons on their territory. It was alleged that: 'Already bases for storing heavy weapons have been made available to the US Army by Norway. Denmark has been included in US plans to deploy medium-range nuclear weapons. US nuclear-capability planes are using the air force base in Keflavik, Iceland . . . Sweden is also coming under attack. Defence Secretary, Caspar Weinberger tried during his recent visit to Stockholm to subvert the idea of establishing a nuclear free zone in Northern Europe in general, and to erode the principles of Swedish neutrality in particular. . . . He described the establishment of a nuclear free zone as unilateral disarmament.' But the effect of these warnings was undermined when on the same day, 27 October, a Soviet submarine with nuclear capabilities was stranded in restricted waters near the Swedish naval base at Karlskrona. This drew a strongly publicised protest from the Swedish Government which was echoed in the other Scandinavian countries and led to Soviet acceptance of responsibility for the incident and payment of compensation. A further setback to Soviet efforts resulted from publicity surrounding the case of the Danish author Arne Petersen who had sponsored advertisements in two Danish newspapers, *Information* and the Communist paper *Lang og Folk*, in 1981 calling for a Nordic Nuclear Weapons Free Zone. Shortly after the grounding of the Soviet submarine, the Danish government announced that he had been charged with violating the security of the State: the money for the advertisements had come from a Soviet diplomat, Vladimir Merkulov, who had been expelled from Denmark (see Chapter 6). The charge against Petersen was dropped by order of the Danish Ministry of Justice.

By this time much of the steam had gone out of the Campaign

for a Nordic Nuclear Free Zone. In Norway the Labour Party lost the election in September 1981 to the Conservatives, and in opposition turned their efforts to stopping the Norwegian contribution to the NATO infrastructure costs of INF basing. They failed, by one vote, to achieve this in November 1982. But the Social Democratic Opposition in Denmark had greater success against the Conservative minority government; by majority vote on 26 May 1983 the Danish Parliament resolved that the Danish contribution should be suspended and called on the government to press NATO to defer the deployment of INF and to continue the negotiations beyond December 1983. The Danish Government suffered a further setback in December when Parliament passed a resolution specifically instructing them to oppose deployment at the NATO Ministerial meeting, despite the Soviet withdrawal from the Geneva negotiations. Meanwhile, during the visit to Moscow of the Finnish President, Koivisto, in June, Andropov attempted to revive the nuclear-free zone proposal by offers intended to meet two objections: he said the Soviet Union was ready to discuss the possibility of giving nuclear-free status to the Baltic (a point which the Swedish Prime Minister, Olof Palme, had emphasised): and to consider 'quite substantial' measures concerning the nuclear status of nearby Soviet territory (a repetition of Brezhnev's 1981 offer). Neither of these gestures aroused much interest in official circles in the Scandinavian countries. Nevertheless, the idea of a Nordic Nuclear Free Zone had long been the rallying cry for the front organisations in Scandinavia; it is likely that it will continue to provide a focus of interest and effort for the peace movements in all the Nordic countries, especially Sweden, and that it will be presented as the first step towards a wider European nuclear free zone. There is no doubt that the Soviet Government will continue by all means open to it to promote this interest.

GREECE

Since the election victory of PASOK (the Socialist Party) in October 1981, the Prime Minister, Andreas Papandreou, has claimed that the Greek Government is the only one in Western Europe which embraced the 'peace movement' and did not consider it as forming part of the opposition. Papandreou has long been a proponent of a nuclear free zone for the Balkans, a project which has had warm Soviet support, and he has consistently reserved Greece's position on the 1979 INF modernisation decision at NATO and European Community meetings.

The project received a set-back in July 1982 when Papandreou announced his decision temporarily to shelve it. This followed a visit to Bulgaria for talks with President Zhivkov. Papandreou said that he would accept no timetable for a removal of nuclear arms from Greece, despite his statement after his election in October 1981 that Greece, after the necessary consultations, would be the first to implement the principle of a Balkan nuclear-free zone by removing nuclear weapons from its territory. He is believed to have been influenced by intelligence, passed to him during his visit to Belgrade in June 1982, that Bulgaria had installed missile launching pads that could easily be converted to accommodate a Soviet nuclear capability. In view of Yugoslav and Rumanian misgivings, the plan for a Balkan nuclear free zone was postponed, as Papandreou put it, to 'a distant and happier future'. Moscow Radio, evidently disappointed, observed that 'in the view of the Soviet Union, it is important not to postpone indefinitely the implementation of a nuclear-free zone'.[15]

By 1983 Papandreou was still at odds with several aspects of established NATO policy, including INF modernisation, Poland and East-West relations generally. Greece was the only NATO member to vote in favour of the resolution on a nuclear arms freeze at the UN General Assembly on 14 December 1982. At a Conference in Athens on Nuclear Free Zones in Europe also in December 1982, Papandreou referred to his continued attempts to negotiate a joint agreement with Bulgaria, Rumania and Yugoslavia while stressing that 'the matter is not that simple, as each of these countries has its own alliances, obligations and policies'. In June 1983, it was reported that the Greek Government had invited all Balkan countries to a further conference in Athens later in the year, at which proposals for a Balkan nuclear-free zone would be discussed. Albania refused but Bulgaria and Rumania accepted, and Yugoslavia expressed cautious interest. The meeting eventually assembled in Athens on 16 January 1984. Bulgaria, Rumania and Yugoslavia took part all at the level of Ambassador. The Turkish Government, which opposes the idea of a Balkan nuclear-free zone, sought and received an invitation; after insisting that denuclearisation be placed low on the agenda, the Turks secured an adjournment of the meeting. When it reconvened on 13 February, it was clear that, without Turkish participation, the project would be pointless.[16]

This followed a conference on the denuclearisation of Europe, in which the WPC was closely involved, from 6–9 February 1984. Representatives of official East European peace committees (including Zhukov) as well as of Western peace movements took part. The conference broke up in disarray, having failed to accept a strongly pro-Soviet draft communiqué.[17]

Papandreou is likely to be under continuing pressure from the Greek Communist party to fulfill his repeatedly declared intention of securing the removal of all nuclear weapons from Greece even if a nuclear free zone is not established. A major demonstration organised by the Communist party but supported by many non-Communists took place in Athens on 8 August 1983 to mark the anniversary of Hiroshima. It concluded with the issue of an 'Acropolis Appeal', which demanded the abandonment of the NATO plans for INF deployment, a freeze on all nuclear weapons and the designation of Athens as a nuclear free city. No reference was made to Soviet missiles.[18]

ITALY

Compared with other West European countries, the 'peace movement' in Italy was slow to take off. Some momentum was gained after the Government's decision in August 1981 to construct a base at Comiso, Sicily, for the 112 cruise missiles which Italy is due to receive under the NATO decision of 1979. A 'March for Peace' from Perugia to Assisi was organised on 27 September 1981, which attracted some 50 000 participants, mostly supporters of the Italian Communist Party (PCI). In the following weeks, demonstrations took place in Rome, Milan, Naples and Turin as part of a campaign coordinated by the National Committee for disarmament, which includes the PCI and its youth organisation (FGCI), the *Partito di Unita Proletaria* (PDUP), *Democrazia Proletaria* (DP), the Radical Party and various anti-militarist groups. A demonstration in Rome on 24 October 1981 was one of the largest in recent years, the PCI taking the leading role and bringing supporters from all over

Italy; a smaller scale march organised by the Radical Party and the extreme left, was held in Rome on 5 June 1982 as a prelude to President Reagan's visit (the PCI again helped to provide transport to bring marchers from all over Italy). Although lip service was paid to the need for disarmament by both East and West, the tone was anti-American. The PCI was represented at a low level and, unlike the October 1981 demonstration, the trade unions did not collectively participate, although some members of the Communist-controlled CGIL were present. Local demonstrations in Comiso have had some success and a petition against the designated cruise missile base gathered over a million signatures in the area in 1982, but the national peace movement seems unlikely to make further headway unless and until the PCI decides more actively to promote it. The PCI may be expected to organise further rallies, but its position has been complicated by its continuing open argument with the CPSU over ideological uniformity in the world Communist movement, and its reluctance, for electoral reasons, as a party supporting Italian membership of NATO, to exploit its full potential as an opposition force.

Indeed from the Soviet point of view, the attitude of the PCI has proved wholly unsatisfactory. Its leader, Berlinguer (who died on 11 June 1984), has urged that the peace movement should not be solely anti-American and anti-NATO, but should extend its condemnation to the Soviet SS-20 missiles as well, and should recognise that in a nuclear age even capitalist states can be in favour of peace. Soviet mistrust of the PCI could only have been reinforced at the end of October 1982 when the Party expelled Roberto Napoleone, the publisher of *Interstampa*, which had challenged the orthodox policy of the present leadership. The timing of this event was also significant in that it took place on the day before Berlinguer saw Vadim Zagladin, Ponomarev's deputy, during his first visit to Italy to test the loyalty of the PCI.[19]

It was not until January 1983 that the fragmented Italian peace movement held its first national meeting in Rome. This was organised by the '24 October Committee' which had been formed to organise the mass demonstration held on that date in Rome in 1981. The Committee's subsequent inability to unite the different components of the movement was shown in a report in the left-wing magazine *Pace e Guerra*, which criticised a recent vote by PCI members at the European Parliament in Strasbourg in

January 1983 in favour of a motion for closer collaboration within NATO and attacking independent peace movements in the West as a menace to European security. The Rome meeting, however, rejected attempts by Nino Pasti, on behalf of the pro-Soviet *Lotta per la Pace* (Struggle for Peace) to promote a motion condemning NATO nuclear modernisation (but not the Soviet SS-20s).

Peace camps similar to that at Greenham Common in England but not confined to women were established at Comiso. They attracted some international publicity and support, and there have been plans to develop the main camp as a centre for the Italian peace movement. The remoteness of the site area from mainland Italy, combined with local Sicilian appreciation of the construction contracts involved, tended to minimise the impact of these activities. The day of protest – 22 October 1983 – did however see a large demonstration in Rome, for which estimates of the size varied between 300 000 and 500 000.

FRANCE

In France the anti-nuclear movement was active in the 1960s in opposition to the development of the French *force de frappe* under General de Gaulle. The Communist Party (PCF) played a leading role through the Mouvement de la Paix (MDP). The PCF and the Socialist Party shared an anti-nuclear platform in the early 1970s. But in 1977 the two parties reversed their positions. From then on they accepted the Gaullist policy of 'independence' of both blocs, East and West, buttressed by medium sized national nuclear forces, which had acquired widespread popular support. When President Mitterrand took office after the elections of May 1981, he moved even further from the policy his party had followed ten years earlier. The presence of four Communist ministers in the Government, in which the PCF is the junior partner, did not prevent him from strongly supporting the NATO 1979 decision to deploy cruise and Pershing II missiles in Europe to balance the Soviet SS-20. At the same time the Foreign Minister, Claude Cheysson, poured scorn in public on what he described as the 'defeatism' of the peace movement.

So the MDP, still depending on support from the PCF, has been through a difficult period. Its National Secretary, Michael Langignon, is a former member of the WPC Secretariat. His assistant, Jacques Denis, the PCF's specialist on international affairs, and Pierre-Luc Seguillon, the editor of the Socialist *Temoignage Chrétien*, were both in 1982 officials of the WPC, but their performance was somewhat erratic, as shown by the MDP's condemnation in early 1980 of the invasion of Afghanistan (which Jacques Denis later corrected).[20] Even so, the demonstration in Paris organised on 25 October 1981 by the MDP against NATO nuclear modernisation and the 'neutron bomb' was, in common with its successors in 1982 and 1983, feeble compared to its counterparts elsewhere. The original demonstration was supported by the PCF and by the Communist-dominated trade union federation (CGT), *La Jeunesse Ouvrière Chrétienne* and the ecological movement, Greenpeace. But it could only muster some 50 000, hardly more than the standard PCF turn-out on such occasions. On 25 November 1981, six of the Generals for Peace and Disarmament, led by Admiral Sanguinetti, published a memorandum claiming that the 1979 NATO decision on cruise and Pershing II deployment had nothing to do with a response to Soviet SS-20 missiles, but was part of a Pentagon effort to gain a first-strike capability. This failed to stimulate much interest. A 'peace weekend' in Nimes in May 1982 also failed to attract much support apart from PCF and CGT members. On the other hand, a march for peace in Paris on 20 June 1982 was the largest such demonstration for many years, although the figure of a quarter of a million demonstrators, claimed by the organisers, was undoubtedly an exaggeration. It took place in response to an appeal from a hundred prominent personalities, mainly members or supporters of the PCF, and was preceded by massive daily coverage in the PCF newspaper, *L'Humanité*. The nucleus of the organisation and the majority of the marchers were from the PCF and the CGT; its objective was described in very general terms, all criticism of the Soviet Union being rigorously excluded. *Le Monde* saw it as a relatively successful attempt by the PCF to unify its political base and to rally to its other groups such as Christian organisations, independent Gaullists and the extreme left.

Despite these efforts, by 1983 there was still little sign of a major peace movement emerging in France. The MDP complained of 'racism' being applied against it by its non-Communist and non-aligned rival CODENE (Committee for Nuclear Disarmament in Europe), which was blamed for MDP's failure to receive an invitation to the END convention in West Berlin in May.

CODENE was formed as a coordinating organisation in order to challenge the monopoly of the Communist MDP and to bring France into the mainstream of European peace movements. But it has so far remained no more than a small group of intellectuals. Its organising secretary, Jean Barthelet, has said: 'if we joined forces with the *Mouvement de la Paix* we should be swamped. It is all right in Britain, Holland or West Germany for large peace movements to accommodate small Communist parties. Here the Communists are just too big'.[21] So the peace movement in France has remained ineffective partly because it is identified with and dominated by the PCF, but also because it does not at present appear to reflect any deeply or widely felt need among French people. The support given to CODENE by the Catholic-trade union federation, CDFT, for a rally on 23 October 1983 may herald a change in this situation. But there has been no subsequent indication of mass support.

BELGIUM

The peace movement in Belgium is divided into two parts, reflecting the linguistic division of the country. The umbrella organisation for Flemish peace groups is VAKA (*Vlaams Aktiekomitte tegen Atoomwapens*), that for French-speaking groups CNAPD (*Comité National d'Action pour la Paix et le Developpement*). VAKA has developed links with the official East German Peace Council with which it has exchanged visits. CNAPD on the other hand has been at pains to differentiate itself from the official peace committees of Eastern Europe; it opposes cruise missile deployment in Belgium but calls also for dismantling of the Soviet SS-20s.

In this it is at variance with the Belgian Union for the Defence of Peace (UBDP), the WPC's affiliate in Belgium, which maintains that nothing should divert the peace movement from its main aim, preventing the basing of American missiles in Belgium. But the UBDP has not been totally compliant. In March 1983 its Secretary, Jean du Bosch, a former WPC Presidential Committee member, told the Belgian Communist Party newspaper, *Le Drapeau Rouge*, that at its recent conference the UBDP had voted to withdraw from the WPC. He explained that historically the Union had strong ties with the WPC, but that the latter had 'not moved with the times' and 'no longer provided a framework in which new forms of East–West dialogue could be sought'. He added that the withdrawal should not be seen as a final breach – the UBDP would still participate in WPC events and activities 'in so far as they met his movement's aims and interests'.

A demonstration on 23 April 1983 at Florennes, the proposed site for deployment of 48 cruise missiles in 1985, which 10 000 people from all over Belgium attended, was supported by VAKA and CNAPD. They demanded rejection of NATO's plans for cruise missiles and no preparations for stationing at Florennes.[22] In July the Belgian Bishops issued a 'Disarmament for Peace' declaration which stated that deterrence, based on balance, is morally acceptable, but not as a goal in itself and on condition that it is a means towards disarmament. This was criticised by the peace movement for not firmly opposing the basing of missiles in Belgium. All groups in the movement came together for a major demonstration in Brussels on 23 October, claimed to number 300 000.

TURKEY

It is not the purpose of this book to assess the events which led to the suspension of political parties in Turkey in 1980 nor the subsequent internal political developments, including the strictly controlled restoration of limited democratic freedoms in 1983. The Turkish Government has maintained its adherence to the NATO Double-Track decision of 1979 and has supported arms control proposals since adopted by the Alliance. No Turkish representative appears among the profiles of international front organisations in Annex II. On the other hand members of the Turkish 'peace movement' have been subjected to arrest and imprisonment. However justified the circumstances may be, the result is that they are deprived of the freedom to dissent and demonstrate which as emphasised in Chapter 1 is among the most prized of Western values. This inevitably is how it is seen by peace movements in Western Europe.

11 The Freeze Campaign in the United States and the Bishops' Letter

The peace movement in the United States is a fragmented one, largely based on a few long-standing organisations such as the War Resisters League, the American Friends and the Committee for a Sane Nuclear Policy (SANE), all pressing for different aims. These groups, however, have never attracted widespread national sympathy. The account in Chapter 7 shows that, although the international front organisations were actively involved in the protest movement against the Vietnam War, they had little success in promoting their disarmament and anti-nuclear campaigns in the United States. The vast majority of American citizens, who still believe in the United States role as the champion of democratic principles, support the policy of nuclear deterrence as the means of preserving peace. This has been the policy of successive Administrations since the announcement of the 'Truman Doctrine' in March 1947.* There is no significant or coordinated unilateralist opposition to it. There is however a vast range of institutes and organisations throughout the country engaged in the serious study of disarmament problems. Many of them are critical of established defence and arms control policies and aim to promote new initiatives with a view to achieving a genuine breakthrough in negotiations. One issue in recent years has attracted the interest of these bodies and a wider and more spontaneous groundswell of popular support throughout the country than anything experienced since the mass protests at the time of the Vietnam war. This is the concept of a 'nuclear freeze' as the basis for halting the 'arms race' and preserving peace.

---

* President Truman said: 'It must be the policy of the United States to support free peoples who are resisting attempted subjugation by armed minorities or outside pressures.'

The freeze is seen as an alternative to traditional and current methods for achieving multilateral arms control. There are many variations. All of them envisage a verifiable bilateral agreement between the United States and the Soviet Union which would freeze the testing, production and deployment of nuclear weapons and delivery systems and would be followed by progressive reductions. It is claimed, and indeed is intended, that this would in no way undermine deterrence, the validity of which is accepted by those who advocate the freeze. The simplicity of the concept, as compared with the complex nature of what often appear to be the arcane theories of experts, has appealed to public imagination.

The concept of a freeze is not new. It was first proposed by President Johnson in January 1964, at a time when the United States still had a clear majority of strategic nuclear weapons and delivery systems, and was then turned down flat by the Russians. During President Nixon's Administration, a resolution calling for a freeze, in the form of 'an immediate suspension . . . of the further deployment of all offensive and defensive nuclear strategic systems', was adopted by an overwhelming majority in the Senate in April 1970. But the Administration preferred to stick to its existing negotiating basis in the Strategic Arms Limitation Talks (SALT) which led, in 1972, to the conclusion of the SALT I agreements. Neither of these initiatives however derived from popular pressures. These did not emerge until some years later. The search for an alternative approach to arms control stemmed initially from the concern of individuals about what they regarded as the inadequacies of the SALT process and the half-hearted reception given to the SALT II Treaty, signed by President Carter and President Brezhnev in Vienna in June 1979 after five years of negotiation. Although the Treaty was sent forward to the Senate in November by the Foreign Relations Committee, with a majority recommendation in favour of ratification, it was evident that there was little prospect that it would secure the necessary two-thirds majority, at least without a demand for amendments which would effectively kill the Treaty. Extraneous events, especially Soviet military activities in Cuba and the invasion of Afghanistan, extinguished any remaining hopes of ratification and, in January 1980, President Carter asked the Senate to suspend action on the Treaty. In practice this was seen as implying that nothing would be done until the next Administration took office in January 1981. Meanwhile consideration was being given, parallel with the SALT ratification process, to the deployment of MX missiles intended to close the so-called 'window of vulnerability' (primarily the supposed Soviet first-strike threat to the American Minuteman ICBM force), which had been exposed – and to some extent exploited – by opponents of SALT II. The large Ohio Class submarines and the long range Trident missiles were under development, and NATO was moving towards the Double-Track decision on INF. Although all this was taking place in response to what was perceived as a major increase in the Soviet nuclear threat – and was considered by many critics not to go far enough – it created the impression that there would shortly be a massive escalation of nuclear capabilities, with little apparent effort on the part of the United States Administration to prevent it and little concern about its implications for world peace.

These developments prompted a reaction from the AFSC which, in the summer of 1979, adopted proposals for a 'Nuclear Moratorium' involving a cessation by the United States of the production and deployment of new nuclear weapons for three years.[1] The proposal was unilateral and as such found few followers. Soon afterwards, however, proposals were being prepared by quite a different source; these were to form the basis for the Freeze Campaign. Randall Forsberg, founder of the Institute for Defence and Disarmament Studies, a research centre modelled on the Stockholm International Institute for Peace Research (SIPRI) where she had previously worked, saw the need for an initiative which would both capture the public's imagination, and yet at the same time gain the suppport of experts on arms control and members of the defence community. In April 1980, she published a four-page document, *Call to Halt the Nuclear Arms Race*, a revised version of which was issued in April 1982. This called for the adoption by the United States and the Soviet Union of a 'mutual freeze on the testing, production and deployment of nuclear weapons and of missiles and new aircraft designed primarily to deliver nuclear weapons'. It was claimed that verification of the suspension of underground tests, of missile production and deployment and of increases in MIRVs could be carried out 'with high confidence' by national means. Two further measures – a halt on weapon production and on the production of fissionable material for weapon purposes – were if possible to be included, although they could not be verified by national means with the same confidence. The freeze would be achieved by a mutual announcement of a moratorium, to be followed by negotiations to incorporate the moratorium in a Treaty. The basis for this proposal was the assumed existence of parity between American and Soviet nuclear forces and the importance of preventing further dangerous escalation of the 'arms race' in the form of a new generation of ICBMs by both sides and the deployment of cruise missiles.

With public attention focused on the approaching Presidential election in November and the calamity of the Iranian hostage crisis, 1980 proved an inopportune time for launching a national campaign. However, developments in the latter part of the year led to an increase in support for the freeze concept. One was the publication in August of Presidential Directive (PD) 59, announcing the policy of selective options for retaliatory nuclear strikes (see Chapter 2). Another was the suspension of the Comprehensive Test Ban (CTB) negotiations during the autumn. The goal of six previous Presidents, a CTB had been given a high priority by President Carter. Its abandonment was therefore seen as a major blow to the prospects for arms control.

A further source of concern was the rhetoric displayed by Governor Reagan prior to his inauguration as President in January 1981. For many people, his statement that SALT II was 'fatally flawed' was a message of despair. This apparent lack of interest in arms control, coupled with his commitment to a massive rebuilding of United States defence capabilities, increased anxieties. Most disturbing of all was the impression given by some members of his Administration, and even in some loosely worded statements by President Reagan himself, that they could envisage the possibility of fighting and 'winning' a nuclear war. As one observer later said when reflecting on the cause of public protest against the new Administration's policies: (President) Reagan spoke of controlling nuclear war, not of controlling arms. He seemed to think that nuclear wars can be won. . . . More generally, the President stood for a vision of America in which power had pride of place. This vision was perfectly expressed in his budget, which called for a radical expansion of the military and a radical extraction of everything else.'[2]

Since the publication of the *Call to Halt the Nuclear Arms Race*, Randall Forsberg had been active in gathering support from existing peace and church organisations through lectures and seminars. By 1980, such diverse organisations as the Fellowship of Reconciliation, Pax Christi, Sojourners, CALC and the previously unilateralist AFSC were united in making a freeze their highest priority. In addition, arms control specialists such as George Rathjens, chief scientist of the Department of Defence under the Eisenhower Administration, and Bernard Feld, chairman of the Pugwash Conferences and Editor-in-Chief of the *Bulletin of Atomic Scientists*, has also endorsed Forsberg's calls.[3]

One of the people the freeze message reached at this embrionic stage was Randall Kehler, a Harvard graduate and co-founder of the Traprock Peace Center in Deerfield, designed to promote the non-violent resolution of conflicts. Kehler had also been active in the anti-Vietnam War movement, which has provided a ready source of freeze campaign activists. He began to organise support for a nuclear freeze in three state senate districts in western Massachusetts, and the freeze appeared as a ballot proposition for the first time in November 1980. This, although non-binding, was upheld in 30 out of 32 towns by a two-to-one margin, despite the fact that Reagan had simultaneously carried the same areas against Carter by a similar margin.[4] Although the ballot went largely unnoticed at national level, a great deal of interest was shown locally. By the time the National Freeze Campaign was officially launched in Washington, in March 1981, some 300 activists from 33 states were drawn to the inaugural conference.[5] As noted in Chapter 7, there were some adversaries among them, but these were not to prove the dominant elements in the freeze movement.

A National Freeze Clearing House was established in Missouri, together with a highly organised series of task forces in such fields as fund-raising, media handling, education, relations with Congress and the Administration, and coordination with other organisations. The problems of running a national campaign were largely overcome by holding regular inter-state telephone meetings through the 'conference call' system, whereby all participants are connected at the same time by the operators. But it was widely recognised that the strength of the Nuclear Freeze Campaign came largely from the independent efforts of local groups in attracting 'grass-roots' support.

Existing and previously redundant civic groups began to join forces with the peace organisations, holding 'teach-ins' on the dangers of nuclear war and the need for a freeze which soon also embraced town meetings and council debates. Support received a special boost in the summer of 1981 when, after 5 years of virtually uncritical support for US defence policy by the major newspapers and television, a major network, CBS, screened a five-part series called 'The Defence of the United States' which examined what would happen if a nuclear missile hit Omaha, Nebraska and questioned the rationale behind the Administration's planned 7% real increase in defence expenditure while concurrently speaking of 'winnable' nuclear war.[6]

Thereafter local radio, newspapers and television were used extensively to advertise the campaign, together with household visits and the use of direct mail. The last involved the distribution of a letter pledging support for a freeze which the recipients were asked to sign and return with donations. Together with a small number of wealthy backers, this remains the principal basis for countryside campaigning and support and has a useful measure of the kinds of people who support the freeze. They are said to include a large proportion of women, environmentalists, non-union members, homeowners, educated and professional people with average income running over 25 000 dollars, fiscal conservatives, non-interventionists and supporters of national parks, abortion and the Equal Rights Amendment![7]

The freeze proposal undoubtedly contains an element of emotional appeal, as evidenced by the popularity of Jonathan Schell's book, *The Fate of the Earth*, published in 1982. The author creates a utopian vision of a new world without the threat of nuclear catastrophe and planetary doom. He argues that only freeze provides the means to leap from the present to utopia. 'Two paths lie before us. One leads to death, the other to life. . . . Either we will sink into the final coma and end it all or, as I trust and believe, we will awaken to the truth of our peril, a truth as great as life itself, and, like a person who has swallowed a lethal poison but shakes off his stupor at the last moment and vomits the poison up, he will break through the layers of denial, put aside our fainthearted excuses, and rise up to cleanse the earth of nuclear weapons.'

The official organisers of the freeze campaign claim that much of its support is either morally or religiously based, and many stress the part that parental fears play in motivation. Most of the organisers are white, academic and middle class. Randall Forsberg herself was an English teacher in Pennsylvania and had studied military policy at Massachusetts Institute of Technology. Helena Knapp, co-chairman of the Nuclear Weapons Freeze Campaign, is the daughter of a civil servant, educated at St Hilda's College, Oxford and a research graduate of the University of Pennsylvania. She has been described as bringing to the nuclear debate, 'less the fervour of the Greenham Common supporters than dry, peculiarly English practicalities of the British academic world'. Dr Helen Caldicott, the president of Physicians for Social Responsibility (PSR), an organisation which has played a major part in contributing to the national freeze campaign, gave up the prospects of research in cystic fibrosis in order to 'work for peace'. She speaks of 'a tremendous untapped majority out there – women. . . . I think if we get moving we can save the earth'. On the other hand, she claims, 'This isn't just a feminist issue. You don't have to be liberated to understand your children may not survive the year 2000, let alone the next five years.'[8] Helen Caldicott's efforts, and those of her colleagues in advertising the health dangers of nuclear war and its aftermath, together with the organisation's breadth of appeal, led to an increase in PSR's membership from 10 in 1979 to 12 000 in 1982.[9]

Complementary to the organisers' aim of evoking a massive display of grass roots support, are their efforts to persuade Congressmen and the Administration to accept the freeze proposal. Early in 1982, freeze supporters began bombarding representatives in the Senate and House of Representatives with letters, telephone calls, visiting delegations and questions at public meetings as to their position on the issue. In Washington DC, the Nuclear Freeze Foundation was established and has worked closely with the national campaign, briefing members of Congress, arms control experts and defence specialists. The Foundation also functions as a centre of information about freeze activities in Congress and how they relate to state and local effort.[10]

At the end of 1981, after Congress had adjourned, two Senators, Mark Hatfield of Oregon (Republican) and Edward Kennedy of Massachusetts (Democrat), were already struck by the 'compelling public feeling for the freeze . . . and by its range of support among constituents of every age, faith, race, philosophy and sex'.[11] They were moved by the apparent public concern about the Administration's policies to seek a new arms control initiative, and in doing so they consulted leaders of the freeze movement and many experts in arms control. Among those who were prepared to support the idea of a freeze were former Under Secretary of State George Ball, retired Chief of Naval Development Admiral Thomas Davies, former Deputy CIA Director Herbert Scoville, John Steinbruner of the Brookings Institution, Jeremy Stone of the Federation of American Scientists (FAS), and the former arms control negotiator, Paul Warnke. Discussions with them convinced Senators that the freeze was a practical and verifiable proposal worth trying, and that it might well prove successful in negotiations with the Soviet Union.

On 10 March 1982, Hatfield and Kennedy introduced a short Resolution in the Senate which asserted in its preamble that 'the nuclear arms race is dangerously increasing the risk of a holocaust', and that 'a freeze followed by reductions in nuclear warheads, missiles, and other delivery systems is needed to halt the nuclear arms race and to reduce the risk of war'. As an immediate objective, the resolution proposed that the United States and the Soviet Union should 'pursue a complete halt to the nuclear arms race; decide when and how to achieve a mutual and verifiable freeze on the testing, production and further deployment of nuclear warheads, missiles, and other delivery systems; and give special attention to destabilizing weapons whose deployment would make such a freeze more difficult to achieve'. Finally, it urged, that 'proceeding from this freeze, the United States and the Soviet Union should pursue major, mutual, and verifiable reductions in nuclear warheads, missiles and other delivery systems, through annual percentages or equally effective means, in a manner that enhances stability'. An identical resolution was introduced in the House of Representatives by Edward Markey (Democrat), Silvio Conte (Republican) and Jonathan Bingham (Democrat). Shortly afterwards, Senators Jackson (Democrat) and Warner (Republican) countered the Kennedy-Hatfield resolution with one closely aligned with the Administration's viewpoint. It warned of Soviet superiority in nuclear weaponry and called for a freeze at 'equal and sharply reduced levels'.

President Reagan made his position clear in a speech in early March to the National Association of Evangelists. He characterised the freeze proposal as 'a very dangerous fraud . . . merely the illusion of peace', adding that 'a freeze at current levels of weapons would remove any incentive for the Soviets to negotiate seriously and virtually end our chances to achieve the major arms reductions which we have proposed'. In his view, Moscow would only agree to substantial reductions if faced with the clear prospect of a US build-up in nuclear weapons: 'the reality is that we must find peace through strength'.[12] On 9 May, he announced his proposals for Strategic Arms Reduction Talks (START), which were promptly endorsed by a resolution of the Senate Foreign Relations Committee.

Though they involved radical reductions in the nuclear weapons of both sides, these proposals did not satisfy the leaders of the freeze movement who, despite the opening the START in June, clearly had little confidence in the prospects for their acceptance by the Soviet Union. In April a revised version of the *Call to Halt the Nuclear Arms Race* was published (described above). Then on 12 June, a peaceful rally was held in Central Park, New York, claimed to be the largest protest demonstration in American history, in which more than 500 000 people took part. The rally had been planned as far back as September 1981 to coincide with the United Nations Second Special Session on Disarmament (UNSSOD II), and its size contrasted remarkably with the 10 000 protestors who had turned out for the First Special Session four years earlier. The massing of freeze supporters in one place showed the variety of people who were committed to 'halting the arms race'. Besides political figures and established bodies concerned to promote arms control, they included new professional organisations such as Dancers for Disarmament and Nurses for a Non-Nuclear Future; and individuals such as the 27 year-old flautist who said he had hitch-hiked from Kentucky to try to ensure that his three year-old son would have a peaceful world to grow up in, and the pied piper, bearded, ponytailed, with a knapsack, bearing the signs of earlier 'peace' campaigns.[13] Among them of course were also many who represented front organisations and their American affiliates.

By June, as many as 600 city and town councils, and 12 state legislatures had adopted freeze initiatives, and a New York Times/CBS News Poll showed that 72 per cent of the American public supported the idea of a freeze.[14] The majority of Democrats endorsed the freeze at the Party's mid-term convention in Philadelphia from 25–7 June. However, when the Markey resolution came up on the floor of the House of Representatives on

5 August 1982, it was narrowly defeated by 204 votes to 202. An amendment was passed – on the lines of the Jackson–Warner resolution in the Senate – which favoured a freeze only after the US and USSR had sharply reduced their strategic forces to equal levels. Thus, the majority in the House supported the Administration, with the emphasis on the establishment of equal ceilings at reduced levels before a freeze could be considered. The freeze supporters had to wait until the 98th Congress before making further efforts to get their proposal adopted.[15]

During the rest of the year, the freeze campaign concentrated its efforts both on strengthening its grass-roots support, and on persuading officials of the importance and negotiability of a freeze. At the mid-term Congressional elections in the autumn of 1982, 30 per cent of the population had the opportunity to vote in state referendums and numerous local ballots, on proposals calling for a US–Soviet freeze on the nuclear arms race. The process began in Wisconsin on 14 September and culminated with many freeze referendums held on 2 November. In order to qualify for a ballot, areas initially had to collect 346 000 signatures. A major drive in California to gain grass roots support had already resulted in more than 600 000 signatures by April 1982. There were similar successes in other States and areas. The freeze proposals eventually passed in 44 out of 49 locations, 34 out of 37 cities and counties, eight out of the nine states in which referendums were held, and in the District of Columbia. The total count was approximately 11.6 million in favour and 7.9 million against, a majority of 60 against 40% of those who had the opportunity to vote.[16] Referendums in only 9 states out of a total of 55, could not be interpreted as constituting a national appeal for the freeze. Nevertheless, the ballot results demonstrated the extent to which the campaign had managed to reach across the whole country. Support cut right across traditional conservative–liberal and Republican–Democrat divisions.[17]

An important element in the campaign to convince expert and official opinion of the merits of the freeze was the hearings organised in Washington by the Federation of American Scientists (FAS) in September and December 1982 and in March 1983. These were conducted by panels of prominent foreign affairs and strategic analysts, who heard presentations from, and questioned, witnesses who testified in favour of the freeze and some who were opposed to it or to various aspects of it. Randall Forsberg, at the first hearing, chaired by Dr Alton Frye of the Council on Foreign Relations, described the freeze as representing a 'slight first step forward toward that world in which we maintain peace without the threat of annihilation'. It would have two components: stopping the production of nuclear warheads; and stopping the steady advance in technology of the delivery systems associated with nuclear weapons. She foresaw that it would be introduced 'by negotiated agreement, tacit or formal, more or less public, with some sort of brief discussions conducted over a period of perhaps several months preceding announcement of a moratorium on all of those things which the freeze is intended eventually to stop'. The moratorium would be sustained during the subsequent period for negotiation of a treaty, which might last between six and eighteen months.

During the negotiation of the treaty, issues such as confidence tests of nuclear warheads and nuclear missiles, possible supplementary verification measures over and above national technical means of verification and machinery for dealing with violation of the agreement, would be discussed. In response to critics of the feasibility of verifying by national means a ban on the production of nuclear weapons, Forsberg argued that production facilities in the Soviet Union, if anything like those in the United States, would involve a relatively small number of large, highly specialised facilities, capable of being monitored for even small signs of activity. Moreover, new warheads could not be deployed on major delivery systems, because the production and joining together of these systems with the warheads would be virtually impossible without detection. So there would be little to gain from violation. The critics remain sceptical.[18]

The second hearing concentrated on the plausibility of negotiating a comprehensive freeze based on SALT II, which was taken as a 'starting point' since it would be too complex a process to scrap and replace it. The idea would be to close the 'loop-holes' in SALT II, for example freezing the 'one new land-based missile' permitted to each side by the SALT II treaty. Thus, the MX missile or any possible substitute for it would be traded off for the one new land-based missile which the Soviet Union has repeatedly tested. Dr Jeremy Stone, director of the FAS, who presented these proposals, described them as a plan to 'Freeze SALT II and Shrink'. He claimed that, if the ceilings in SALT II were frozen and then through annual percentage reductions 'shrunk' by 50%, this would approximate to the Reagan START plan, and would do so in a manner which would be more readily negotiable with the Russians. The plan also envisaged dealing with the problem of the SS-20 and American cruise and Pershing II missiles in Europe by deferring the introduction of Cruise and Pershing missiles in return for reductions in Soviet INF. Thus, the interim freeze package would entail US acceptance of limited deployment of SS-20s in Europe in return for Soviet acceptance of the Reagan START plan, although within the context of a 'new types' freeze and a shrinkage of SALT II.[19]

The third hearing concentrated mainly on the prospects for bringing within the freeze concept a halt to the production of fissionable material for weapons purposes and a comprehensive test ban, and on the problems of verification. In its closing stages it was suggested that the basic difference between the 'freeze approach' and the traditional 'arms control approach' to stopping the 'arms race' was one of presumption: the presumption of the freeze was that all activities should be stopped, as a starting point for negotiations; the arms control presumption was that all activities would continue except those which it proved possible, through negotiation, to control. The conclusion, expressed by Stone, was that a Treaty based on the former approach stood a greater chance of securing the political support needed for ratification.[20] This was an impressive series of discussions in which the views of the witnesses were seriously argued in each hearing and thoroughly probed by the panels. They demonstrated that those who were advocating a freeze as an alternative policy were able to make a respectable case for the sophisticated proposals which they advanced. Although their critics and representatives of the Administration have been quick to point to defects in the proposals and aspects of them which could impact adversely on American and NATO security interests, the hearings represented a significant advance in the efforts of the freeze campaigners to make a convincing case to a wide spectrum of informed opinion.

The latter part of 1982 brought with it new developments which were thought, by many commentators, to portend rifts in the freeze movement, leading to possible loss of direction and weakening of its impact. Differences of opinion began to appear between those, particularly amongst the more militant peace groups, who felt that the campaign ought to attack individual weapons programmes, and the leaders of the national campaign who wanted to continue to concentrate on persuading the House of Representatives to back the freeze resolution in the first half of 1983. When Congress was voting on production funds for the MX missile in December 1982, SANE and the United Church of Christ, together with several environmental organisations, engaged in a campaign of lobbying local members of Congress, which contributed to Congressional rejection of the Administration's proposal for the MX dense-pack basing mode. Then in February 1983 at a strategic conference in St Louis, the campaign reaffirmed the call for Congressional approval of a bilateral freeze resolution, and decided to work in parallel for 'interim restraints' on certain US weapons, on the grounds that the prospects for a bilateral freeze would be undermined by their deployment. The conference specified three such steps: a cancellation of funds to test new nuclear weapons, contingent upon a Soviet halt to such tests; a one-year delay in the production and deployment of Pershing II missiles and GLCMs; and a freeze on the rate of production of nuclear materials needed to make warheads.[21]

On 3 January 1983, a new freeze resolution was introduced into the House of Representatives by Clement Zablocki, a Democrat from Wisconsin and chairman of the House Foreign Affairs Committee. This contained a number of modifications and qualifications aimed at satisfying some of the critics of the simpler Markey resolution. Starting from the premise that 'essential equivalence in overall nuclear capabilities' should be maintained, the Zablocki resolution proposed that the objective of the Strategic Arms Reduction Talks should be the negotiation of 'an immediate, mutual, and verifiable freeze' to be followed by the further negotiation of 'substantial, equitable and verifiable reductions'. Any suggestion of a moratorium during the negotiations (a point on which the Markey resolution was ambiguous) was specifically ruled out; pending full ratification of the freeze agreement, the United States would have no obligation to discontinue the modernisation and deployment of weapons required to 'maintain the credibility of the United States nuclear deterrent'. When the freeze was in force, one-for-one replacements of weapons and delivery vehicles would be permitted. Similarly, although the resolution called for a merger of the START and INF negotiations, in the absence of a freeze agreement the deployment commitments in the NATO Double-

Track decision of December 1979 would remain in force. Commenting on the effect of the resolution, Zablocki emphasised that no item would be frozen unless both sides agreed, any item that could not be verified would not be frozen, and nothing would be frozen while negotiations were being conducted or until the freeze agreement was signed and ratified by both sides.[22]

When opening discussion in the Foreign Affairs Committee, Zablocki reminded his colleagues that freeze resolutions had been passed by 8 state referendums, 11 state legislatures and hundreds of other jurisdictions. His proposal was adopted on 8 March, by 27 votes to 9, after heavy lobbying by freeze supporters which culminated in a rally on Capitol Hill immediately after the vote attended by approximately 5000 people. The mid-term Congressional elections had considerably increased the majority of Democrats in the House of Representatives, so that, whereas during the 97th Congress there had been 242 Democrats and 189 Republicans, there were now 267 Democrats as against 167 Republicans. The increase in Democrats, who have generally shown greater support for the freeze idea than the Republicans, was reflected in the vote on the floor of the House on 4 May, when the resolution was adopted by 278 votes to 149, a majority of 129 in favour, in contrast to the rejection of the Markey resolution by two votes in August 1982. This was a considerable success for the freeze supporters although the form of the proposal fell far short of the ideal promoted by the campaign. However, without Senate endorsement, the House's resolution would carry little weight with the Administration.

The Senate, with its Republican majority, had been slow to take up consideration of the freeze, on the basis of the Kennedy–Hatfield resolution which had first been introduced in March 1982, in parallel with the introduction of the identical Markey resolution into the House. On 2 August 1983, the Senate Foreign Relations Committee blocked an attempt to force an immediate vote on the Kennedy–Hatfield resolution: the majority favoured a proposal by Senators Cohen (Republican) and Nunn (Democrat) that reductions should be achieved by the withdrawal of two existing warheads for each new one deployed. Eventually, on 23 September, a vote was taken on a resolution calling on the United States and Soviet Governments to decide when and how to begin an immediate, mutual and verifiable freeze: the resolution was rejected in the Committee by 7 votes to

10.²³ When the Kennedy–Hatfield resolution at last came to a vote in the Chamber on 1 November (in the form of an amendment to a Bill to raise the national debt ceiling), it was defeated by 58 votes to 40, 12 out of 45 Democratic Senators voting with the Republican majority. At the same time the Senate adopted a resolution supporting the Cohen–Nunn proposal, the so-called 'build-down', which was incorporated in revised proposals put forward by President Reagan in the START in October.²⁴

Freeze supporters have not abandoned all hope of drafting amendments to current freeze resolutions so as to make them attractive to a majority in the Senate. The House Zablocki resolution has not been considered in the Senate and there is no sign that it will be. However the focus of action by the end of 1983 had changed, with the prospect of elections in 1984. The aim had become, in the words of Chaplain Morrison, an official of the Freeze Campaign, 'to get every Senator on record with a vote for or against freeze as we move into the electoral year 1984'.²⁵

Concurrently with the development of the freeze campaign a debate has been going on within the Roman Catholic Church in the United States, specifically among the American Catholic bishops, about the moral and ethical dilemmas involved in the possession of nuclear weapons and the policy of deterrence. The debate, though not related to, or directly resulting from, the freeze campaign, has been inspired by the same basic concern, the desire to give practical effect to the ringing plea by Pope Paul VI to the United Nations in 1965: 'No more war! War never again!' Of the 285 American bishops, 60 are members of Pax Christi, and they have been the principal advocates of the pacifist position in the debate.²⁶

The debate has however represented a new departure for the US Catholic bishops as a body. With the possible exception of the stand they took against the Vietnam War in 1971, when they called upon the government to end the war on the grounds that any good that might be gained by fighting on was outweighed by the destruction of human life and moral values, they have hitherto steered clear of passing judgement on American defence policy. Perhaps one of the most important factors contributing to the change in this attitude was the 1973 Supreme Court decision to allow abortion virtually on demand, which they strongly opposed. Archbishop Bernardin of Chicago put the issue succinctly: 'if you take a strong stand against abortion as the unjust taking of human life, then you cannot remain indifferent to nuclear warfare'.[27]

In November 1981 Archbishop Bernardin was appointed by the annual Bishops' Conference as chairman of a committee charged with drafting a pastoral letter on war and peace. The committee was selected so as to be representative of 'liberal' and 'conservative' branches of catholic opinion; its other four members included Bishop Thomas Gumbleton of Detroit, a prominent member of Pax Christi, and Bishop John O'Connor of New York, the head of the Catholic military chaplains. While during the latter part of the 1970s individual bishops had begun to take a more outspoken stand on the issues of peace and the arms race, the committee did not set out to challenge the Administration but rather to expound and interpret christian teaching in relation to these issues. They made it clear that they did not intend their treatment of these issues to 'carry the same moral authority as our statement of universal moral principles and formal church teaching'. But they insisted that 'any claim by any government that it is pursuing a morally acceptable policy of deterrence must be scrutinised with the greatest care'. For this reason they were 'prepared and eager to participate in our country in the ongoing public debate'. The committee received testimony from a large number of theologians, peace activists, and leading defence experts, including James Schlesinger, Eugene Rostow, Herbert Scoville and Edward Rowney. It also received advice and comment from senior members of the Reagan Administration. The progress of the committee's deliberations was known by the publication of successive drafts of their report. The second draft was presented to the Bishops' Conference in Washington in November 1982 and, after debate and further revision, was approved by the bishops in May 1983 in Chicago. The final version was issued in the form of a lengthy pastoral letter entitled 'The Challenge of Peace: God's Promise and Our Response'.[28]

The bishops based their definition of moral standards in the nuclear era on Just War Principles which essentially state that war must be waged by legitimate authority; it must be in a just cause, proportionate to the evils caused by the fighting; it must be undertaken with the intention of achieving a just and lasting peace; it should be a last resort, when all peaceful remedies are exhausted; it should have a reasonable expectation of success; and it should be fought by morally legitimate methods, for example, there must be no indiscriminate killing of non-combatants. In the past there had been a tendency to let the state take precedence over the individual conscience. Memories of Auschwitz and of the passivity of German Catholicism in the face of fascism, however, together with the moral problems raised by indiscriminate civilian bombing during the Second World War and also in Vietnam, encouraged the bishops to try to refine the requirements of the Just War Theory.

The bishops found little difficulty over their attitude towards fighting a nuclear war. In the final document, they came out firmly against it, saying: 'Traditionally the church's moral teaching sought first to prevent war and then to limit its consequences if it occurred. Today the possibilities for placing political and moral limits on nuclear war are so minimal that the moral task ... is prevention. As a people, we must refuse to legitimate the idea of nuclear war.' The doctrine of deterrence, in the age of nuclear weapons, however, raised questions of risks and consequences, for which there were no clear guidelines. Archbishop Bernardin was the first to acknowledge this in November 1982, when he said, 'when we realised the awesomeness and complexity of the problem, we grew humble about the presuppositions each of us had brought to the task'.[29] The fact that it took three drafts to achieve a satisfactory position reflects this dilemma.

It was one thing to inveigh against the rhetoric of 'winnable nuclear wars' and of strategies of 'protracted nuclear war', and to condemn the indiscriminate targetting or use of nuclear weapons with the deliberate object of destroying civilian populations or non-combatants. Such views were unlikely to arouse open controversy. But finding a satisfactory definition of deterrence proved very difficult; the first draft spoke of a 'marginally justifiable deterrent policy', which was patently unsatisfactory. Then in June 1982, Pope John Paul II included in his statement to the Second United Nations Special Session on Disarmament a formulation which, in the bishops' words, 'provided new impetus and insight to the moral analysis':

In current conditions 'deterrence' based on balance, certainly not as an end in itself but as a step on the way toward a progressive disarmament, may still be judged morally acceptable. Nonetheless, in order to ensure peace, it is indispensable not to be satisfied with this minimum which is always susceptible to the real danger of explosion.[30]

This statement was incorporated into the second and third drafts, and, extrapolating from it, the bishops proposed specific prohibitions and requirements, in relation to nuclear strategy and disarmament, which were designed to reinforce the acceptability of deterrence.

When the second draft was published in October 1982, the bishops were aware that a great deal of work on it was still needed. Nevertheless it aroused intense criticism from the Administration on a number of counts; in particular for its implicit support for the freeze campaign, and its condemnation of the first use of nuclear weapons in any circumstances. Both were in conflict with the Reagan Administration's policy and considerable efforts were made by the Administration to persuade the bishops to alter the draft. The most notable was an open letter of November 1982 from William Clark, the President's then National Security Adviser, who is also a Catholic layman.[31] Clark said that the President agreed with the Pope's statement of June 1982 on deterrence, but was 'especially troubled' that the Bishops' draft ignored American proposals 'on achieving steep reductions in nuclear arsenals and, through a variety of verification and confidence-building measures, on further reducing the risks of war'. Noting the Soviet arms build-up in the last decade, he argued the moral case for the United States to make certain that US forces remained sufficiently strong and credible to assure effective deterrence, and claimed that the bishops' opposition to the new MX missiles 'would reduce the prospects of limiting a nuclear war'. Concern was also expressed by the Germans: Alois Mertes, State Secretary in the Foreign Ministry in Bonn, speaking on behalf of Chancellor Kohl, said the position adopted by the bishops would have a negative impact on Germany's debate on nuclear weapons because it favoured the strategy of the neutralists, the pacifists and the Soviet Union.[32] Clark, in a further letter of January 1983, confirmed that 'the United States does not target the Soviet civilian population as such' but went on to explain that 'it would be impossible for us to issue policy statements which might suggest to the Soviets that it would be to their advantage to establish privileged sanctuaries within heavily-populated areas'.

The third draft expanded and redeveloped several sections,

producing in the final result, a more 'moderate' position. Although urging that flexible response be replaced rapidly by an adequate non-nuclear alternative, it gave recognition to the role that NATO's flexible response strategy had already played in deterring Soviet aggression in Western Europe. Moreover, specific reference to the MX missile, which the second draft said might fit into the category of a first-strike weapon, was relegated to a footnote. An important addition was made to the 'first use' section, recognising 'the responsibility the United States has had and continues to have to protect allied nations from either conventional or nuclear attack'.[33] A small, but significant, amendment was made to the passage which appeared to support the 'freeze': the call for agreements to 'halt' the development of nuclear weapons was changed to 'curb'. Clark was then able to say of the third draft that 'while we do not share all of the bishops' specific judgements, we believe this document is an important and responsible contribution to the discussion of this issue', and the draft was given some praise for appearing 'no longer' to advocate a nuclear freeze.[34]

Nevertheless, while Cardinal Bernardin could say that the bishops had 'misunderstood' the Administration's position and that Clark's letters had 'clarified' it, the final version of the pastoral letter shows that some important underlying differences remained. Despite the greater understanding shown for the temporary need for NATO to retain the nuclear option in its strategy, the bishops' state unequivocally their adherence to 'no first use', saying that they 'do not perceive any situation in which the deliberate initiation of nuclear warfare on however restricted a scale can be morally justified'. They therefore urge NATO 'to move rapidly towards the adoption of "no first use" policy'. Moreover, the bishops revert to the earlier text on negotiations with the Soviet Union, which now recommends 'support for immediate, bilateral, verifiable agreements to halt the testing production and deployment of new nuclear weapons systems'. As regards targeting policy, the pastoral letter, although welcoming the fact that declared United States policy now excludes the targeting of civilian populations, notes that such a target plan does not, by itself, make the policy moral, since many military targets are within civilian population centres. The principle of proportionality, which requires that the damage inflicted by a particular military action must be proportionate to the good expected to be achieved, would be violated. Thus, the bishops say: 'We cannot be satisfied that the assertion of an intention not to strike civilians directly or even the most honest effort to implement that intention by itself constitutes a "moral policy" for the use of nuclear weapons.' This leads the bishops 'to a strictly conditioned moral acceptance of nuclear deterrence' for the sole purpose of 'preventing the use of nuclear weapons or other actions which could lead directly to a nuclear exchange'. But they are emphatic that they do not consider nuclear deterrence 'adequate as a long-term basis for peace'. The bishops harbour no illusions about the Soviet military threat and the repressive nature of the Soviet system, but they insist that the two super powers have a mutual interest in negotiation. While the letter rejects a policy of unilateral disarmament, it calls upon the United States to take further initiatives with the aim of encouraging a 'constructive Soviet response'. For all its authoritative argument and guidance, 'The Challenge of Peace: God's Promise and Our Response', leaves the issues ultimately to be resolved by the individual conscience. The special problems of those in the armed forces or who work in the defence industries are recognised: 'Those who in conscience decide that they should no longer be associated with defence activities should find support in the Catholic community. Those who remain . . . should find in the Church guidance and support for the ongoing evaluation of their work.'

Many criticisms may be, and have been, made of the analysis and judgements in the pastoral letter. It has however served as a focus for serious debate, in which its ambiguities and inconsistencies have been scrutinised. One of the most glaring, the contradiction between the bishops' acceptance of deterrence and their moral condemnation of any plans for using nuclear weapons even in retaliation, was attacked by Albert Wohlstetter, a leading expert on security matters, in a lengthy study of deterrence policy published in June 1983. In the same study Wohlstetter also argued that a nuclear freeze would prevent the United States from exploiting the potentialities for technical improvements which would enable deterrence to be maintained at a much lower level of numbers and destructiveness of weapons.[35] Though not intended as a stimulus to militancy, some activists took the bishops' publicly-reported deliberations as a basis for protest. Possibly the most notable incident occurred while the Bishops were considering the second draft in November 1982, when two nuns were convicted of forging government passes in order to enter the Rocky Flats nuclear weapons plant and erect signs reading 'Dachau' and 'Death Factory'.

Any idea that the 'peace movement' in the United States is in some way an extension of the 'peace movements' in Western Europe is misconceived. The freeze movement and the bishops' letter, the principal manifestations, are essentially indigenous in form and content and owe nothing to transatlantic migration. The freeze movement developed out of disillusionment with the prospects for the SALT process, following the failure of efforts to achieve the ratification of the SALT II Treaty, and with what was perceived to be the uncompromising attitude towards arms control adopted by the Reagan Administration. Its aims are almost exclusively directed at influencing the Administration's policies. There is little support in the US for unilateralism. Another marked contrast with the campaigns in Western Europe is the extent to which the freeze is supported and advocated by a large body of highly experienced and respected defence and arms control experts and leading political figures. Ideas which have the backing of such people as Averell Harriman, George Kennan and Thomas Watson, all former American Ambassadors to the Soviet Union, of former Secretaries of State Dean Rusk and Edmund Muskie, former Secretary of Defence Clark Clifford and CIA Director William Colby, and of former head of the Arms Control and Disarmament Agency and SALT I negotiator Gerard Smith, to mention only a few of the freeze's supporters, cannot but merit serious consideration.[36]

There is nothing new in the idea of the American churches taking a position on political issues where moral judgements are involved. Other churches have at various times taken a public position on aspects of nuclear strategy. For the normally conservative Roman Catholic Church to do so collectively underlines the extent to which the issue of nuclear weapons was increasingly seen to raise far-reaching moral and ethical questions on which it was incumbent on the Church to provide guidance. To describe this as merely a reaction to national and international concern about nuclear weapons would be to underestimate the seriousness and caution with which the bishops collectively approached the very difficult task they set themselves. The outcome for all its defects was a profoundly significant document of high theological and intellectual content. The Administration, as Clark's letter of November 1982 showed, were clearly concerned about the impact the letter might have on public opinion generally and not only on the Roman Catholic Community (which alone is said to number more than 51 millions).[37]

These two developments, the freeze and the bishops' letter, undoubtedly have had an impact, as the public debate which they have stimulated has shown. How far they have been effective in influencing the policies and rhetoric of President Reagan and members of his Administration is hard to say. It would be difficult for any politician to ignore the support for the freeze shown by the 1982 referendums and by subsequent opinion polls. The leading aspirant for the Democratic presidential nomination, Walter Mondale, former Vice-President in the Carter Administration, announced his support for negotiations for a mutual and verifiable nuclear weapons freeze in a major speech on 3 January 1984.[38] The fact that this resembled the position announced by Brezhnev in his message to UNSSOD II in June 1982 and reafirmed by the Russians on subsequent occasions is certainly not a conclusive argument against a proposal, more of which is likely to be heard during the 1984 Presidential campaign. But the crucial questions about the freeze proposal are, first, its effect on the nuclear balance; second, whether it could be adequately verified; and third, whether it would improve the prospects for substantial reductions. On all these points, the Reagan Administration has taken issue with its critics and has pursued its policy of going straight for deep cuts in strategic nuclear weapons in parallel with measures to correct what it perceived as American inferiority in certain important areas of the strategic balance. Soviet actions helped to secure domestic support for this position in 1983. The shooting down of the South Korean airliner on 1 September was followed two weeks later by Congressional approval by large majorities in both houses of the 1984 defence authorisation bill, which included provision for such items as the MX missile, the BI bomber and binary chemical weapons, which had previously met with strong resistance in the House of Representatives. (Congress has so far denied appropriation of funds for chemical weapons.) When this was followed in November by the abrupt withdrawal of the Soviet representatives from the START as well as the INF negotiations, there was little inclination to challenge the Administration's view that the responsibility for breaking off the dialogue lay with the Russians.

When Senator Kennedy wrote, in April 1982, that 'in a matter of months, the two superpowers, assuming their goodwill, could reasonably work out verification procedures for a freeze',[39] he could not have foreseen the total lack of goodwill which was to be displayed by the Soviet Government over existing arms control negotiations in the closing weeks of 1983. Nevertheless the impression persists that in the United States, to a much greater extent than in Western Europe, the main lines of the debate between the opponents and supporters of established policies are about means within the context of the same agreed ends rather than about fundamental differences of approach.

Part IV
Conclusion

12 Unofficial Peace Activities in Eastern Europe

The subject of this chapter goes beyond the main theme of the book. It is not primarily concerned with Communist attempts to manipulate opinion and policies in the West, through international front organisations and peace campaigns; nor does it deal directly with the aims and activities of the indigenous peace movements in Western countries. It is included for three reasons. The first is that it illustrates the sharp contract between the situation in the West and that in the East. In Western countries the peace movements are movements of protest. Their purpose is to campaign against existing defence policies (or their interpretation of those policies) and what they see as being the consequences of decisions taken under them. They claim to champion 'peace' with the implication that those who disagree with them are working against peace, even when not positively in favour of war. This often brings them into sharp confrontation with Western governments. But they are free to promote their views, however unpalatable these may be to their governments.

In the Warsaw Pact countries, the only officially tolerated peace movements are those which are in effect controlled by the authorities. Whatever the latter may claim about the spontaneity of such movements, assertions that they have any independence of action are transparently false. When G. A. Zhukov, chairman of the Soviet Peace Committee, claims a membership for his Committee of 80 millions and announces that a petition against the deployment of American neutron weapons in Europe was signed by 'more than 180 million people' (out of a total population of 270 million), that is tantamount to saying that the purpose of the Committee is to provide public demonstration of support for Soviet policies. This is not surprising, since Communist doctrine emphasises the 'unity of peace and socialism'. Lenin's views that 'democratic peace' will only be secured through 'the victory of socialism' and that disarmament is not acceptable to socialism short of the defeat of imperialism remain Moscow's guiding principles. Since therefore 'socialist countries' are by definition committed to 'peace', everything they do in regard to their armaments is, *ex hypothesi*, done for the purpose of preserving peace on Moscow's terms.

The second reason for including this Chapter is that it underlines the fundamental difference between unofficial peace activities in the East and the Western peace movements. The efforts of the latter can be devoted to mobilising public support and organising demonstrations; whatever their leaders may claim, criticism of Soviet policies plays a relatively small part on such occasions. In the East, comparable public demonstrations would be inconceivable. The first priority for the unofficial campaigners in the East is to attempt to establish their right to exist, something which the Western peace movements are able to take for granted but which the authorities in the East are determined not to concede to the unofficial groups in these countries. In the East, even to suggest that blame for the arms race rests equally with the Soviet Union and the United States is heresy, which results in physical and psychological harassment, imprisonment or exile. The more heinous sin of attributing the whole, or principal, responsibility to the Soviet Union, which would be more directly comparable to the position of the peace movements in the West, would be tantamount to blasphemy. So the activities of these unofficial groups have often to be undertaken clandestinely and, despite the claims of growing support, the KGB and its counterparts are in a position to ensure that the numbers do not grow beyond manageable levels. A partial exception has been East Germany, whose population has direct and frequent links with the Federal Republic, and access to West German television. In these special circumstances the authorities have, according to one observer, been concerned to embrace grass roots initiatives as far as possible 'within a unified socialist movement in which there is room for everyone to take part in the broad dialogue'.[1] While this may result in greater licence for dissent, it does not necessarily make the struggle for identity and survival easier, nor does it preclude the use of repressive measures against activists.

The final reason is the dilemma which such a situation poses for all Western peace movements. The episode of the Zhukov letter (see Chapter 9) highlighted this. The official Eastern committees are ready to support fully the Western movements' criticisms of their own Governments, but not to accept any criticism of the policies of the Soviet Union or its allies. So the Western movements cannot expect to make any headway in their attempts to influence the policies of the East European Governments through the official peace committees. They are on less equivocal ground in maintaining contact with the unofficial peace groups in Eastern Europe. Here they can rightly claim that they are helping to 'keep freedom alive' and that it is in long-term European interests to 'hold the space for dialogue open' (to quote E. P. Thompson). No one interested in the future prospects for these Communist countries as part of Europe is likely to dispute the importance of such arguments. But what END and their allies have so far been able to do in this respect is a long way from the realisation of the aims of the European Appeal which the official Soviet Peace Committee has refused even to publish.

EAST GERMANY

The Protestant (Lutheran) Church in East Germany (the German Democratic Republic) embraces about 8 million out of the $9\frac{1}{2}$ million Christians (about 46 per cent of the population), most of the rest being Catholics. In 1971, when Honecker replaced Ulbricht as First Secretary of the ruling Socialist Unity Party (SED), the regime relaxed its previous hostile attitude to the Church in the hope that, if the explicitly atheistic propaganda was toned down, the valuable social role of the Church could be used to the advantage of socialism. There was no intention of allowing the Church to share political power, but from then on it was increasingly recognised as the main forum for discussion of unofficial ideas. The evolution of the government's attitude was demonstrated by the official celebration in 1983 of the 500th anniversary of Martin Luther's birth, which would have been unheard of a few years earlier. By 1980 contacts between the East and West German Churches had been revived, especially on issues of peace and disarmament. That these links were officially condoned even after the NATO Double-Track decision of

December, 1979, implied that they were regarded as usefully complementing the hard-line reaction to the decision dictated by Moscow and dutifully adopted by the East European Governments. There was, however, a hardening of Communist policy towards the churches after the Gdansk strikes in August 1980, which raised the spectre of the East German Lutheran church playing a role similar to that of the Roman Catholic Church in Poland. In November 1980, the East and West German Protestant churches organised a ten day action programme, to take place simultaneously in both countries, under the West German peace slogan 'Make peace without Weapons' (*Frieden schaffen ohne Waffen*), which was used in East Germany for the first time. It was planned to end the week by ringing church bells throughout East Germany (which is often used in Poland as the signal for a strike); but the authorities decided to drown the effect of this by testing the nation's sirens at precisely the same moment.[2]

In August 1981 the Protestant Church gave signs of overstepping the limits of its permitted autonomy. This was when it supported an initiative by young East Germans for a 'social peace service' (*Friedensdienst*) as an alternative to compulsory military service for those aged 18 to 25. Although conscientious objection to military service, which is against Marxist–Leninist principles, is not recognised in any of the Warsaw Pact countries, objectors in East Germany had, since 1964, been allowed to serve in quasi-military Construction Units (*Bausoldaten*), provided that they wore military uniforms and took the oath of allegiance. The purpose of the initiative was to extend the range of permitted alternatives to military service and remove the obligation to wear uniform. A petition with over 4000 signatories in support of *Friedensdienst* was sent to the church leadership. It was strongly endorsed by the Saxon regional church Synod, which also expressed disapproval of a report that 11 year-olds were being given pre-conscription instruction in the use of hand grenades and that 17 and 18 year-olds were being forced to sign on for five years military service instead of the compulsory two years. An immediate effect of the *Friedensdienst* initiative was that the numbers applying to serve as *Bausoldaten* increased rapidly; by early 1982 some of them were even permitted to work in hospitals.[3]

The official attitude to *Friedensdienst* was one of strong disapproval. Addressing a meeting at Humboldt University in East Berlin in September 1981 Klaus Gysi, the East German State

Secretary for Church Affairs, categorically rejected the implication that military service was anti-social, since military strength was 'the greatest and most genuine contribution' that East Germany could make to secure world peace. The party line was reinforced by Werner Walde, a candidate member of the Politburo, in his statement to the third plenum of the SED Central Committee in November 1981 that 'the enemy has no chance to create a front with the phrase of so-called peace service against the necessary military strengthening of socialism ... these people forget that the whole of our Republic is social peace service'.[4]

The authorities' counter-offensive against the Church's initiatives was continued by the broadcast of a programme on East German radio on 10 November, immediately after the morning service, which emphasised Martin Luther's militancy on matters concerning peace and asserted that such concepts as neutralism and pacifism were totally alien to his thinking. By then, the target was a wider one than *Friedensdienst*; the regional church synods in Saxony and Mecklenburg had passed resolutions calling on the Warsaw Pact countries to take 'unilateral and coordinated steps towards disarmament, such as reducing the SS-20s aimed at the West'. The synods also criticised the growing number of civil defence exercises involving first-year schoolchildren. Another provocation was the practice adopted by some youngsters of wearing on their jackets badges carrying the words 'swords into ploughshares' (Isaiah 11:4) and depicting a man beating a sword into a ploughshare. Although the same image is embodied in the statue which the Soviet Union has placed outside the United Nations building in New York, the badges drew a sharp rebuke from State Security officials who pronounced them contrary to East German's 'peace policy'. Two months earlier the slogan 'make peace without weapons' had been used in East Berlin at a peace demonstration which was broken up by the police: and when supporters of the peace movement in the Federal Republic, on visits to East Germany, drove in cars with stickers bearing this slogan, they were ordered by the East German border guards to remove them.

That the Honecker régime took a serious view of these events, and felt the need to reaffirm its support for Soviet peace policies, was shown by a meeting of intellectuals, artists and musicians organised by the authorities in East Berlin, from 13 to 15 December 1981. Although the participants were mainly East

Germans it was attended by intellectuals from the West such as Günter Grass, Luise Rinser and Peter Hartling, and by others from Eastern Europe. As intended, it provided an opportunity for the East German and other East European participants to express support for the peace policies of their governments and to condemn Western attitudes, particularly those of the US, as the main cause of East–West tension. But although the East German media mainly reported those speakers who expressed orthodox opinions, such as Soviet academician and former atomic research spy at Harwell, Klaus Fuchs, who claimed that the Church's aim of *Friedensdienst* as an alternative to regular military service would be tantamount to unilateral disarmament by East Germany and not in the interests of peace, the authorities did not have it all their own way. The East German writer, Stefan Heym, whose books only appear in the West, stated that 'today there is no longer a just war, as there are no just atomic bombs. There can be no such thing, because there is no just nuclear war with weapons which destroy all life and transform this earth into a dead star. The SS-20 is as unjust as the Pershing II'. Günter de Bruyn, an East German novelist, expressed his uneasiness over official East German support for the Western peace movements as long as the Government prevented 'the anti-war struggle by Christians, pacifists and conscientious objectors within its own borders'; he also warned that if the unofficial East German peace movement was 'driven underground, East Germany will not only lose valuable forces for peace, but it will also detract from East Germany's credibility'.[5]

The regime had, however, to face something more serious than *Friedensdienst* and the views of dissident intellectuals when a document, called the Berlin Appeal and bearing 35 signatures, appeared in East Germany on 7 February 1982.[6] It began: 'There can only be one war in Europe: a nuclear war. The weapons piled up in the East and in the West will not protect us but destroy us. We will all be dead when the soldiers in their tanks and missile bases and the generals and politicians in their defence bunkers – those whom we trust for our defence – continue to live and go forth to destroy whatever remains. . . . If we want to live, then away with the weapons'.

The Appeal proposed the removal of all nuclear weapons from East and West Germany as the first step towards a European nuclear-free zone; the conclusion of peace treaties with the two

German states as envisaged in 1945 at Potsdam and withdrawal of the 'occupation troops'; and official recognition of the right freely and publicly to debate such questions as the replacement of military instruction in schools with instruction about peace, of military parades on state holidays by peace demonstrations, and the introduction of *Friedensdienst* for conscientious objectors.

Although the Lutheran Church denied direct responsibility for the Berlin Appeal, a leading signatory was Pastor Rainer Eppelmann, one of the principal promoters of *Friedensdienst*. Another was the dissident writer and scientist, Robert Havemann, who in March 1982 (a month before his death) called on writers, scientists and churchmen in the Federal Republic to put pressure on the West German media to publicise the Berlin Appeal, and thereby bring it to the attention of the population in East Germany.[7] Havemann was anxious that the Berlin Appeal should be compared with the earlier Krefeld Appeal which had played so large a part in the West German peace movement (see Chapter 10). Another Church official to sign the Berlin Appeal was Pastor Hans-Jochen Tschiche who, in an open letter in December 1981, had countered Werner Walde's criticism of *Friedensdienst* as a 'tool of the enemy' directed against 'socialism'. Tschiche said that 'it is the enemy within ourselves, the fear of our influence, of our power, of our human intolerance, and of our ideological dogmatism which will destroy us. In this country we must turn away from the cult of the military . . . the death dance of those without imagination begins, yet we don't sound the alarm bells'.[8] The original signatories of the Berlin Appeal included three pastors, two deacons and five theology students.

Pastor Eppelmann was detained and interrogated by State Security officials on 9 and 10 February 1982. His release was ordered by the SED Politburo following pressure from church leaders. The homes of several of his associates were searched. Some 700 people are believed to have added their signatures to the Berlin Appeal; others are said to have signed copies circulating throughout East Germany.[9]

Despite government and party hostility to the Berlin Appeal, the local peace campaign continued. On 13 February 1982 the customary celebration was held in Dresden to mark the 37th anniversary of the bombing of the city during the Second World War. This anniversary has traditionally been celebrated in East Germany by official statements deploring the Allied raid in which the city was destroyed. But the 1982 commemoration was unique in that it marked the first unofficial, independent and public peace demonstration in East Germany, when between five and six thousand people, mostly young, attended a service in the Kreuzkirche, and thereafter took part in a Peace Forum organised by the Lutheran Church in Saxony. Many participants brandished the prohibited slogans, 'make peace without weapons' and 'swords into ploughshares'. A number of prominent ecclesiastics took part in the Forum including Johannes Hempel, Bishop of Saxony and Kurt Domsch, president of the Office of Regional Churches. Discussion in the Forum mainly revolved round the questions raised by the Berlin Appeal. Several thousand people subsequently moved in procession to the ruined Frauenkirche, where candles were lit and peace ballads were sung. The demonstration passed without incident under the eyes of the security police, who made no attempt to intervene; the young people disappeared as quietly as they had come.[10]

Although the authorities had so far responded with restraint, they clearly felt that the time had come when they had to make a firm stand against the growing unofficial peace movement to prevent it getting out of hand. In March the movement was denounced as an 'illegal political association' and its ploughshares emblem was banned as an 'expression of a mentality hostile to the State'. A law passed on 25 March, at the time of an intensive campaign in schools and youth organisations, required all state enterprises, factories and social and educational organisations to help prepare citizens for military service. When introducing this law in the *Volkskammer* (Parliament), the Defence Minister, General Heinz Hoffmann, said that 'peace and socialism are inseparably linked to each other . . . Socialism and peace still need our ploughshares and our swords'. This reflected the Soviet line that since 'socialism and peace' are indivisible, an independent peace movement is unnecessary in a 'socialist state'. But the slogans had made their impact and more was needed to counteract them. At Whitsuntide large rallies were organised throughout the country by the official youth organisation, the *Freie Deutsche Jugend*, which adopted, in evident parody of the unofficial movement's slogan, the strange formula: 'make peace against NATO weapons'.

The Church as an institution did not formally support either the Peace Forum in Dresden or Pastor Eppelmann's Berlin Appeal, although it used its influence to secure his release from detention. Its traditionally cautious attitude has so far enabled it to keep just to its side of the bargain of the Church-State compact of the 1970s. It intercedes when its followers come into conflict with the authorities, as many of them do. But its officially neutral, if sometimes equivocal, stance on controversial issues does not allow it to escape from the dilemma of supporting many of the objectives, while disapproving of some of the methods, of the unofficial movement. At the synod of the Federation of East German Churches, from 29 to 31 January 1982, the Moderator expressed regret at the government's decision to prevent Western journalists from following its proceedings as deviating from 'the practice of previous years'. When the speech of the chairman of the Federation, Bishop Werner Krusche, became available it showed that although not expecting any concessions from the Government on such issues as *Friedensdienst*,[11] the Church would continue its attempts to negotiate a compromise. In the meantime, individuals affected by the current regulations would have to make their own decisions whether or not to obey them: the task was to prevent young people from becoming resigned or embittered. 'Demonstrations', Krusche said 'will not help us in our situation.' In a later article in *Idea*, the information bulletin of the German Evangelical Alliance, he was quoted as saying that the government had refused to meet the desire of young people for *Friedensdienst* as an alternative to military service, but the Church, at the request of all its synods, would go on trying to find some solution to this demand.[12]

The synod of the East Berlin regional church on 20 April moved on to more dangerous ground, when it issued a statement which underlined its opposition to both US and Soviet nuclear missiles by calling for a reduction in the level of SS-20s targeted on Western Europe, while at the same time backing Brezhnev's offer of a moratorium. The Church, the statement asserted, would continue to support young East Germans who were harassed for wearing peace emblems. But it urged the government not to misinterpret criticism of the militarisation of East German life, and support for peace campaigners, as representing political opposition. The synod also sent a letter to Churches in the Berlin–Brandenburg area authorising the open discussion of previously forbidden military–political topics.[13] In June, East Berlin churchmen organised a 'peace workshop' which again raised the idea of a social alternative to military service: four of the organisers were expelled to the West. Further demonstrations of dissent took place later in the year. In October a group of 150 Women for Peace sent a letter to Honecker, declaring their refusal to be included in military conscription. In November, the Protestant Church organised its third annual 'Peace Week', involving 10 days of discussions with young people under the forbidden slogan 'swords into ploughshares'.

Further evidence of broadened support for independent peace initiatives in East Germany was the text of the pastoral letter of the Roman Catholic bishops published in the *Frankfurter Allgemeine Zeitung*, 4 January 1983. In this, the Roman Catholic Church, addressing its 1 300 000 members for the first time on peace issues, criticised the official Warsaw Pact policy of 'just wars' and denounced as unjustified wars fought with nuclear, chemical and biological weapons. The pastoral letter, while acknowledging the existence of the 'construction soldier' (*Bausoldat*) option for conscientious objectors, supported the introduction of *Friedensdienst* and criticised military education and indoctrination in schools. The official East German press agency, clearly acting under orders from the regime, did not report the content of the Catholic bishops' letter.

Despite attempts to suppress the unofficial peace movement by legislative and administrative measures and to distract attention from it by organising demonstrations in support of the official line, it is clear that the East German regime has not been able to eliminate 'pacifism', especially among the Churches. So long as it accepts the need to maintain the existing delicate *modus vivendi* between Church and State, in which the churches have an equal interest, it is unlikely that it will ever do so. The most that the regime can hope for is to contain the effects, although the process will remain an uneven one. The official East German Peace Council declined the invitation to attend the second END convention in West Berlin in May 1983 in conformity with the Soviet Peace Committee's decision to boycott it. The régime also prevented a group of unofficial East German peace campaigners from taking part by denying them exit visas; although not able to participate in person, 35 of their number met in East Berlin with representatives from Western peace movements and sent a message to the convention setting out their demands for the establishment of nuclear-free zones in Europe, the withdrawal of foreign troops and the creation of free democratic societies throughout Europe; and insisting that 'the credibility of peace proposals of the Soviet Union and the German Democratic Republic is undermined by their refusal to allow us to take part in the open dialogue of your conference'.[14] In July, an estimated 100 000 people supported a Lutheran rally in Dresden, said to be the largest since 1954, at which the church leaders declared their support for young East Germans who opposed induction into the armed services. In November a petition, the Rostock Appeal, initially signed by 100 individuals, Christians and non-Christians, protested against the government's acceptance of the deployment of Soviet nuclear missiles in East Germany. But although this new protest began to spread, with support from Roman Catholic priests and Protestant pastors, it was discouraged by the church hierarchies, who clearly saw the dangers. Predictably, it resulted in a harsh, security crack down against those known to be actively involved.

HUNGARY

In Hungary a movement within the Roman Catholic Church, which comprises over 55% of the population, has also been campaigning since 1979 for recognition of the right of conscientious objection to military service. Although it has been condemned by the Roman Catholic hierarchy, which upholds the official position of the Communist authorities, the founder of the movement was a priest, György Bulányi. By the end of 1981, the Bishop of Pecs estimated its membership at over 20 000 including 40 priests, two of whom, László Kovács and András Gromon, were suspended at that time by Cardinal László Lékai, the Primate of Hungary, a strong opponent of conscientious objection. Five other priests, who protested against the suspensions, were transferred to other parishes.[15] Bulányi was forbidden by the Cardinal to officiate in June 1982, soon after an official warning that the Government would 'not tolerate religious debates as a pretext for camouflaging violation of the law'. The compliance of the church authorities has enabled the government to leave it to the Bishops to discipline dissenting priests who might otherwise face arrest.

In 1981 and 1982 a number of spontaneous peace groups came

into being in Hungarian schools and universities. They had no fixed programmes, but they shared two characteristics: they kept their distance from the official Hungarian National Peace Council and they criticised the efforts of both East and West in the field of disarmament. The most prominent was the Peace Group for Dialogue, founded by Ferenc Köszegi, a researcher in peace studies at Budapest University. Köszegi published a personal statement in the *New Statesman*, of 2 July, 1982, in which he wrote that: 'For a nation which already has an official and institutionalised peace movement, the development of a new and independent peace movement is not easy. ... Peace is now perhaps the tritest word in our journalistic vocabulary. We have to endow such words with new meaning.... Our efforts to form a new peace movement under present conditions have encountered difficulties. One example: last year some students from the faculty of arts wanted to organise a peace march against the deployment of Cruise missiles in European countries. Of course against Soviet missiles too. At first, the authorities supported this plan, but later they organised an ('official') peace rally in the new gigantic sports hall with official speakers, with official slogans and with official attendants. The students wanted their own peace march with their own slogans. Unfortunately, the opportunities are not equal.' The article concluded: 'In Hungary most of the so-called dissidents are opposed to the Western European peace movement which ... they view as a puppet of the Soviet Union, resulting in a weakening of Western military capacity.'

In September 1982, E. P. Thompson visited Hungary at the inivitation of the Peace Group for Dialogue, particularly Ferenc Köszegi, Ferenc Rusza, László János and Eva Forgács, to give a lecture, an extract from which was published in the *Guardian* on 25 October 1982. Although it had originally been proposed that Thompson would speak at Budapest University, official permission was refused at the last moment. Instead he was able to give his talk to an audience of predominantly young people in the flat of the writer György Konrad. His theme was the importance of being able to answer critics of the peace movement in the West who asked for evidence of a similar movement in the East. He went on: 'If it is answered that the Soviet Peace Committee and certain other national peace committees and councils in the East have organised their own demonstrations and petitions, the critic replies: yes, but these were directed against NATO weapons, not against the weapons and militarism of their own States. If the Western peace movement is to break through this barrier, then we must be able to clasp hands with a non-aligned movement, totally independent of the State, on your side also.'

Next day, Thompson took part in a round table discussion attended by Ferenc Köszegi and other members of the Peace Group for Dialogue, Andras Hegedüs, former Prime Minister and founder-signatory of the Warsaw Pact, and the dissident writer Miklós Haraszti were present. While Hegedüs favoured working with such official organisations as the National Peace Council (whose representative declined to participate), Köszegi outlined his views on building a movement to be neither official nor in opposition but that could be simultaneously authorised by and independent of the régime.[16]

It was reported in the *Guardian*, on 1 December 1982, that the Peace Group for Dialogue had met in November on the premises of the National Peace Council, attracting an audience of 300 to 400 people, including about 25 with official connections whose hostile questioning interrupted the proceedings. Ferenc Köszegi and the other speakers discussed possible independent peace initiatives, including the removal of Soviet missile launchers which could be equipped with nuclear warheads at short notice, a non-aggression pact with Austria and Yugoslavia and an expanded 'Rapacki Plan' under which Hungary would be included in a Central European nuclear free zone. It was also reported that in the same month the Group had held an official meeting with György Aczél, the Hungarian Communist Party Secretary, and had organised a meeting under the auspices of the Centre for Peace Research at the Hungarian Academy of Sciences at which Mary Kaldor of END and Mient Jan Faber of the Dutch IKV had spoken.

In a subsequent message to the Conference on Nuclear-Free Zones organised in Athens by Greek peace movements in December 1982 (which members of the Peace Group for Dialogue were not permitted to leave Hungary to attend), the Group pressed for a Central European nuclear-free zone and called for the withdrawal of Soviet troops from Hungary. Nevertheless the Group has seemed anxious not to be regarded as a dissident body, and its contacts with the authorities have prompted speculation that the latter might be aiming to compromise its 'independence'. So far this has not been borne out by developments. In a letter to

Western peace movements in March 1983, its present leader, Ferenc Rusza, said it was having a difficult time and that its meetings with the authorities had brought few benefits: by then there were groups in seven cities and a newsletter (another member quoted a figure of 2000 for those wearing the group's badges). At the end of a large procession of young people taking part in an official 'Youth Peace Festival' organised by the National Peace Council in Budapest on 7 May, 450 members of the Peace Group for Dialogue separately marched through the city.

In July 1983, the Group attempted to organise a temporary 'peace camp' in Budapest. However Western visitors, including four women from Greenham Common, were picked up by the police and deported. Shortly afterwards the Western press reported that the Group had decided to disband although smaller, informal meetings and discussions would continue.[17]

Although the unofficial movement is small scale and, unlike East Germany, lacks the sympathy of the Church, the Hungarian authorities have evidently found it hard to produce convincing arguments against its demands. A report on the State television on 8 February 1983 referred to 'views, particularly among young intellectuals lacking in political experience, according to which, if the Dutch can demonstrate against American missiles, why should we not demonstrate against Soviet missiles?' The reasons why not, it was suggested, were that there were no nuclear missiles on Hungarian territory and that 'both the Hungarian and Soviet Governments want to see ... that there should be no nuclear weapons targeted on Europe ... including the European territory of the USSR'.

CZECHOSLOVAKIA

Charter 77 was founded in 1977 by 240 leading writers, academics, journalists and politicians who had been banned from public life after the Soviet suppression of the 'Prague Spring' in 1968. Its purpose was to monitor the implementation by the Czech Government of the provisions of the international conventions on human rights and of the 1975 Helsinki Final Act. It was not until the end of 1981 that it began to concern itself with peace issues. In an open letter to the peace movements in Western Europe in

March 1982, it proclaimed that 'since the threat to peace in Europe is an urgent issue and since official social structures may be suspect in the matter of peace because of too close a tie between them and political groups or state authorities, we believe that these questions should everywhere be the province of unofficial action by ordinary citizens'. In a subsequent letter to the Czech Federal Assembly in August, Charter 77 proposed that the withdrawal of the Soviet forces stationed 'temporarily' – since 1968 – on Czech territory 'would constitute a sign of goodwill and contribute towards *détente* in Central Europe'. Two months later, a letter was published which had been sent by members of Charter 77, including Dr Jiri Hajek, the Foreign Minister at the time of the Prague Spring in 1968, to the Czech Government and the Czech Peace Council. This contained the following passage:

> Our continent faces the threat of being turned into a nuclear battlefield, into the burial ground of nations and of its civilisation which gave birth to the very concept of human rights, amongst which the right to live occupies the supreme place. It is difficult to regard as champions of these rights, including the right to live and to be free from the fear of war, those who only criticise their ideological opponents and rival powers for violating these rights while they themselves tolerate such violations.[18]

In April 1982 Charter 77 sent a message of support to the organisers of the Berlin Appeal, especially mentioning Havemann (see above). Charter 77 has always seen peace as indivisible from human rights: one of its members wrote that 'without the existence of human rights in the East there is no possibility of a disarmament in those countries'.[19]

Ladislav Lis, a leading member, was arrested on 5 January 1983, the day on which the Warsaw Pact Political Consultative Committee, meeting in Prague, announced their official 'peace' proposals. (He was released on 6 March 1984.) Members of Charter 77 were refused permission to attend the World Assembly for Peace and Life against Nuclear War in Prague in June. But some representatives of Western peace movements succeeded in making contact with members of Charter 77 in the company of Western press and television reporters. When their meetings were broken up by the Czech security police, the Western representatives experienced at first hand the lengths to which the Communist authorities will go to prevent free discussion. The Charter members said that they were under constant surveillance, that some of them had lost their jobs and about 20 out of a total membership of 1100 were in prison.[20] The three representatives of the West German Green party left the Assembly in protest at what had taken place. The Soviet decision to deploy new missiles in Czechoslovakia, allegedly in response to the NATO deployments, aroused a flood of protests from young people, not confined to Charter members. *Rude Pravo*, the Communist party newspaper, took an unprecedented step of referring publicly, on 9 November, to the concern expressed in many letters it had received. As in East Germany, many young people were held for interrogation and stern warnings were issued to Charter members.

Early in February 1984, three Bishops representing dioceses in predominantly Roman Catholic Slovakia issued a joint pastoral letter condemning nuclear weapons, which, in the hands of leaders interested in world domination but not in human rights, threatened the world with annihilation, On 12 February, a joint statement issued in Prague and Warsaw by members of Charter 77, of the Polish KOR (Committee for Workers' Defence) and of Solidarity warned that so long as the human rights and civil freedoms of these organisations continued to be suppressed there would be 'no genuine peace in Europe and the World'.[21]

SOVIET UNION

In the Soviet Union itself there have been signs that 'pacifism' has in recent years begun to be seen as a problem by the authorities. The Soviet media have given continuous coverage to the growing strength of Western peace movements, though they have reported only the evidence of protest against 'militarist, aggressive and expansionist Western policies' and ignored all criticisms of Soviet policy, also omitting to publish demands by Western peace movements which would impose obligations on the Soviet Union as well as the West. But 'pacifism' in official Soviet terms is very different from Western pacifism. The 1978 edition of the Soviet Military Encyclopaedia described it as being 'as unscientific now as it was at the time of its inception' and warned that 'the overwhelming majority of participants in the pacifist movement do not perceive the true causes and the class-political nature of war. The danger of pacifism was that it distracted the masses from the true means of outlawing war'. The attitude of Marxist–Leninist parties towards pacifism is 'determined by its objective role in the struggle between the world's progressive and reactionary forces ... Lenin recognised the necessity of using pacifism as a means of strengthening the positions of the Soviet Republic and repelling imperialist aggression'.[22] Articles in the Soviet press nonetheless suggest that anti-militarism has recently been making unwelcome progress among young people. On 30 November 1981, it was stated in the course of a long article in *Pravda* that 'our propaganda must ... decisively rid itself of the traces of pacifism that are occasionally found in some instructional or propaganda materials.... The Soviet people's interest in questions of war and peace is natural.... Recently, however, the resolution of these questions has become more complicated as a result of the policies of the aggressive imperialist circles.... It would be a mistake to create the impression that nuclear war is unavoidable.'

In January 1982, *Izvestia* published an article by Anatoly Marchenko,[23] attacking 'the rotten, thoroughly harmful idea that years of service in the army are wasted years'. He called for an increase in 'military–patriotic literature' to help parents 'inculcate in their children respect and love of the army', and told Soviet writers not to worry if the stress laid on military themes in Soviet literature led bourgeois propagandists to allege that Soviet society was becoming militarised. 'Military–patriotic literature' was a necessary weapon against external enemies; Marchenko denounced the sort of book that portrayed 'hysterical hesitation between duty and personal selfishness'. In this connection, cases have been reported of mothers lobbying recruiting boards to prevent their sons being sent to Afghanistan.[24]

Marshal Nikolai Ogarkov, Chief of the Soviet General Staff and First Deputy Defence Minister, also referred to the dangers of pacifist and anti-militarist sentiments in an article published in July 1981 when he warned that 'questions of the struggle for peace are sometimes perceived in a simplistic way: any peace is good, any war is bad. This may lead to carelessness, complacency and smugness and to an underestimation of the threat of a possible war'.[25] In February 1982, he published a booklet aimed at a mass readership which included a call for a decisive struggle against 'complacency and elements of pacifism' among Soviet youth.

After two generations of peace, he warned that some young people had no idea what war was really like: 'peace is for them the normal state of society. Some of them think that continuing and strengthening peace does not require any personal effort on their part'.[26] In May 1982 the head of the armed forces' political wing, General Alexei Yepishev, also criticised signs of pacifism (and indiscipline) among recruits to the army and navy: speaking at a congress of the Soviet Young Communist League (Komsomol), he referred to 'instances – be they only isolated – where young people entering the army show elements of political naïveté, pacifism and a carefree attitude when assessing the threat posed by our class enemies'. The Komsomol's First Secretary, Boris Pastukhov, stressed in his own report to the Congress that 'in the world of today, love for the socialist fatherland is impossible without class hatred'.[27]

While the Soviet authorities are understandably determined to draw the maximum advantage for their cause from Western peace movements, these pronouncements show that they are also aware of the danger that developments abroad which they can claim as successes may be 'misinterpreted' at home. Hence the swift represssion by the KGB of what would appear to be, judged by Western criteria, no more than minor political incidents, but which the Soviet authorities view quite differently because they break the cardinal rule of security by demonstrating independent political initiative critical of Government policy.

In April 1982, a small group of West European pacifists unfurled a banner in Red Square with the words 'Bread, Life and Disarmament', and distributed pamphlets with the message that the Soviet Union should devote 0.7% of its gross national product as aid to developing countries, this being the target figure set by the United Nations. They were immediately seized by the KGB and expelled from the country.[28] In June Soviet tugboats towed a ship carrying members of the Greenpeace environmentalist group, including the American activist Daniel Ellsberg, out of Leningrad harbour, after they had released 2000 balloons calling for a halt to Soviet nuclear tests.[29] In July, the Soviet authorities tried a different tactic. The authorities had felt constrained to admit the Nordic Women's Peace March into the Soviet Union (see Chapter 10), but they took steps to control its activities and to prevent the participants making contact with ordinary Russians, especially with members of Batovrin's Group for Establishing

Trust (see below). They also tried to exploit the march for their own ends by directly linking it with a second march, organised by the official Soviet Peace Committee, from Moscow to Vienna by way of Kiev, both marches being reported under the same title of Peace March 1982. The Soviet news agency *Tass* announced on 31 July, after most of the Scandinavian women had left, that 'Peace March 1982 . . . which began in Stockholm, is now in its 15th day on Soviet territory in Kiev. The march will pass through Budapest, Bratislava and Vienna where a mass international rally against the threat of nuclear war will be held on 6 August. The peace march, organised by peaceful public organisations and movements, gathered together representatives of 30 countries of Europe, the Americas, Asia and Africa.' The participants travelled by train from demonstration to demonstration before finally arriving in Vienna, where they joined another group from Berlin and the members of an associated Balkans 82 Peace March from Greece and Romania. It hardly needs to be added that, unlike those of the Nordic Women, the slogans and demands of this second march were exclusively directed against United States and against NATO policies and there was no suggestion that any reciprocal modification of Soviet policies was needed.

No one should have been surprised at the way in which these events were handled by the authorities. Soviet policy had been authoritatively set out in a statement by Valentin Kopteltsev, a member of the ID of the CPSU, in an interview in Vienna on 22 April 1982: 'In the Soviet Union there are also peace movements and demonstrations and there are reports about them in our press. Of course, we understand that some circles in the West would welcome it if the peace movement in our country were adulterated and turned into an anti-State and anti-socialist movement, even with the use of the slogans of peace. That, however, will not happen in our country, because according to our law and constitution, it is not permitted to attack the foundations of socialism and the social system, no matter what the slogans.'[30]

Six weeks after this statement was made, an initiative was launched which threatened the Soviet policy of confining 'peace activities' to officially controlled bodies. This was the formation of an independent Group For Establishing Trust between the USSR and the USA. The founders were eleven young Soviet intellectuals, including a psychiatrist, two engineers, two mathematicians and two physicists, led by a freelance artist, Sergei Batovrin, who announced the movement's aims at a press conference in his Moscow flat on 4 June to which Western correspondents were invited.

Batovrin's inaugural statement appealed to politicians to exploit 'the enormous potential of the general public in the search for disarmament and peace'. The group's ultimate aim, he said, was 'the total liquidation of nuclear arms and other stocks of weapons of mass murder, and the limitation and reduction of conventional arms'. The statement called for an 'exchange of opinions between the USA and the USSR' and for 'informing the public of both countries about disarmament issues'. Among its proposals were holiday exchanges between the children of Soviet and American leaders and US-Soviet television debates to be screened in both countries. Batovrin's group stressed that its members were not dissidents and that its activities were not directed against the Soviet authorities but, in answer to telephoned questions from a French left-wing periodical, Batovrin admitted that his movement's position on peace issues was close to that of the human rights activist, Andrei Sakharov, and that 'Soviet pacifism has only just come to life . . . there are very few of us, but our numbers are increasing . . . we are in contact with the Baltic group, which on 10 October 1981 addressed a letter to the governments of the USSR and the USA advocating a nuclear-free zone in Western Europe to include the Baltic states, and we hope this group will join us. We know that other groups in Moscow and the Ukraine will soon make known their existence.'[31]

The group claimed to be working in the spirit of the policy of the Soviet government, which regularly advocates the promotion of mutual trust between East and West, as was made explicit in Brezhnev's message to the United Nations Special Session on Disarmament (published by *Tass* on 15 June), which said that 'one objective of the Soviet Union's initiative [in undertaking not to be the first to use nuclear weapons] is to raise the level of trust in relations between States'. The same policy was reaffirmed by Soviet endorsement of the Final Document of the Madrid European Security Review Conference on 7 September 1983. Nevertheless official reaction to the group has been predictably hostile, one reason being that the group's initial and subsequent statements have put the USSR and the USA on the same level instead of extolling the USSR as the champion of peace. Another is that its views are inconsistent with those of the Soviet Peace

Committee. Batovrin and Sergei Rosenoer, a mathematician, the two chief spokesman at the inaugural press conference, were detained on 11 June and reminded that all organised groups were required by law to be formally registered with the authorities. Another member, Vladimir Fleischgakker, was threatened with prosecution under Article 200 of the Russian Republic's criminal code which prescribes a sentence of up to six months imprisonment for 'the unwarranted exercise, in violation of the legally established order, of real or supposed rights'. All the group's members were kept under house arrest from mid-June onwards and Western journalists were warned against reporting their activities. A report in July that two members of the group, Yuri Medvedkov, the geographer, and Yuri Khronopulo, a physicist, had been sentenced to imprisonment provoked a letter to *The Times*, on 19 July 1982 from E. P. Thompson and his wife protesting against the 'outrageous behaviour' of the Soviet security services and warmly defending Batovrin's activities. They made a further protest in a letter to the *Guardian* on 18 August: 'what is absurd is the suggestion (from Soviet sources) that the Moscow peace group is a "provocation". How can a group of intellectual workers, who want to get into direct touch with peace workers in the West, be seen as a threat to the security of the Soviet state? What has been a provocation and an action damaging to the cause for peace, has been the foolish over-reaction by the Soviet authorities to an unlicensed initiative by their own citizens: the arrest of two distinguished scientists on charges of "hooliganism" and the harassment of the rest'. In a further letter to *The Times*, on 28 October, the Thompsons claimed that in response to a message in July from a member of the persecuted group calling for world-wide support, 'vigorous representations to the Soviet authorities were made by Western peace movements (including CND and END) and by United States peace organisations, as well as by many individuals. Early in September, Batovrin was released'. However, on 1 November Soviet plainclothes men barred Western reporters from attending Batovrin's attempt to hold a news conference after leaving a Moscow psychiatric hospital.[32] Soon after in a letter to *The Times*, on 8 November, Dr Oleg Popov, claiming to be one of Batovrin's original advisers and subsequently his spokenman in the West after emigrating to Italy in July, challenged the Thompsons' suggestion that as a result of representations from CND and

END, KGB pressure on the Moscow peace group had been reduced: indeed Popov pointed to the recent arrest of another member of the Moscow group, Oleg Radzinski, and suggested that the group's prospects were hopeless since no independent initiative could survive 'under the existing power structure in the Soviet Union'. The earlier suppression by the Soviet authorities of the Helsinki human rights monitoring group gives credence to this view. However in an article in *The Times*, on 17 November, the Thompsons again referred to evidence of growing support for Batovrin's group 'which had expanded its activities to form new groups in Novosibirsk, Odessa and Leningrad . . . and had collected 900 signatories by early October'. They questioned both Popov's information and his credentials as a representative of the group, and asserted that he had not only misinterpreted the group's views and aims but also totally misrepresented the attitude of CND and END towards unilateral disarmament.

In their article, the Thompsons stressed the importance of END's efforts to keep alive and, if possible, to extend the scope for dialogue with the Batovrin group and other independent groups in Eastern Europe. But they admitted the obstacles posed by the action of the Soviet authorities. They ended by saying that 'if there are to be changes in Soviet policy following upon the death of President Brezhnev, many of us in Western (and some Eastern) peace movements will be looking for an ending of represssion against this group as the first signal of a new course'. There have been no such changes. Indeed the first evidence since Andropov succeeded Brezhnev that the Soviet authorities were continuing to regard Batovrin's group as a serious nuisance appeared in a Reuter report from Moscow on 27 November. This quoted a *Tass* commentator, Yuri Kornilov, who not only described the group as renegades and criminals but added the charge – a particularly grave one – that Batovrin, Medvedkov and their accomplices were 'supporters of Israel', although no member of the group had made any public statement referring to the Arab–Israeli conflict. Nevertheless, according to an interview which Batovrin gave to the *New Statesman* in January 1983, his group was continuing to expand its membership and activities despite repression and its lack of contact with Western peace groups. In February, Batovrin and Rozenoer began a month-long hunger strike in protest at the restrictions placed on their activities. Soon afterwards, following renewed harassment of Batovrin and his wife by the KGB, he was offered (according to Thompson for the third time) the choice between imprisonment and exile. He chose the latter and arrived in Vienna in May. Thompson, who met him there, reports that, in reply to the question whether 'if Britain were to initiate disarmament' there would be a Soviet response, Batovrin replied that: 'he did not know. He could give no certain assurance. But if Britain were to halt cruise missile deployment, the Soviet people would see that as "an act of peace". It might make more possible the real work, the work of establishing trust'.[33] This begs the key question of who is to trust whom; however welcome the small chink of independence provided by the Batovrin group may be, it is hardly likely to shake the all pervasive power of the KGB.

The authorities maintained their harassment of the Group after Batovrin's departure. One of its founder members, Oleg Radzinsky, was sentenced in October 1983 to a year's imprisonment to be followed by five years exile in Siberia. At his trial he deeply repented his actions.[34] Olga Medvedkova, wife of Yuri Medvedkov, was charged, after an interrogation lasting six and a half hours, with striking a policeman while trying to attend the trial. Several other original members of the group have resigned. In the climate of 1984, it is hard to believe that the group has any prospect of doing more than managing to avoid suppression. Even that is problematical, but if it does, its very existence may be a portent of importance.

CONCLUSION

The marked deterioration in East–West relations in the final weeks of 1983 increased the difficulties of the unofficial peace campaigners. In both East Germany and Czechoslovakia there were protests at the deployment of new Soviet missiles; Charter 77 contrasted this action with the Czech Government's earlier support for the Western peace movements' opposition to the NATO missiles. In both countries, as well as in the Soviet Union, repression was stepped up. These events underlined the importance of 'holding open the space for dialogue'. In a letter published early in 1983, one Charter 77 member defined the 'long term strategy of the democratic peace movement' as being to 'end the division of Europe into two opposing systems and unify this articifially divided continent 'and quoted approvingly President

Mitterrand's remark that 'anything that would allow us to go beyond Yalta is welcome, so long as we do not mistake the desire for reality'.[35] The same thought is reflected in the European Appeal. Moreover, it is not inconsistent with US Secretary of State Schultz's statement on 17 January 1984 at the Stockholm Conference on disarmament in Europe: 'The United States does not recognise the legitimacy of the self-imposed division of Europe. This division is the essence of Europe's security and human rights problems'. But short of major changes in the pattern of intergovernmental relations between East and West and in the attitude of the Communist Governments in the East towards civil rights, no amount of dialogue with the unofficial peace groups in the East is likely to bring the unity of Europe any nearer. In 1984, such changes seem as far off as ever.

13 Future Conditional

That the origins and motives of the adversaries are quite different from those of the critics should by now be clear. The aims of the adversaries are fundamentally inimical to the Western purpose of maintaining peace in freedom and security under the rule of law, and their activities are directed to undermining the instrument which, with the support of all Western governments, has served this purpose since 1949, the North Atlantic Alliance. The success of the Alliance lies in its capacity to demonstrate in peacetime the determination of its members to provide collectively for their defence in support of this purpose. This lesson from the 1930s has been learned. Moreover the association of the United States with the defence of Europe is as vital to this success in 1984 as it was in 1949; in present and foreseeable circumstances, the prospect of Western Europe alone providing a viable deterrent remains illusory. No doubt many of those working with or alongside the adversaries would repudiate any intention to weaken the basis of Western defence and would deny that they were serving anything other than the cause of peace. But the question which has to be put to them is: peace on whose terms?

There is no reason to impugn the motives of the genuine critics. Their concern at the lack of success of current and past efforts to limit and reduce the growing nuclear armouries on both sides, and their fear of what they claim to see as the probable consequences of this failure are entirely respectable. But they face two problems. One is to formulate a coherent policy which will not only lead to the reductions in nuclear armaments which they rightly demand but will at the same time avoid weakening the structure of security on the basis of which peace between East and West has been maintained for the past 35 years. So far they have not succeeded in reconciling these two requirements. What the American Roman Catholic bishops call 'peace of a sort' is no substitute for the ultimate goal of a world which no longer has to rely on the 'balance of terror'. But to abandon deterrence without putting any viable alternative in its place cannot provide a constructive route to achieving the Western purpose. The only deterrent to the use of nuclear weapons is the probability of nuclear retaliation. Stronger conventional defence, desirable though it may be (and expensive), is no substitute. The stark fact is that so long as the Soviet Union has nuclear weapons, the West must have them too. This is why, for all the massive crowds the critics are able to muster at public demonstrations throughout Western Europe, a broad-based majority for their policies has so far eluded them.

The critics' other problem is to avoid being influenced and penetrated by the adversaries. Just as there are critics who, perhaps unwittingly and often naïvely, align themselves with the adversaries, there are also many adversaries who, with deliberate intent, involve themselves in the activities of the critics. Many of the leaders of the Western peace movements recognise the dangers and have made efforts to counteract them. The Zhukov letter and the treatment of the Moscow Group for Establishing Trust were rude awakenings; in an apt phrase, E. P. Thompson spoke of the Western peace movement 'sleepwalking into a situation of extraordinary complexity' and called upon it to 'wash the sleep out of its eyes'. But, however sincere their motives may be, the critics will continue to be open to exploitation by the adversaries until they have found some way of resolving the internal contradictions in their policies.

The NATO Double-Track decision of 1979 was a watershed. In a negative sense, it provided the adversaries with a concrete issue on which, in the West, they were able to claim common cause with the critics. But it also had the useful effect of starting, throughout the countries of the Alliance, a major public debate on nuclear weapons policy. Although the debate has often been acrimonious, one side being self-righteous and demagogic and the other at times inflexible or insensitive, the result has been to open up the discussion of a subject of vital concern on which, hitherto, Governments have been generally uninformative and publics lamentably uniformed. As a result nuclear disarmament and arms control are now firmly fixed, so far as the West is concerned, at the head of the international agenda.

But the benefits from this have been marred by two things. One is that, on the side of the critics, the public debate has often been conducted on the basis of prejudice, and even distortion of facts, rather than rational argument. Much has been made of the horrors of nuclear war, with the wholly unfounded implication that NATO and its member governments are prepared to contemplate them with equanimity. This has had the unfortunate effect of diverting public attention from the central issue, which is to find the most effective means of preventing war of any kind. The other negative factor is the critics' emphasis on unilateral disarmament by the West. They claim to believe that the unilateral steps they demand can be taken without reducing Western security and that, if such steps are taken, the Russians will reciprocate.

NATO has never rejected unilateral measures as a matter of principle. In the 1950s Britain unilaterally abandoned chemical weapons; the United States stopped manufacturing such weapons in 1969 and has not added to her stocks since then. The US stockpile of nuclear weapons in Europe was reduced by 1000 in 1980 and a further planned reduction of 1400 was announced in October 1983 (see Chapter 2). None of these measures has been reciprocated by the Russians. The steady and continuing increase in their nuclear weapons targetted against Western Europe has already been described; they have also built up their capability in lethal chemical weapons to a point where it now represents a serious threat to NATO.

Soviet policy was clearly expressed in President Andropov's much quoted statement in November 1982: 'let nobody expect us to disarm unilaterally. We are not naïve. We do not demand that the West disarm unilaterally'. This should leave no room for doubt that the only way to secure a reduction in Soviet nuclear weapons is through multilateral (or bilateral) negotiations. Certainly there is no evidence on the basis of experience that the Russians recognise any obligation or incentive to respond to unilateral reductions or restraints by the West. The unilateralist demands of the critics would not improve the prospects for achieving agreed mutual disarmament. At the same time they would deny NATO the ability to take decisions needed to maintain the effectiveness of the deterrent. This is why they are unacceptable, and why they are strongly supported by the adversaries.

One issue of concern almost exclusively to the British peace movement is the United Kingdom nuclear deterrent. It has together with the French deterrent, provided the Russians with the basis for their INF proposal, which would allow them to keep a large proportion of their SS-20s while eliminating NATO's cruise and Pershing II missiles. The reasons why the British deterrent is not, even by Soviet definition, comparable to the SS-20 are summarised in Annex I. The purpose of the British deterrent is now, as it always has been, to deter the threatened use of any Soviet nuclear weapons either for blackmail or for attack against the United Kingdom. The SS-20 has no corresponding role in relation to the Soviet Union. For those who do not accept this purpose, the logical answer to the Soviet proposal should be to abandon the British (and French) deterrent in return for the total dismantling of the SS-20s; but the CND's unqualified unilateralism inhibits them from using the British deterrent even to secure the Soviet reductions which they claim to want. What should have been a serious debate about the military case for and the 'opportunity cost' of the British deterrent has been distorted by the moral-emotional bias of so many of its opponents. As CND have recognised, abolition grounded on this bias would not be consistent with continued membership of an Alliance in whose strategy nuclear weapons play a crucial part. But this is not a position which has any appeal for the great majority of people in Britain.

It is perhaps not surprising that in their propaganda directed to the West, the Soviet authorities should define Western deterrence as 'containment by terror or intimidation', while describing Soviet military policy as being 'centred exclusively on maintaining an equilibrium of strength'.[1] This is the mirror image of NATO's position. In December 1983, the NATO governments jointly declared: 'We do not aspire to superiority, neither will we accept that others should be superior to us'.[2] This was no mandate for the much-criticised concept of 'negotiating from (superior) strength', but it equally rejected the absurd notion of 'negotiating from weakness'. When the Warsaw Pact leaders declare their aim as 'the maintenance of military and strategic balance at increasingly lower levels',[3] NATO can but echo the same sentiment. This was precisely the purpose of President Reagan's 'Zero Option' proposal in November 1981 (to abandon NATO's INF plans in return for the dismantling of Soviet intermediate range missiles) and the subsequent interim offer of equal ceilings at the lowest acceptable level. When the Russians rejected both proposals as 'propaganda', they relied on pressure from the adversaries and critics in the West to get NATO's plans cancelled without having to reduce their own SS-20s. Soviet miscalculation of NATO's resolve and of the critics' influence, and failure to engage in serious negotiations, resulted by the end of 1983 in the event which the Russians had hoped, (and NATO would have preferred) to avoid, the initial deployment of cruise and Pershing II missiles.

The Soviet use of propaganda thrives on an asymmetry which operates to the disadvantage of the West. The Soviet authorities have exploited to the full their freedom to address Western public opinion on the INF issue. But, despite Soviet commitments to the free flow of information in the 1975 Helsinki agreement, the West has no comparable facility in the Soviet Union. The Russian people hear much of the iniquities of NATO's INF plans but nothing of the concern which NATO has expressed constantly since 1977 about the deployment of the SS-20. In any case, the Soviet Government is under no domestic pressure to translate its peace proposals, frequently reiterated and deceptively simple, into concrete results and the Russian people are unaware that it is so often Soviet intransigence in actual negotiations which has prevented progress. Since so many of these proposals are patently designed with the express purpose of securing military advantage for the Soviet Union, it is difficult to Western Governments to take them at their face value.

The Soviet propaganda campaign presents a major challenge to NATO which Western Governments are only now beginning to face up to. The events of 1983 revealed how much needs to be done, both within the West and in relations with the East. First, Governments need to do more to explain the basis of Western policies. There was little preparation of Western public opinion for the 1979 Double-Track decision, with the result that the reasons for it were widely misunderstood. With some help from Soviet errors, some of the lost ground has been recovered. But the Alliance has still not found the way to project the positive aspects of its policies: the 1982 Summit undertaking that NATO would never be the first to use force of any kind was buried in a forgotten communiqué, whereas the more limited Soviet declaration on 'No First Use' of nuclear weapons, which lacks credibility through being unenforceable and unverifiable, caught the headlines; and despite the growing public concern about the need to reduce NATO's reliance on nuclear weapons, little has been done by the

Alliance to explain how this is being tackled and with what priority. A more concerted Alliance effort is also needed to expose not only the onesidedness of many Soviet peace initiatives but also the deliberate distortions, such as the demonstrable absurdity of allegations that the 108 Pershing single-warhead II missiles, with their strictly limited number, range and target coverage, will have a 'first strike' capability. Secondly, it is a truism to say that the West needs to be ready, and to show itself ready, to seek and seize opportunities for dialogue with the East. But if the Alliance is to retain the confidence of Western public opinion in its conduct of this dialogue over what may prove to be a very long haul, it must be seen to be united behind policies which are consistent, flexible and imaginative. This will not be, and never has been, easily achieved. The transatlantic disputes over many East–West issues in recent years have too often given an impression of disarray. But throughout its life the Alliance's salient characteristic has been its resilience. Herein lies the significance of the study of East–West relations put in hand by the Alliance in December 1983. The published conclusions, in the Washington Statement of May 1984, are a classic restatement of the Alliances approach but contain little to inspire. What is important is that the private consultations which have taken place during its preparation should succeed in generating a real sense of urgency and purpose on both sides of the Atlantic. Unless this is demonstrated in 1985, the study will be seen in the West as yet one more opportunity missed.

The challenge to the West from the Soviet political offensive is as formidable as the challenge from the Soviet military threat. The two challenges are mutually reinforcing in that the aim of the former is to reduce Western resistance to the latter. The West's future security is conditional on the Alliance's collective will and ability to meet both these challenges. The final words are from NATO's new Secretary-General: 'NATO is essential for peace, but a NATO which knows not only where it has come from but where it is going.'[4]

Annex I   The United Kingdom Nuclear Deterrent

1. During the Second World War the British, American and Canadian Governments collaborated closely in the development of the atom bomb. This collaboration was terminated in 1946. The decision to manufacture a British atom bomb was taken by the Labour Government of Prime Minister Clement Attlee in January 1947. By the time the first British nuclear test took place in October 1952, Winston Churchill was again Prime Minister of a Conservative Government. The first British thermonuclear (hydrogen bomb) test took place in 1957.
2. The order to produce the first V-Bombers, the first British aircraft specifically designed to carry nuclear weapons, was placed by the Labour Government early in 1951. Delivery of the full complement of V-bombers to operational units was completed by 1960. In December 1962 at Nassau, Prime Minister Harold Macmillan obtained from President Kennedy an undertaking to supply Polaris missiles, which would be armed with British-made warheads and deployed in British-made submarines. The Polaris construction programme was carried out under the Labour Government of Prime Minister Harold Wilson (1964–70); the fourth and last Polaris submarine became operational in 1970.
3. The Chevaline project for improving the ability of the Polaris missile to penetrate Soviet defences was initiated by the Conservative Government in 1973. The decision to go ahead with development of Chevaline was taken by the Labour Government in 1974. Chevaline became operational in 1980, under the Conservative Government.
4. After prolonged studies the decision to replace the Polaris in the 1990s by the Trident (C4), to be purchased from the United States and fitted in the British-made submarines, was announced by the Conservative Government in July 1980. In

March 1982 it was announced that the longer-range Trident II (D5) missile was to be substituted for the C4, primarily because the C4 would have been replaced by the D5 in the United States shortly after the first British Trident submarine entered into service.
5. Since 1947, the British nuclear weapons programme, from which evolved the British nuclear deterrent, has been maintained by successive British Governments, under six Conservative and four Labour Prime Ministers. The Labour Party in opposition has announced that, in office, it would cancel the Trident programme and phase out the British deterrent.
6. The Government has explained the rationale for the British deterrent (in Defence Open Government Document 80/23) as follows:

The Government has great confidence in the depth of resolve underlying the United States commitment (to the defence of Europe). But deterrence is a matter of perception, and perception by a potential adversary. The central consideration is what that adversary may believe, not what we or our Allies believe; our deterrence has to influence possible calculations made by leaders whose attitudes and values may differ sharply from those of the West. The decision to use United States nuclear weapons in defence of Europe, with all the risk to the United States homeland this would entail, would be enormously grave. A Soviet leadership . . . might believe that it could impose its will on Europe by military force without becoming involved in strategic nuclear war with the United States. Modernised US nuclear forces in Europe help guard against any such misconception; but an independent capability fully under European control provides a key element of insurance. . . . The nuclear strength of Britain or France may seem modest by comparison with the superpower armouries, but the damage they would inflict is in absolute terms immense. . . . An adversary assessing the consequences of possible aggression in Europe would have to regard a Western defence containing these powerful independent elements as a harder one to predict, and a more dangerous one to assail, than one in which nuclear retaliatory power rested in United States hands alone.

7. The British Polaris force is a strategic nuclear deterrent with a purpose comparable to that of the US strategic nuclear deterrent, although it is only about 2.3% of the size of the Soviet strategic forces, whether measured by launchers or by warheads. The Polaris submarines are in the same category of weapon system as the US and Soviet strategic ballistic missile submarines included in the SALT and START. This was explicitly recognised by the Russians during the negotiation of the SALT I agreement in 1972. The British Polaris submarines are, by Soviet definition, as well as by NATO's, excluded from the INF talks. The Soviet purpose in seeking to include them in the INF equation is to secure the elimination of existing and planned American INF missiles, thus converting Soviet current superiority at this level of forces into a monopoly legitimised by formal agreement.

Annex II Profiles of the Principal International Front Organisations

World Peace Council
Afro-Asian Peoples Solidarity Organisation
Christian Peace Conference
International Association of Democratic Lawyers
International Federation of Resistance Fighters
International Organisation of Journalists
International Institute for Peace
International Radio and Television Organisation
International Union of Students
Women's International Democratic Federation
World Federation of Democratic Youth
World Federation of Scientific Workers
World Federation of Trade Unions

WORLD PEACE COUNCIL (WPC) (HQ: Lonnrotinkatu 25A, Helsinki 18, Finland)

Membership

Affiliates in over 135 countries; total membership, organised on a national basis, never published.

Organisation

Council: c. 1600 members, includes representatives of international organisations, national peace committees; provision for honorary members and observers (individuals) and associate members (organisations).

Presidential Committee

Elected by Council, runs organisation between Council sessions, meets annually and in emergencies. Presidents of Honour can take part in all WPC meetings (currently: Hortensia Allende (Chile), Gusta Fucikova (Czechoslovakia), Heinrich Hellstern (Switzerland), Dolores Ibarruri (Spain), Pastor Martin Niemöller (FGR – died March 1984) and Yannis Ritsos (Greece). 39 Vice-Presidents, and over 176 members including one observer. Elects Bureau of the Presidential Committee, which meets three or four times yearly, made up of President, Vice-Presidents and national peace movements' representatives.

Secretariat, executive body of Presidential Committee and appointed by it, carries out decisions of Council, Presidential Committee and Bureau. Members: Executive Secretary, c. 20 Secretaries, (most are Communists) and other Secretariat staff.

Leading Secretariat Officials

Executive Secretary: Frank Swift (UK); Secretaries: Daniel Cirera (France); Nathaniel Hill Arboleda (Panama); Kosta Ivanov (Bulgaria); Karoly Lauko (Hungary); Karel Lukas (Czechoslovakia); Rolf Lützkendorf; Max Moabi (ANC-South Africa); Bahig Nassar (Egypt); Arsenio Rodriguez; Carl Rosschou (Denmark); Mamadou Sako (Mali); Sana Abu Shakra; Tair Tairov (USSR); Karen Talbot (USA); Ryszard Tyrluk (Poland).

The WPC has representatives at the UN (New York and Geneva) and UNESCO (Paris).

Presidential Committee Members

President: Romesh Chandra (India, appointed 1977, having been Secretary-General since 1966; member of Indian CP Central Committee). Vice-Presidents: Severo Aguirre del Cristo (Cuba); Olga Aviles Lopez (Nicaragua); Richard Andriamanjato (Malagasy); Phan Anh (Vietnam); Eduardo Arevalo Burgos (Colombia); Ali Badeeb (Yemen); Mohammad Jaber Bajbouj (Syria); Vital Balla (Congo); Freda Brown (WIDF); Martha Buschmann (FRG); Josef Cyrankiewicz (Poland); Camara Damantang (Guinea); Jacques Denis (France); Günter Drefahl (GDR); Luis Echeverria (Mexico); George Georges (Australia); Dawit Wolde Giorgis (Ethiopia); Francisco da Costa Gomes

(Portugal); Matti Kekkonen (Finland); James Lamond (UK); Pascal Luvualu (Angola); Khaled Mohei El-Din (Egypt); John Hanley Morgan (Canada); Gus Eugene Newport (USA); Alfred Nzo (ANC-South Africa); Camilo O. Perez (Panama); E. M. Primakov (USSR); Nadim Abdul Samad (Lebanon); Ilona Sebestyen (Hungary); Blagovest Sendov (Bulgaria); Aziz Sherif (Iraq); Filifing Sissoko (Mali); T. B. Subasinghe (Sri Lanka); Amerigo Terenzi (Italy); Mikis Theodorakis (Greece); Emma Torres (Bolivia); Tomas Travnicek (Czechoslovakia); Alfredo Varela (Argentina – died in Feb 1984); Ibrahim Zakaria (WFTU). Members include Zhukov and Shaposhnikov (USSR).

Information Centres

In Helsinki, Havana, Addis Ababa, and New York (for Puerto Ricans).

Subsidiaries

Subsidiary bodies include: International Campaign Committee for a Just Peace in the Middle East, International Commission of Enquiry into Israeli Treatment of Arab People in Occupied Territories, International Commission of Enquiry into the Crimes of the Chilean Junta, International Committee of Solidarity with Cyprus and International Commission of Enquiry into Israeli Crimes against the Lebanese and Palestinian Peoples.

Commissions: Culture, Development, Disarmament, Education and Science, Human Rights, Imperialist Policy of Destabilisation, International Solidarity, Mass Media and Information, Non-Alignment, Parliamentarians, Racism, Religious Peace Forces, Scientific Research for Peace, Trade Unions, Transnational Corporations, Women and Youth.

Funding

Contributions from national peace committees, special collections and World Peace Fund, but in practice 'has received large-scale financial support from government sources, and has gone to great lengths to conceal that fact from the committee' (ECOSOC Report, 16 March 1981). Soviet Peace Fund helps WPC's and others' 'large public initiatives'.

Other Front Organisations

Most represented on Presidential Committee and/or Council – WPC attempts to coordinate their activities, e.g. they met Prague (October 1978) 'to coordinate their efforts in the struggle for peace'; Budapest (March 1979) on anti-racial policy; East Berlin (December 1979) to discuss NATO's INF proposals; Nicosia (April 1980); Prague (September 1981) on ways of averting a nuclear war; Prague (March 1982) on mobilising world public opinion against the arms race; Prague (October 1983) to coordinate action against the deployment of US missiles in Western Europe; Prague (February 1984) to assess 'possibilities for further strengthening cooperation'. The WPC and the theoretical magazine World Marxist Review held an international symposium on *détente* in 1982 and on international conflicts in Helsinki in February 1983. Cooperation agreement with WFTU, April 1979; both have an interest in the International Trade Union Committee for Peace and Disarmament (also known as the Dublin Committee).

Cooperation since 1973 with ostensibly independent (but WPC-run) International Liaison Forum of Peace Forces (ILFPF), Executive Secretary, Oleg Kharkhardin (USSR). Under Chandra's chairmanship, ILFPF Vice-Presidents included: Sean MacBride (Ireland), President, International Peace Bureau, and Edith Ballantyne (Canada), General Secretary Women's International League for Peace and Freedom (WILPF).

Non-Aligned Movement

Elena Gil (Cuba) heads WPC Committee on Non-Aligned Movement established at East Berlin, February 1979. At International Seminar on the Non-Aligned Countries (Kingston, Jamaica, March 1979), Chandra emphasised 'the identity of views between the WPC and the Non-Aligned Movement'.

British Peace Assembly (BPA)

A WPC Vice-President, James Lamond, is President of BPA, set up April 1980 and 'pledged to promote and support initiatives from the World Peace Council' (*New Worker*, 2 May 1980).

Origins

World Congress of Intellectuals for Peace at Wroclaw, Poland, August 1948, led to World Peace Congress, Paris, April 1949, at which World Committee of Partisans for Peace was established: became November 1950 the World Peace Council (WPC).

Subsequent History

Based Paris, until expulsion by French Government in 1951 when it moved to Prague, then to Vienna, 1954. Banned in 1957 by Austrian Interior Minister for 'activities directed against the interest of the Austrian State' but continued operations in Vienna under cover of IIP until moved to Helsinki, September 1968.

Security and Disarmament

Stockholm Appeals

First appeared March 1950, demanded absolute ban on atomic bomb, second in June 1975: 'to make detente irreversible, stop the arms race . . .'. 500 million signatures claimed, representing 700 million people, over half from Eastern Europe and USSR.

European Security Conferences

Presidential Committee members 'among principal organisers' of preparations for European Assembly of Peoples, Brussels, June 1972, which set up permanent International Committee for European Security and Cooperation in support of Soviet proposals at governmental level.

Disarmament

Conferences: International Forum on Disarmament, Helsinki, September 1976; participation UN Special Session on Disarmament, New York, May–June 1978 (and support for next session, June 1982); Seminar on Alternatives to Arms Productions (intended for trade unionists), London, November 1978; Forum on Disarmament and *Détente*, Vienna, May 1980 and January–February 1982, (organised by the International Liaison Forum of Peace Forces); Conference against the Arms Race and for Confidence and Security in Europe, Stockholm, June 1981.

Religion and Human Rights

World Conference of Religious Leaders for Peace, Moscow, June 1977 (planned by 1973 World Congress of Peace Forces). World Conference of Religious Leaders for Peace, Moscow, May 1982 (convened on the initiative of the Russian Orthodox Church).

Human rights in Communist countries are never subject of WPC resolutions (despite western European Communists protests) but rather Northern Ireland, Chile, South Africa, El Salvador.

International Activities and Meetings

Africa

As part of close collaboration with 'national liberation movements', WPC conferences include: Emergency Conference in Solidarity with the South African Liberation Struggle, Geneva, July, 1978 and (with AAPSO), International Conference against Apartheid, Lisbon, June 1977, when International Committee on South Africa (ICSA) originated.

Asia

In support of WPC campaigns for 'elimination of war bases in the Indian Ocean' and for designation of area as 'Zone of Peace'; WPC conference on 'Zone of Peace', Sydney, July 1979. Paris Agreement 'a glorious victory' (for which WPC claimed much credit): WPC Stockholm Conference on Vietnam; international Conference on Vietnam (Helsinki, March 1979) condemned Chinese invasion; Special Conference in Hanoi marked Ho Chi Minh's anniversary; International Conference for a Zone of Peace in the Indian Ocean, New Delhi April 1982.

Europe

WPC International Conference for Peace, Security and Cooperation in the Mediterranean, Athens, February 1978, particular emphasis on Cyprus: 'foreign aggression fomented by US imperialism', no mention of enmity between Greek and Turkish communities (*Tass*, 10 May 1975, reporting final resolution of WPC's Conference of Solidarity with Cyprus, London).

Latin America

Allende helped WPC activity in Chile: Presidential Committee met in Santiago, October 1972; Meeting of Central American Peace Forces, June 1973. WPC campaigned against Pinochet with meetings in Moscow (September 1973) and Helsinki (latter set up International Commission of Enquiry into the Crimes of the Military Junta in Chile). Strong support for World Conference of Solidarity with Chile, Madrid, November 1978; involved in International Conference on Argentine Sovereignty over the Malvinas and for Peace, Buenos Aires, August 1982.

Middle East

Cooperation with League of Arab States, strong condemnation of Israelis as 'tools of US imperialism'. WPC conferences included International Conference for Peace and Justice in the Middle East, Bologna (May 1973), Paris (May 1975 – set up International Campaign Committee for a Just Peace in the Middle East, still active), Paris (October 1977). International Conference on Solidarity with the Palestinian People, Basle (May 1979, set up International Committee for Solidarity with the Palestinian People); World Conference on Solidarity with the Arab People and their central cause – Palestine, Lisbon (November 1979, organised with WPC help) set up International Committee of Solidarity with the Arab People and their central cause – Palestine (with its International Secretariat based in Tripoli) which organised International Conference of Solidarity with the People of Lebanon, Paris, June 1980, and Vienna, September 1982. International Commission to investigate Israeli Crimes against the Lebanese and Palestinian Peoples, many of whose members have WPC connections, established in Nicosia, August 1982, under the chairmanship of John Platts Mills (UK), an

Annex II

IADL Vice-President. International Conference on the Arms Build-up and the Middle East, Aden, February 1982.

'Third World'

WPC backs campaign for 'a new international economic order'. WPC conferences: World Conferences on Development, Budapest (October 1976), and Tripoli (April 1978), and Mexico (1981); Seminar on Problems and Socio-Economic Transformation in Developing Countries, Aden, January 1978. International Conference on Socio-economic Development, Kabul November 1982.

World Peace Congresses

Paris and Prague (April 1949)
Warsaw (November 1950)
Vienna (December 1952)
Helsinki (June 1955)
Stockholm (July 1958)
Moscow (July 1962)
Helsinki (July 1965)
East Berlin (June 1969)
Budapest (May 1971)
Moscow (October 1973)
Warsaw (May 1977)
Sofia (September 1980)
Prague (World Assembly for Peace and Life, Against Nuclear War) (June 1983)

International Conferences of Peace Committees:
Prague, December 1974
Leningrad, November 1975

Regional Conferences: Socialist Countries:
Ulan Bator, October 1975
Havana, November 1976
Prague, November 1977
Sofia, December 1978
Warsaw, January 1980
Gordony, October 1981
Kiev, October 1982

'European Socialist countries':
Lvov, May 1979

Europe:
: Sofia, February 1977
: Kosice, October 1981

Latin America:
: Bogota, June 1976

Latin American and Caribbean:
: Havana, April 1981

Emergency Consultative Meeting of Latin American Peace Committees on Falklands Conflict:
: Panama, May 1982

Meeting of West European countries, USA, Canada and Australia:
: Moscow, January 1983

Publications

Six times yearly, *New Perspectives* (in English, French, Spanish, German, Japanese); monthly, *Peace Courier* (in English, French, Spanish, German); twice yearly, *Development and Peace* (in English, with Hungarian National Peace Council); quarterly, *International Mobilisation* (in English, with UN Centre against Apartheid); monthly, *Disarmament Forum* (in English); monthly, *Sintesis Informativa* (in Spanish, published by the WPC Information Centre for Latin America and the Caribbean). Regional Bulletins, irregularly published, e.g. *Solidarity with Cyprus*, *Palestine Solidarity Newsletter*, *Latin America Today* and *Solidarity with Chile*.

AFRO-ASIAN PEOPLES' SOLIDARITY ORGANISATION (AAPSO)
(HQ: 89 Abdul Aziz Al Saoud St., Manial, Cairo)

Membership

Some 90 African and Asian 'Solidarity Committees' and 'national liberation movements' are affiliated. Associate members in East and West Europe, USA and Canada.

Organisation

Conference met in: Cairo (December 1957), Conakry (April 1960), Moshi (February 1963), Winneba (May 1965), Cairo (January 1972). (6th Conference scheduled for Baghdad, 1979, re-scheduled for Algiers, May 1984.)

Council: representatives of each member organisation, meets between and acts on behalf of Conferences; elects, every 2 years, Executive Committee (designed to meet twice a year). Permanent Secretariat: deals with routine business. Presidium (set up March 1974) mainly to devise a programme, has met 12 times.

Leading Officials

President: Abdul Rahman Al-Sharkawi (Egypt); Secretary-General: Nuri Abdul Razzak Hussein (Iraq); Deputy Secretaries-General: Chitta Biswas (India), Abdul Galil Gailan (PDRY), Abdel Rashid Issakhodjaev (USSR), and an unnamed representative from Guinea. Deputy Chairmen: Abdul Aziz (Sri Lanka), Mme Binh (Vietnam), Mirza Ibragimov (USSR), Vassos Lyssarides (Cyprus), Abdul Mohsen Abu Meizer (PLO), Alfred Nzo (ANC – South Africa), Anahita Ratebzad (Afghanistan), Aziz Sharif (Iraq). Head of Women's Section: Bahia Karam (Egypt). Secretaries: eleven from Africa, three from Arab States, three from Asia, one from GDR. Presidium members: 35.

Subsidiaries

With WPC, set up (June 1977) Continuation Committee of the World Conference Against Apartheid, Racism and Colonialism, now renamed the International Committee Against Apartheid, Racism and Colonialism in South Africa (ICSA), which has held International Conferences in London, Paris, Stockholm and Lisbon.

International Commission of Enquiry into Crimes of the Racist Regimes in Southern Africa (following decision of AAPSO Conference on South Africa, Addis Ababa, October 1976); Chairman: Sean MacBride (Ireland, Lenin Peace Prize winner (1976) then Vice-Chairman of International Liaison Forum of Peace Forces); Secretary-General: Paulette Pierson-Mathy (Belgium, a WPC and IADL member).

Funding

Constitution states finance is by membership fees from affiliates, and donations. Member organisations expected to give some £2,000 pa, (Secretary-General's report to 12th Council session, Moscow, September 1975: without help of Egyptian, Iraqi and Soviet 'Solidarity Committees', 'the Permanent Secretariat would not have been able to assume its duties and implement its programme of action').

Origins

Formally inaugurated at Second Afro-Asian Solidarity Conference, Conakry, Guinea, April 1960, as culmination of Soviet efforts to reassert influence in Africa and Asia after exclusion from non-governmental Afro-Asian Conference, Bandung, Indonesia, April 1955. An Asian Conference on the Relaxation of International Tension, New Delhi, April 1955, set up a Committee of Asian Solidarity in New Delhi, and other Solidarity Committees elsewhere in Asia: 38 of these, with African support, organised the First Afro-Asian Solidarity Conference, Cairo, 1957 in the 'Bandung spirit'.

Subsequent History

Incorporation of Latin American bodies

First mooted at Bandung, 1961; proposal to change name to Afro-Asian Latin American Peoples' Solidarity Organisation (AALAPSO) opposed by Cubans and Chinese at first Tricontinental Conference, Havana, January 1966 (Cubans set up AALAPSO separately).

Struggle for Control

Originally under Soviet/Chinese control, with Egyptian Secretary-General (Yusuf El-Sibai, assassinated Nicosia, 1978), but this arrangement ended with Chinese refusal to attend Council meeting, Nicosia, February 1967. Iraqis subsequently prominent; Afro-Asian Development Centre set up in Baghdad;

Soviet Afro-Asian Solidarity Committee now provides main impetus. AAPSO Information and Development Centre in Nicosia and Asian Information Centre in Hanoi established by 1982.

International Meetings and Activities

Meetings: International Conference Against Imperialist Bases, Valletta, March 1980; International Conference for Independence, Solidarity and Security, Colombo, May 1980; Solidarity Conference with People of Afghanistan, Kabul, June 1980; International Conference Against Imperialist Conspiracies in the Indian Ocean and Gulf Area, Nicosia, October 1980; International Conference on Solidarity with the Kampuchean People, Phnom Penh, May 1981; Colloquium on Problems of Developing Communities, Grenoble, July 1981; International Conference in Support of the Syrian People, Damascus, February 1982; Second International Conference on Multinationals, Addis Ababa, April–May 1982; Conference on Peace, Security and Cooperation, Hanoi, September 1982; International Conference on Palestine and Lebanon, Athens, April 1983, International Seminar on Regional Cooperation, Brazzaville, Summer 1983.

Publications

Monthly, *Solidarity* (in English and French); quarterly, *Development and Socio-Economic Progress* (in English, Arabic and French); numerous booklets. WPC usually handles publicity for joint ventures.

CHRISTIAN PEACE CONFERENCE (CPC)
(HQ: Jungmannova 9, Prague)

Membership

Claimed in 86 countries, including regional associations.

Organisation

All-Christian Peace Assembly (ACPA) met in 1961, 1964, 1968, 1971, 1978 in Prague; the sixth Assembly is to be held in Prague in July 1985. Committee for the Continuation of Work, elected by Assembly, with about 100 members, functions between Assemblies and meets about every 18 months; 46-member Working Committee includes the President and Secretary-General, meets twice yearly. International Secretariat (22 members) meets at least thrice yearly. Study Commissions meet at least yearly and have sub-commissions on e.g. European security, disarmament, Vietnam, Middle East, the UN, racism, youth and women, economics and politics.

Leading Officials

President: Dr Karoly Toth (Hungary). Vice-Presidents: Rev Richard Andriamanjato (Madagascar), Professor Sergio Arce-Martinez (Cuba), Professor Gerhard Bassarak (GDR), Dr Nicolae Corneanu (Romania), Rev Charles Gray (USA), Metropolitan Paulos Mar Gregorios (India), Dr Jan Michalko (Czechoslovakia) Pham Quang Phuoc (Vietnam), Bernadeen Silva (Sri Lanka). Honorary Presidium Members: Bishop Tibor Bartha (Hungary), Dr Heinrich Hellstern (Switzerland), Dr Herbert Mochalski (FRG), Abraham K. Thampy (India). Secretary-General: Lubomir Mirejovsky (Czechoslovakia). Deputy Secretaries-General: Sergei Fomin (USSR), Rev Christie Rosa (Sri Lanka). Director of Central Office: Rev Tibor Görög (Hungary).

Subsidiaries

Asian, African, Latin American CPCs set up at Asian and African Christian Peace Conferences (January 1975 and December 1977) and First Latin American Study Congress (April 1978).

Funding

All activities and administrative costs financed from voluntary contributions of Churches, regional committees, groups and individuals associated with CPC.

Annex II

Origins

Originated in Prague in 1958, as a result of which it was formally constituted June 1961 at the first All-Christian Peace Assembly, Prague; two Czechs became President and Secretary-General: Prof. Joseph Hromadka (Lenin Peace Prize winner and WPC member), and J. Ondra. '. . . the generation which was in the vanguard of the World Peace Movement included Christian personalities such as Professor Joseph Hromadka and Martin Niemöller (West Germany, a WPC Honorary President) . . . It was certainly no accident that these very men and others close to the World Peace Council were responsible for the creation of the Christian Peace Conference . . .' (Bishop Tibor Bartha, member of WPC Presidential Committee, in WPC's *New Perspectives*, no. 4, December 1974).

Subsequent History

'. . . we had better admit without further prevarications that our Eastern brethren are being used for Communist policy, and that through them we are being used in the same way' (Richard K. Ullmann, a former Vice-President, in his book *The Dilemmas of a Reconciler*, 1963.)

Internal Problems

Soviet influence paramount, despite internal crisis over 1968 invasion of Czechoslovakia; Hromadka forced to resign 1969 after his open letter opposing Soviet action (Ondra had already been forced out.) CPC meeting in Paris condemning the invasion (October 1969) and subsequent resignations at Warsaw meeting, 1970, failed to diminish Russian control, although a collective leadership was then arranged by seven Vice-Presidents under the late Metropolitan Nikodim of Leningrad.

Developing Countries

'More militants from these regions should be recruited for the CPC. . . . Our militants went to Africa, America, Latin America and India in 1971. . . . Representatives of the Third World have never been so numerous as today, when they constitute nearly 40 per cent of this assembly' (Secretary-General at 4th Assembly, September 1971).

Meetings

Helped WPC organise (on Russian Orthodox Church's initiative) International Peace Conference of Religious Figures, Moscow, June 1977, and World Conference of Religious Leaders for Peace, Moscow, May 1982. The CPC held a consultation on disarmament in Budapest in May 1983.

Publications

Quarterly *Christian Peace Conference*, circulation c. 10 000 in 1972 (in English and German), and a bulletin, *CPC Information*, circulation about 3000 (in English and German, about three times a month).

INTERNATIONAL ASSOCIATION OF DEMOCRATIC LAWYERS (IADL) (HQ: 263 avenue Albert, Brussels 1180)

Membership

Total about 25 000; national groups claimed in 64 countries (1980).

Organisation

Congress, the main IADL body elects the Council (meets annually) and Bureau. Congress meetings:

  Paris (October, 1946)
  Brussels (July, 1947)
  Prague (September 1948)
  Rome (October 1949)
  East Berlin (September 1951)
  Brussels (May 1956)

Sofia (October 1960)
Budapest (March 1964)
Helsinki (July 1970)
Algiers (April 1975)
Valletta (November 1980)

Leading Officials

President: Joe Nordmann (France), WPC member; John Platts-Mills (UK) one of some twenty-five Vice-Presidents. Secretary General: Amar Bentoumi (Algeria). Secretaries: Eduardo Barcesat (Argentina), Tudor Draganu (Romania), Ahmed El Hilaly (Egypt), Lennox Hinds (USA), Sergio Insunza (Chile), Semion Ivanov (USSR), Lorand Jokai (Hungary), Pierre Lavigne (France), Nelly Minyerski (Argentina), Ugo Natoli (Italy), Phan Anh (Vietnam), Kazuyoshi Saito (Japan), Jitendra Sharma (India); Roland Weyl (France). Treasurer: Henrich Toeplitz (GDR).

Subsidiaries

Commission on Neutrality and Aggression (1960); Commission for the Investigation of the Re-employment of Nazis in the West German Legal System; and International Commission for the Investigation of American War Crimes in Vietnam (1963), later replaced by Stockholm Conference on Vietnam (WPC subsidiary); International Committee of Lawyers for Democracy and Human Rights in South Korea, set up in Paris, October 1976, under IADL aegis; IADL/IOJ Committee for the Defence of Journalists' Rights set up October 1981; Permanent International Legal Commission on the Middle East set up October 1982.

Origins

Founded October 1946, Paris, at International Congress of Jurists, held under aegis of (Communist-controlled) Mouvement National Judicaire.

Subsequent History

Most non-communist lawyers resigned by 1949. No IADL observers at trials in Communist countries; protests over false imprisonment and arrest confined to non-Communist governments. IADL protests about detention without trial in Brazil led a Brazilian lawyer to write to *Le Monde* (Paris, 1 August 1969): 'I do not believe in the IADL's sincerity since it does nothing for political prisoners from Socialist countries, where it has great prestige.' In 1978, IADL International Tribunal on the British Presence in Ireland.

Foreign Policy

Consistent support in Congress for Soviet line on e.g. decolonisation, human rights, disarmament.

Recent Conferences

International Colloquium on Disarmament and Security, Brussels, February 1980; International Conference Against the Threat of War and in Support of the Initiatives in Favour of Peace and International *Détente*, Moscow, June 1981; Symposium on the policy of forced disappearances (in Latin America), Paris, January-February 1981; Multidisciplinary Conference on the Transition Towards a New International Democratic Order, Mexico City, September 1981; International Lawyers' Peace Conference, Frankfurt (Federal Republic of Germany) March 1982; International Lawyers' Conference on the Indian Ocean, New Delhi, September 1982; International Conference on Mediterranean, Algiers, December 1982. Three International Seminars for European Trade Union Lawyers (with WFTU Legal Commission). Conference on Human Rights in Namibia, January 1976 (with IOJ and International Institute of Human Rights).

Publications

Twice yearly *Review of Contemporary Law* (in English and French); irregularly published *Information Bulletin*, often with specific theme; pamphlets on many subjects.

INTERNATIONAL FEDERATION OF RESISTANCE FIGHTERS (FIR) (HQ: Castellezgasse 35, 1021 Vienna 11)

Membership

Claims 5 million members (3 million full members) active in 64 organisations in 25 countries. With the exception of Israel, all member organisations are from Europe (the Yugoslav body has observer status).

Organisation

The supreme body is the Congress which has met:

June 1951	Vienna
November 1954	Vienna
March 1959	Vienna
December 1962	Warsaw
December 1965	Budapest
November 1969	Venice
November 1973	Paris
May 1978	Minsk
September 1982	East Berlin

FIR also has a general Council, a Bureau, a Secretariat, a Finance Control Commission and Historical, Medical, Legal and Social Commissions.

Leading Officials

President: Arialdo Banfi (Italy). Secretary-General: Alix Lhote (France). Vice Presidents: Marcos Ana (Spain), Dr Vladimir Bonev (Bulgaria), Jean Brack (Belgium), Jacques Debu-Bridel (France), Otto Funke (GDR), Maron Ispanovits (Hungary), Helge Theil Kierulff (Denmark), Spyros Kotsakis (Greece), Alexei Petrovich Maresiev (USSR), Andrei Neagu (Romania), Dr Josef Rossaint (FRG), General Frantisek Sadek (Czechoslovakia), Wlodzimierz Sokorski (Poland), Dr Ludwig Soswinski (Austria), Umberto Terracini (Italy), Robert Vollet (France).

Funding

No details published. FIR claims to be financed by affiliation fees, gifts, legacies and other subventions.

Origins

Founded at a congress organised in Vienna June 1951 by its predecessor, the International Federation of Former Political Prisoners of Fascism (FIAPP), which did not include resistance fighters. FIR has always mainly comprised Communist groups. Breakaway groups from the FIAPP formed the non-Communist World Veterans' Federation (WVF) in Paris in November 1950.

Subsequent History

The FIR supports Soviet initiatives on world disarmament. In conjunction with non-Communist bodies such as the WVF, organised a European Symposium on Disarmament, Paris, November 1975. This set up a Coordinating Committee to organise a World Conference on Disarmament in Rome in October 1979.

In May 1978, FIR decided to set up a 'permanent commission to investigate neo-Nazi activities'. This commission organised an International Symposium on the Struggle against Nazism and Fascism, and for Defence for Democracy and Peace, Frankfurt (FRG) October 1980.

The non-Communist International Union of Resistance and Deportee Movements (UIRD) has consistently rejected appeals for joint action with the FIR on the grounds that the latter is 'an instrument of agitation and propaganda' sympathetic to the USSR.

Publication

Résistance Unie/Service d'Information in French and German.

INTERNATIONAL ORGANISATION OF JOURNALISTS
(IOJ) (HQ: Parizska 9, 1101 Prague 1)

Membership

Over 180 000 in 120 countries.

Organisation

Congress: Copenhagen (June 1946), Prague (June 1947), Helsinki (September 1950), Bucharest (May 1958), Budapest (August 1962), East Berlin (October 1966), Havana (January 1971), Helsinki (September 1976), Moscow (October 1981).

Executive Committee, elected by Congress; Presidium, also elected by Congress carries out routine business.

Leading Officials

Hon. President: Jean-Maurice Hermann (France); President Kaarle Nordenstreng (Finland). Secretary-General: Jiri Kubka (Czechoslovakia). Secretaries: Kosta Andreev (Bulgaria), Miguel Angel Arteaga (Cuba), Sergiusz Klaczkow (Poland), Boris Sakharov (USSR), Victor Stamate (Romania), Leopoldo Vargas Fernandez (Colombia), Manfred Weigrand (GDR). Treasurer: Andras Kiraly (Hungary).

Subsidiaries

Social Commission (established 1967) and Professional Commission (1968); Vietnam Commission (1970); International Committee for Cooperation of Journalists (established 1965); Commission for Training Journalists from Developing Countries (established 1981); International Committee for Defence of Journalists' Rights (established 1980 with IADL); Commission for Studies and Documentation (1981),

Other Sections: International Photo-Section (1962), Interpress Motoring Club (1965), Interpress Graphic Club (1967), International Club of Agricultural Journalists (1970) and International Club of Science and Technology.

Branch Offices: Budapest, Paris.

Funding

Affiliation fees: c. $75 000 p.a. Other sources: largely from an International Solidarity Fund (receives 10% of affiliation fees); donations; proceeds of International Solidarity Lottery (only USSR, Eastern bloc countries and Vietnam take part). Accounts seldom published; in reply to Inter-American Press Association claim that it was 'publicly known' IOJ was supported financially by 'the States of the Soviet bloc', IOJ stated it was 'willing at any time' to present accounts (*IOJ Newsletter*, no. 5, 1981).

Origins

Founded June 1946 at Copenhagen when International Federation of Journalists (IFJ) and International Federation of Journalists of Allied and Free Countries disbanded and merged.

Subsequent History

After Communists gained key posts, all non-Communist unions withdrew by 1950 (and revived IFJ, 1952). First President, A. Kenyon, called IOJ 'a branch office of the Cominform' (was set back by Soviet invasion of Czechoslovakia-HQ Prague, Secretary-General Czech and local Czech staff interrupted Soviet control for some time). IOJ now diverted largely to activity in developing countries.

Persecution of Journalists

Ignored Solzhenitzyn, Daniel, Sinyavsky, even own Secretary Ferdinando Zidar (Italy) when expelled from Czechoslovakia, February 1972; and case of Zoya Krakhmanlikova, editor of religious publications, Nadezhda, arrested by KGB, 4 August 1982. Frequent protests in non-Communist countries.

Press Freedom

'The suppression of the reactionary Press marked an important stage in the development of Socialist journalism. Within the peoples' democratic States there no longer existed bourgeois and anti-Communist Press organs . . .' (R. Ovsepyan, *The Democratic Journalist*, no. 1, 1975); 'free flow of information (is) nothing but the free flow of information for imperialist ideas' (ibid, no. 2, 1976).

International Activity

Developing Countries: Since 1961 IOJ courses held in: Afghanistan, Algeria, Cuba, Egypt, Ethiopia, Ghana, Guinea, Iraq, Peru, Somalia, Syria, PDRY.

Leading IOJ-Sponsored Schools: Werner Lamberz Institute (formerly School of Solidarity of the GDR Union of Journalists), East Berlin, for newspaper and magazine journalists; IOJ Centre of Professional Education of Journalists, Budapest, mainly for radio and TV journalists; Georgi Dimitrov International Institute of Journalists, Bankia, near Sofia, established 1978, gives training in agriculture and economics. IOJ involved in setting up Journalists' School of Bucharest; International School of Solidarity, Havana; Arab journalists' training centre, Baghdad. Julius Fucik School of Solidarity, Prague, opened 1983 to train journalists in the field of newscasting. Jose Marti International Institute of Journalism, Havana, opened in 1983 to raise the qualifications of journalists.

Asia

Considering permanent IOJ base in India; financial aid to Association of Vietnamese Journalists; press centre built and equipped in Hanoi; organised World Conference of Journalists Against Imperialism for Friendship and Peace in Pyongyang, July 1983, in conjunction with several regional journalist organisations.

Latin America

Latin American Federation of Journalists (FELAP) constituted at First Congress of Latin American Journalists, Mexico City, June 1976, with IOJ nominee as Secretary-General (Peruvian, Genaro Carnero Checa); cooperation agreements with FELAP and Latin American Institute for Transnational Studies (ILET), November 1978. IOJ President and Secretary-General attended FELAP's Second Consultative Meeting of the International

Organisations of Journalists, Mexico, 1980 (under UNESCO auspices). IOJ set up Latin American Information Centre, Lima 1974.

Publications

Monthly *Democratic Journalist*, editor Oldrich Bures (Czechoslovakia), (in English, French, Russian and Spanish); fortnightly *IOJ Newsletter* (replaced Journalists' Affairs, June 1980), (in English and Spanish); quarterly *Interpressgrafik*; monthly *Interpressmagazin* (in Czech and Hungarian); *Facts about the IOJ* and some 40 other brochures, plus some 82 000 copies of books published in recent years.

INTERNATIONAL INSTITUTE FOR PEACE (IIP)
(HQ: Möllwaldplatz 5, A-1040 Vienna)

Organisation

Presidential Committee contains prominent WPC members, e.g. Professor Gerhard Kade (FRG); WPC President Romesh Chandra on Executive Committee.
President: Dr Georg Fuchs (Austria); Administrative Director: Viktor Vasiliev (USSR).

Origins

Established Vienna 1957 as legal cover for WPC Secretariat after WPC's expulsion for 'activities directed against the interest of the Austrian State'.

Subsequent History

Since WPC moved to Helsinki, in September 1968, IIP has concentrated on problems of disarmament and *détente*, claiming to provide a meeting-point for academics, politicians and scientists from East and West.

Meetings

Symposium on Disarmament, Kishinev, USSR, April 1978.

Publication

Peace and the Sciences (in English and German).

INTERNATIONAL RADIO AND TELEVISION ORGANISATION (OIRT) (HQ: 1 Skokanska 169 56, Prague 6)

Membership

21 radio and television organisations in 16 countries.

Organisation

The General Assembly, which meets every two years, elects the Administrative Council.

Leading Officials

Secretary-General: Milena Balasova.

Subsidiaries

Include Intervision Council, Radio Programme Commission, Technical Commission, Economic and Legal Commission.

Origins

Founded in Brussels in 1946 when many countries joined the organisation. After the Communists gained control, the British Broadcasting Corporation (BBC) initiated the establishment in 1950 of a rival body, the European Broadcasting Union (EBU).

Subsequent History

OIRT activities are mainly technical but, because most of its member organisations are from Communist countries and are State-controlled, it is inevitably used as an outlet for governmental propaganda.

Publications

Radio and Television, six times a year (in French/English (combined), Russian and German;) *OIRT Information* monthly (in Russian, German and English).

INTERNATIONAL UNION OF STUDENTS (IUS)
(HQ: 17th November Street, 11001, Prague 01)

Membership

118 member organisations with ten million members, mostly from Communist countries.

After the 13th Congress (end of 1980), the National Union of Iraqi Students (NUIS), the League of Yugoslav Socialist Youth (SSOJ), and others, withdrew.

Organisation

Congress decides policy, budget, affiliations, elects Executive and Finance Committees: Prague (August 1946), Prague (August 1950), Warsaw (August 1953), Prague (August 1956), Peking (September 1958), Baghdad (October 1960), Leningrad (August 1962), Sofia (November/December 1964), Ulan Bator (March/April 1967), Bratislava (February 1971), Budapest (May 1980), Sofia (April 1984).

Executive Committee limited to implementing 'policies, decisions and projects adopted by the Congress', supervising Secretariat; meets at least once a year. National Student organisations, elected by Congress, nominate own representatives. Secretariat runs day-to-day business.

Leading Officials

President: Miroslav Stepan (Czechoslovakia). Secretary-General: Srinivasan Kunalan (India) (Replaced by Georgious Michaelides – Cyprus – April 1984.) Vice Presidents: Mohammed Bakir (Iraq), José Castillo (Panama), Leonardo Candieiro Celano (Mozambique), Leszek Kaminski (Poland), Dimiter Karamfilov (Bulgaria), Kim Gwang Hub (North Korea), Ravane Kone (Senegal), Witold Nawrocki (Poland), Ong Dung (Vietnam), Antonio Pardo (Cuba), Petrus Schmidt (Namibia), Alexander Zharikov (USSR); Secretaries: Ahmed Al-Wahishi (PDRY), Manuel Coss (Puerto Rico), Nicolae Daravoinea (Romania), John Gallagher (Ireland), Karoly György (Hungary), Gerardo Herrera (El Salvador), Johnny Kwadjo (Ghana), Faysel Mekdad (Syria), Christina Valanidou (Cyprus). Treasurer: Michael Geiger (GDR).

Funding

Stated to be by affiliation fees and by fund-raising activities, but much support from USSR and Communist parties.

Origins

Founded at World Student Congress, Prague, August 1946.

Subsequent History

Within five years, most non-Communists had left and Communists controlled key posts.

Student Rights

Violations in Communist countries, e.g. expulsion of Chinese and Albanian students from Soviet Union 1962, arrests in GDR 1969, ignored; alleged violations in non-Communist countries give rise to IUS protests.

Internal Problems

Criticism especially after invasion of Czechoslovakia in 1968 (IUS President Vokrouhlicky was Czech; 10th Congress postponed.) 'The Soviet Union was always trying to impose its tactical policy of the moment on the organisation. ... Soviet members saw the IUS and similar organisations merely as unofficial instruments of Soviet foreign policy' (Jiri Pelikan, Czech, former IUS President and Secretary-General, in *New Left Review*, January–February 1972).

International Meetings and Activities

'Without IUS influence no single major international or regional student event takes place regardless of whether it is organised within the framework of the IUS, its member organisations or organisations that are not IUS members' (former IUS President Dusan Ulcak, in Czech youth newspaper *Mlada Fronta*, 6 May 1974).

World Youth Festivals: organised with co-sponsor WFDY.

Africa

Meetings: with UN Special Committee Against Apartheid, WFDY and others organised International Youth and Student Conference of Solidarity with the Peoples, Youth and Students of Southern Africa, February 1979, at UNESCO HQ, Paris; (second conference held Luanda, November 1981). Meetings organised in Africa on, e.g. Neo-Colonialism in African Universities, Democratic Education, the Student Press; Disarmament, the Struggle for National and Social Liberation, Illiteracy.

Asia

Activities: International Student Conference on the Struggle Against Illiteracy, New Delhi, (December 1978). 'A Solidarity Train for Vietnam' launched November 1979; 'A Student Cultural Centre for Vietnam' (1980); Asian Student Information Centre set up in India in 1981 on initiative of IUS-affiliated All-India Student Federation (AISF).

Europe

Meetings: Organised World Student Forum on 'Education is a Right, Not a Privilege', Weimar, January 1980; with WFDY, and non-Communist bodies, World Forum of Youth and Students for Peace, Detente and Disarmament, Helsinki, January 1981. IUS initiated European Students' Forum on Education, Technology and Society, Dublin, May 1980; held a 'round-table' on 'Students for Disarmament' in Nicosia, August 1983; supported a Tribunal against US Missiles held by the Students' Union of the Federal Republic of Germany (VDS), Cologne, June 1982; held a seminar on Students in Europe in Espoo, Finland, February 1983; and an International Seminar 'The Mediterranean – a Zone of Peace', Nicosia, August 1983.

Latin America

Meetings: Student meetings organised with IUS: Jamaica, October 1978; Grenada, June 1980; Panama, September 1980. International Student Meeting for Peace, Disarmament and Anti-Imperialist Solidarity, Mexico, May 1982; Central American University Seminar, Costa Rica, August 1982.

Middle East

Meetings: International Seminar on the Contribution of Youth and Students to the Struggle for National Independence in the Developing Countries, Aden, May 1980; International Student Forum on Unity of Action and Solidarity in the Anti-Imperialist Struggle, Damascus, May 1980; International Student Conference for Solidarity with Palestine, Athens, January 1983; International Student Conference in Solidarity with the Struggle of the People and Students of the Syrian Arab Republic, Damascus, November 1983.

Publications

Monthly *World Student News* (in English, French, German, Spanish and Arabic); fortnightly bulletin *News Service* (English, French and Spanish). Others include *Young Cinema and Theatre*, *DE* (Democratisation and Reform of Education); three special bulletins – *Disarmament Bulletin, Democratisation of Education Bulletin* and *Sport Bulletin*. Bulletins on Europe, Middle East conflict, Latin America and specific subjects and conferences.

Secretariat Reports, started in 1982, appears 10 times a year in English, French, Spanish and Arabic.

Arabic editions, published in Beirut, have been temporarily suspended.

WOMEN'S INTERNATIONAL DEMOCRATIC FEDERATION (WIDF) (HQ: Unter den Linden 13, Berlin 108)

Membership

Over 200 million, mostly from Communist countries, claimed in 1966, 131 affiliates in 116 countries, mostly in the major Communist countries.

Organisation

Congress: Paris (Foundation Congress), November 1945; Budapest (December 1948); Copenhagen (June 1953); Vienna (June 1958); Moscow (June 1963); Helsinki (June 1969); East Berlin (October 1975); Prague (October 1981).

Council, meets annually, elected by Congress, elects Bureau and Secretariat, appoints members of Finance Control Commission.

Leading Officials

President: Freda Brown (Australia, Lenin Peace Prize winner, 1978). Secretary-General: Mirjam Vire-Tuominen (Finland); Vice Presidents: Aruna Asaf Ali (India), Luisa Amorim (Portugal), Fatma-Zohra Djaghroud (Algeria), Fanny Edelman (Argentina), Vilma Espin de Castro (Cuba), Issam Abdul Hadi (Palestine), Fuki Kushida (Japan), Salome Moiane (Mozambique), Nguyen Thi Dinh (Vietnam), Valentina Nikolayeva-Tereshkova (USSR), Ilse Thiele (GDR). Secretaries: Mercedes Alvarez Moreno, Evgenia Andrei (Romania), Aurora Barcena (Mexico),

Hanna Busha (Iraq), Helga Dickel (FRG), Olga Gutierrer (Argentina), Norma Hidalgo (Chile), Valeria Kalmyk (USSR), Surjeet Kaur (India), Susan Mnumzana (ANC), Azza el Horr Mroué (Lebanon), Ana-Maria Navarro (Cuba), Jesselina Peytcheva, Maria Taneva (Bulgaria), Wanda Tycner (Poland). Organising Secretary: Sabine Hager. Treasurer: Maria Duschek.

Funding

Affiliation fees and 'special contributions'; one million marks transferred to World Congress of Women (East Berlin, October 1975).

Origins

Founded Paris, December 1945, at Congress of Women organised by Communist-dominated Union des Femmes Françaises.

Subsequent History

'... only Socialism leads to women's complete liberation and offers the most favourable conditions for maximum use of her rights as mother, worker and citizen', (WIDF President Hertta Kuusinen, in World Marxist Review, March 1971).

Internal Problems

Italian affiliate, Union of Italian Women (UDI) withdrew from full membership, 1964, because of Soviet control of WIDF. Chinese protested at 5th WIDF Congress, 1963. Union of French Women (WIDF affiliate) protested that 1968 invasion of Czechoslovakia infringed principles of sovereignty and non-interference.

International Activity and Meetings

International Women's Year and Decade

WIDF's activities in 1975 included 7th Congress, 30th anniversary celebration, promotion of World Congress of Women (all in

East Berlin, October), which it at first promoted at expense of UN Conference on International Women's Year (Mexico, June). Took part in NGO Forum and World Conference on the UN Decade for Women (July 1980). Freda Brown, President of the WIDF inspired International Committee for the UN Decade for Women, which organised World Conference in the International Year of the Child (Moscow 1979).

Seminars

Lima (October 1974, with UNESCO), Havana (September 1975, with UNESCO), Sofia (September 1976), Panama (January 1977), Conakry (February 1977), New Delhi (February 1978), Luanda (April 1978), Vienna (April 1978, with WILPF and others), Budapest (November 1978, with WFTU), Helsinki (June 1979), Nicosia (November 1979), Warsaw (May 1980), Panama (June 1980, with UNESCO), New York (June 1980), Antananarivo (Summer 1980), Aden (November 1980), Kabul (December 1980), Mexico (June 1983).

Welfare and Training Centres

Regional Centre opened Havana, 1979; Orphanage, Beirut (with UNESCO); Welfare centre, Hanoi (1979); literacy centre, Afghanistan (projected, with UNESCO).

Publications

Quarterly, *Women of the Whole World* (in French, English, German, Russian, Spanish and Arabic); Bulletins and pamphlets.

WORLD FEDERATION OF DEMOCRATIC YOUTH (WFDY) (HQ: Ady Endre Utca 19, Budapest 11)

Membership

Over 150 million in 270 organisations in 123 countries, mostly from Communist countries.

Annex II

Organisation

Assembly: London (November 1945), Budapest (September 1949), Bucharest (July 1953), Kiev (August 1957), Prague (August 1959), Warsaw (August 1962), Sofia (June 1966), Budapest (October 1970), Varna (November 1974), East Berlin (February 1978), Prague (1982).

Executive Committee: elected by Assembly to carry out its decisions, meets twice a year. Bureau: 33 members, meets as required; controls activities of Secretariat, commissions and departments for e.g. disarmament, peace, international solidarity, rights of youth.

Leading Officials

President: Walid Masri (Lebanon); Secretary-General: Vilmos Cserveny* (Hungary); Deputy Secretaries-General: Oscar Gonzales (Colombia), Ernesto Suarez (Argentina); Vice Presidents: Khalil Elias (Sudan), Pablo Reyes Dominguez (Cuba), Ranajit Guha (India), Manuel Hernandez (Chile), Thuy Giang Hoang (Vietnam), Alfredo Junior (Angola), Jin Bom Kim (North Korea), Vsevolod Nakhodin (USSR), Francisco Phillipe (Portugal), Jorge Prigoshin (Argentina); Secretaries: Saleem Obaid Altamimi (PDRY), Frieder Bubl (GDR), Andrzej Gerhardt (Poland), Franklin Gonzalez (Venezuela), Ivan Nicolai Joan (Romania), Akira Kassai (Japan), Alan Lopez (Costa Rica), Leonard Mabassy (Congo), Vesselin Mastikov (Bulgaria), Panayotis Michalatos (Greece), Thomas Bo Mogensen (Denmark), Markku Soppela (Finland), Daniel Santana (Dominican Republic), Joe Sims (USA), Mohamed Haji Youssouf (Somalia); Treasurer: Jörg Cezanne (FRG).

Subsidiaries

International Committee of Children's and Adolescent's Movements (ICCAM, or French initials CIMEA), founded Kiev, 1957; Secretary General Sandor Molnari. International Bureau of Tourism and Exchanges of Youth (BITEJ), founded March 1960; Director: Andrzej Checinski (Poland). International Voluntary

---

* 'Charged with performing the tasks of the Secretary-General of the WFDY' from 29 February 1984.

Service for Friendship and Solidarity of Youth (SIVSAJ), founded Moscow, February 1967; Director Vesselin Mastikov (Bulgaria).

Funding

Resources from affiliation fees, subsidies, donations, provision of conference facilities, largely from Communist countries. No accounts published.

Non-Aligned Students' Movement

WFDY represented at First Conference of Non-Aligned Student Organisations, Valetta, January 1979 (prospect of separate student movement for non-aligned countries has concerned WFDY and IUS.) Fear that 'imperialist and Maoist propaganda' might persuade youth in developing countries that in organisations such as WFDY and IUS 'their interests are allegedly disregarded when youth forums and such are held' (*Soviet Radio Peace and Progress*, 27 October 1978).

Council of European National Youth Committees (CENYC)

WFDY and CENYC have organised meetings on European Security. CENYC delegation visited WFDY HQ September 1977; WFDY delegation visited Brussels to meet CENYC, January 1981; bilateral seminars held in Weimar, GDR, August 1981 and Copenhagen, February 1983.

Ecumenical Youth Council of Europe (EYCE)

EYCE invited WFDY to help organise Seminar on *Détente* and Disarmament (first such meeting) Ferch, near Potsdam, May 1980. WFDY delegate attended EYCE's 11th General Meeting, Stockholm, October 1979 and the EYCE's 3rd Conference in Burgscheidungen, GDR, April 1982.

Framework for All-European Youth and Student Cooperation

Officially set up Budapest, October 1980. WFDY and IUS with non-Communist youth organisations (e.g. International Union of Socialist Youth (IUSY), CENYC, Democrat Youth Community of Europe (DEMYC) and the International Federation of

Liberal and Radical Youth (IFLRY)) were founding members. Its various bodies met regularly until December 1982, since when, owing to disagreements, its activities have been suspended.

International Union of Socialist Youth (IUSY)

WFDY and IUSY organised Youth Seminars on Disarmament, Budapest, (November 1978), Helsinki (December 1979) and Budapest (August 1980). European Youth Conference on Disarmament, Budapest, (January 1978), and similar meeting, Helsinki, May 1978, jointly organised by WFDY, IUSY and CENYC.

Nordic Centre Youth (NCY)

Two joint seminars: Siikaranta, Finland (1979) and Senohraby, near Prague (November 1980).

Pan-African Youth Movement (PAYM)

WFDY and PAYM, in Algiers, organised International Conference of Solidarity with the People and Youth and Africa Struggling against Colonialism, Mogadishu, April 1974. PAYM represented on Preparatory Committee for 11th World Youth Festival, Havana 1978, and at World Forum of Youth and Students for Peace, Detente and Disarmament, Helsinki, January 1981.

World Forum of Youth and Students for Peace, Détente and Disarmament

Held Helsinki, January 1981, with WFDY and IUS, and also with non-Communist youth organisations, e.g. IUSY, CENYC, DEMYC, IFLRY.

Origins

Founded London, November 1945 at a World Youth Conference convened by the Communist-controlled World Youth Council.

Subsequent History

Because Communist capture of key posts meant Soviet control, most non-Communists left by 1950. By 1970 'the torch of proletarian internationalism, freedom and peace, held aloft by the Socialist Youth International at the time of its founding, later picked up and carried forward with glory by the Young Communist International, is now in the new conditions borne with merit and in different ways by the WFDY'. (Raymond Guyot, French WPC Presidential committee member, in *World Marxist Review*, January 1970). 'World Campaign of Common Actions – Youth for Anti-Imperialist Solidarity, Peace and Progress', approved by 9th Assembly, 1974 and 'The Youth of the World with Chile'. 11th Assembly, 1984 launched 'World Campaign of Youth Actions against the Nuclear Threat for Peace and Disarmament'.

International Activities and Meetings

World Youth Festivals (co-sponsored with IUS): originally for 'Peace and Friendship', but also for 'Anti-Imperialist Solidarity, Peace and Friendship' in 1973 and 1978. National preparatory committees usually Communist-run; most Festivals held in Communist capitals; attendance between 10 000 and 34 000: Prague (July 1947), Budapest (August 1949), East Berlin (August 1951), Bucharest (August 1953), Warsaw (July 1955), Moscow (July 1957), Vienna (July 1959), Helsinki (July 1962), Sofia (July 1968), East Berlin (July 1973), Havana (July 1978).
The next will be Moscow, 1985.

Publications

Monthly, *World Youth*; bi-monthly *WFDY News*, news bulletin (both in English, French and Spanish); *Disarmament Bulletin*. Others include: *WFDY for Disarmament*; *War and Peace in Lebanon*; *The Freedom Charter of South Africa*; *WFDY and the New International Economic Order*; *WFDY for the Independent and Peaceful Reunification of Korea*; *Afghanistan in a New Phase of its Revolutionary Struggle*; *Youth for Freedom and Democracy* in *Brazil, Argentina, Uruguay, Paraguay. WFDY in the Fight Against the Arms Race in Asia and for the Indian Ocean as a Zone of Peace*; *WFDY for Peace, Détente and Disarmament*; *US Bases of Aggression in the Caribbean*; *Lebanon: Stop the Genocide*; *Halt the Arms Race* (1981) and (1982) – folders containing relevant material. Information bulletins also produced by CIMEA, BITEJ and SIVSAJ.

WORLD FEDERATION OF SCIENTIFIC WORKERS
(WFSW) HQ: 6 Endsleigh Street, London WC1)

Membership

Over 500 000 in affiliated organisations in over 50 countries; corresponding members in 26, many Soviet-aligned.

Organisation

General Assembly, on which all affiliated organisations are represented (designed to meet every two years): London (Constituent Conference) (July 1946); Dobris (Czechoslovakia) (September 1948); Paris and Prague (April 1951); Budapest (September 1953); East Berlin (September 1955); Helsinki (August-September 1957); Warsaw (September 1959); Moscow (September 1962); Budapest (September 1965); Paris (April 1969); Varna (September 1973); London (September 1976); East Berlin (May 1980); Paris (September 1983).

Executive Council: 40-strong, elected as individuals by the Assembly from member organisations but can be recalled and replaced at any time by national organisations. Bureau: i.e. the President, five Vice-Presidents, the Secretary-General, the Deputy Secretary-General, three Assistant Secretaries, and the heads of the regional centres. Deals with routine business, meets regularly.

Leading Officials

President: Professor Jean-Marie Legay (France); Secretary-General John Dutton (UK); Deputy Secretary-General and Treasurer: André Jaeglé (France).

Regional Centres

Algiers, East Berlin and New Delhi. (Peking Centre closed by the Chinese due to Sino-Soviet strains: Cairo Centre, after internal dissensions, was transferred to Algiers, 1980); after 1968, Ivan Malek, Head of the Prague Centre (now inactive) was dismissed.

Permanent Standing Committees

Scientific policy, disarmament, and socioeconomics; *ad hoc* committees on, 'nuclear hazards' (1957), developing countries (1966).

Funding

By subscription from member organisations (percentage of their own subscriptions); 90% from Communist sources, mainly the Soviet Union and GDR. (Communist affiliates assist, e.g. the French edition of *Scientific World*, printed by Romanian affiliate).

Origins

Founded 1946, London, at international conference organised by British trade union, the Association of Scientific Workers.

Subsequent History

Communists soon controlled WFSW; Soviet policies actively supported, e.g. early 1960s major campaigns against US, French and UK nuclear tests, but not Soviet; refused to condemn invasion of Czechoslovakia, August 1968; in 1962 French and UK affiliates accused WFSW of partisan involvement in foreign affairs and threatened withdrawal.

Recent Symposia

International Symposium on the Higher Training of Scientists and Engineers (1980); International Symposium on Disarmament and Development (Varna, October 1980); conference on the Dangers of ABC (atomic, biological and chemical) weapons in Europe (East Berlin, November 1971); international 'round-table' 'The Qualitative Arms Race' (East Berlin, April 1983); International Symposium 'Science and the Crises of Development' (Paris, September 1983).

Publications

Quarterly *Scientific World* (over 20 000 copies in English, Esperanto, French, German and Russian). Arabic, Spanish and Czech editions withdrawn but Arabic and Spanish editions again under consideration; *Bulletin*, c. six per year; pamphlets, e.g. *'Human Progress Depends on Peace'* (disarmament) and *'The Earth Must Not Become a Desert'* (ecology) – both with WFTU; brochure, *'Ending the Arms Race; the Task of the Scientist'*; brochure on the WFSW; brochure cataloguing all the articles published in *'Scientific World'*, WFSW Conferences and other publications. *'Charter for Scientific and Technical Cooperation and Technology Transfer'*.

WORLD FEDERATION OF TRADE UNIONS (WFTU)
(HQ: Vinohradska 10, Prague 2)

Membership

Total claimed 206 million, 90% from Communist countries, over 107 million from USSR. Constitution amended by 1969 Congress: 'right of affiliation could be granted in exceptional circumstances to more than one national centre of more than one trade union' (previously only one national trade union per country could join). 1973 Congress allowed for 'associate membership' and non-member organisations can take part in discussing problems of concern to them, by agreement. Italian CGIL used 1973 decision to loosen WFTU tie and apply to join European Trade Union Confederation (ETUC); CGIL ceased WFTU affiliation 1978.

Organisation

Congress, held every four years: Paris (October 1945); Milan (June 1949); Vienna (October 1953); Leipzig (October 1957); Moscow (December 1961); Warsaw (October 1965); Budapest (October 1969); Varna (October 1973); Prague (April 1978); Havana (February 1982).

General Council and Executive Bureau administer WFTU

between Congresses. General Council (designed to meet every two years) has 170 members from 74 countries and the 11 Trade Unions Internationals (TUIs). (China and Albania have not filled their places since 1966). Meetings: Budapest (October 1969), East Berlin (December 1971), Havana (October 1974), Paris (October 1975), Warsaw (April 1977), Sofia (April 1979), Moscow (October 1980), Budapest (July 1981), Nicosia (April 1983). Executive Bureau: President, six Vice-Presidents, General Secretary, 64 members from 32 countries.

Leading Officials

President: Sandor Gaspar (Hungary) – member of Politburo of Hungarian Socialist Workers' [Communist] Party Vice-Presidents: Elias El Habre (Lebanon); Indrajit Gupta (India); Karel Hoffman (Czechoslovakia); Roberto Veiga (Cuba); Romain Vilon-Guezo (Benin); Andreas Ziartides (Cyprus). General Secretary: Ibrahim Zakaria (Sudan) – member of the Central Committee of the Sudanese Communist Party. Secretaries: Ernesto Araneda Briones (Chile); Boris Averyanov (USSR); Jan Kusnierik (Czechoslovakia); Jan Nemoudry (Poland); Krishna Sriwastava (India).

Subsidiaries

Active 1981: Young Workers' Commission; History Commission, Legal Commission Environment Commission; International Trade Union Committee for Solidarity with the People and Workers of Africa; Commission on Trade Union Education; Advisory Committee on Socio-Economic Affairs; Commission on Engineers, Managerial Staffs and Technicians; International Trade Union Committee for Solidarity with the Peoples and Workers of Chile; Permanent Committee for Printing Industry Trade Unions; Commission on Multinationals; WFTU International Confederation of Arab Trade Unions (ICATU) Joint Committee; Commission on the Constitution; International Trade Union Committee for Solidarity with the People and Workers of Palestine; International Trade Union Committee for Solidarity with the People and Workers of Korea; International Trade Union Committee for Social Tourism and Leisure (formerly International Trade Union Committee for Social Tourism); European Commission. Also associated with the International Trade Union Committee for Peace and Disarmament (known as the 'Dublin Committee'), whose secretary is Brian Price (UK), head of the WFTU West European department.

Funding

Stated to be by affiliation fees, donations, sales of publications. However, USSR and Eastern Bloc provide free travel, conference facilities, 'special donations': 'Bulgaria, Hungary and the Soviet Union are but a few of the countries that have done the maximum to assist us (paying air fares)' (General Secretary of Dockworkers' Union of Dahomey, in *Transport Workers of the World*, no. 4, 1971.

Origins

Founded Paris, October 1945, on British Trades Union Congress (TUC) initiative, after preparatory conference, London, February 1945.

Subsequent History

First General-Secretary Louis Saillant (France), Soviet nominee, ensured that organisation was soon Communist run. By 1948 'the WFTU is rapidly becoming nothing more than another platform and instrument for the furtherance of Soviet policy' (UK TUC Chairman Arthur Deakin); '... completely dominated by Communist organisations which are themselves controlled by the Kremlin and the Cominform' (TUC pamphlet, *Free Trade Unions Leave the WFTU*, 1949). 'Controlled by the KGB' (*The Leveller*) No. 32, November 1979).

Internal Dissension

January 1949 withdrawal of non-Communist unionists, led by UK TUC, US CIO, Dutch NVV, who set up International Confederation of Free Trade Unions (ICFTU), Brussels, 1949. Yugoslavia expelled 1950 after Stalin–Tito dispute. Leading officials replaced after WFTU Secretariat's criticism of invasion of Czechoslovakia 1968. Italian CGIL left WFTU March 1978.

Attitude to Strikes

'... as a class organisation of the workers, the Federation is doing a great deal to develop the strike movement, and if the strike movement in capitalist countries has been growing recently, much of the credit must go to the Federation...' (Moscow Radio, 30 October 1967, commemorating WFTU's 22nd Anniversary). Encouragement of West European strikes but not of e.g. GDR, 1953, and subsequent strikes in Poland, which were subdued by force.

Acting General Secretary Zakaria led delegations to Poland, August 1980, April 1981, for talks with unions: 'Solidarity is something other than a trade union. We still do not have any contacts with Solidarity because the present resolutions of this trade association indicate that it is not yet a trade union' (Zakaria at Warsaw Press Conference, April 1981). Workers would find 'the best solution without any interference in their movement from outside' (WFTU to delegates from old Polish unions, December 1980).

On 8 September 1983, Sandor Gaspar, President, said that Solidarity had to be judged on the results of its activities, not on the intentions of some of its members; these had been mistaken from the start, making demands that were 'impossible to implement under socialism'. The National Coordinating Commission of the Branch Trade Unions of Poland, set up as a successor to the disbanded WFTU member, the Central Council of Polish Trade Unions (CRZZ), affiliated to the WFTU at its first congress in October 1981.

Relations with other TU movements

WFTU aim to set up and control world-wide organisation and lead working class unity, but relations cool with International Confederation of Free Trade Unions and World Confederation of Labour (WCL)' '... we may agree on what we want to destroy but not on what we want to build in its place', (ICFTU journal *Free Labour World*, December 1975); '... as long as the WFTU continues to act as a tool for promoting the foreign policy objectives of the USSR, rather than for advancing the interests of the world's workers, the ICFTU can have no truck with it' (ICFTU's Priorities for the 80's: Programme of Action). ICFTU agree to meet WFTU only on neutral ground under ILO auspices, for non-political and unofficial discussion (first meeting January 1974, subsequently 1975, 1977, 1979, and November 1981). ICFTU has not responded to WFTU appeal to all international trade union organisations to take part in joint action to stop the arms race. WFTU seek to weaken ICFTU by opening ETUC to unions not affiliated to ICFTU, getting Communist-led unions into ETUC.

Trade Unions Internationals (TUIs)

Set up mostly in 1949–50 (formerly Trade Departments) to undermine influence of non-Communist rivals, e.g. of ICFTU's affiliates such as International Trade Secretariats (ITS), gain recruits and support for 'united action'. TUIs represent workers in similar trades and crafts, appear independent with own Secretariats and Constitutions, but close control by TUI Department at WFTU HQ. Regional bodies set up in developing countries where possible, or liaison committees and cooperation with existing organisations, e.g. Teachers' TUI (FISE) agreement with Confederation of Latin American Educators (CEA): joint meetings between FISE and non-Communist teachers unions, Copenhagen, November 1977.

Existing TUIs

Agricultural, Forestry and Plantation Workers
    Membership: 52 million
    HQ: Prague
    President: Andreas Kyriakou (Cyprus)
    General Secretary: René Digne

Building, Wood and Building Materials' Industries
    Membership: 17 million
    HQ: Helsinki
    Hon President: Veikko I Porkkala (Finland)
    President: Lothar Lindner (GDR)
    General Secretary: Mauri Pera (Finland)

Chemical, Oil and Allied Workers
    Membership: 10 million
    HQ: Budapest
    President: Ferenc Dajka (Hungary)
    General Secretary: Alain Covet (France)

Commercial, Office and Bank Workers
   Membership: 20 million
   HQ: Prague
   President: Janos Vas (Hungary)
   General Secretary: Ilie Frunza (Romania)

Food, Tobacco, Hotel and Allied Industries
   Membership: 21 million
   HQ: Sofia
   President: Bertrand Page (France)
   General Secretary: Francisco Castillo (Cuba)

Metal and Engineering Industries
   Membership: 22 million
   HQ: Moscow
   Hon President: Rosario Pietraroia (Uruguay)
   President: Reinhard Sommer (GDR)
   General Secretary: Alain Stern (France)

Miners and Energy Workers
   Membership: 9.5 million
   HQ: Warsaw
   President: Jan Konieczny (Poland)
   General Secretary: Alain Simon (France)

Public and Allied Employees
   Membership: 24 million
   HQ: East Berlin
   President: Alain Pouchol (France)
   General Secretary: Hans Lorenz (GDR)

Textile, Clothing, Leather and Fur Workers
   Membership: 12 million
   HQ: Prague
   President: Gilberto Morales (Colombia)
   General Secretary: Jan Kriz (Czechoslovakia)

Transport, Port and Fishery Workers
   Membership: 18 million
   HQ: Budapest
   President: Georges Lanoue (France)
   General Secretary: Dev Kumar Ganguli (India)

Annex II

World Federation of Teachers' Unions (FISE)
   Membership: 18 million
   HQ: East Berlin
   President: Lesturuge Ariyawansa (Sri Lanka)
   General Secretary: Daniel Retureau (France)

International Activities

Education: Permanent Consultative Group on TU education in Asia, Africa, Latin America. Training schools, in East Europe mainly, e.g. Georgi Dimitrov Trade Union School, Sofia, administered by local affiliates, courses from 4–18 months students often promised financial aid in return for obtaining support for WFTU; International TU College, Moscow; and Fritz Heckert TU College, Bernau, GDR form national groups. Developing countries send students to courses and seminars run by, e.g. Romanian TUC; 'African Workers' University', Conakry, Guinea, set up by WFTU and General Union of Workers of Black Africa (UGTAN) 1960, runs training courses.

Africa

WFTU helped establish All-African Trade Union Federation (AATUF), 1961, originally based Accra, largely Communist financed; after increasing of Communist connections, despite move to Tanzania, it eventually disbanded. Organisation of African Trade Union Unity (OATUU) set up under OAU auspices April 1973, signed cooperation agreement with WFTU August 1976.

Asia

Asian Trade Union Seminar, New Delhi, April 1972, recommended a Regional Office to be set up, initially in India, which would help WFTU influence Asian trade unions: Asian Liaison Office opened November 1978, Ho Chi Minh City, Vietnam, later moved to Hanoi. Fourth Asian Trade Union Seminar, Nagpur, India, September 1975, and another in New Delhi, March 1979, organised by WFTU; cooperation with WPC and other fronts' activities, especially Stockholm Conference on Vietnam. Chinese hinder Soviet and WFTU progress in Asia.

Europe

Expelled from France 'for subversive activities', January 1951, and from Vienna, February 1956, 'for endangering Austrian neutrality', moved to Prague HQ. Main short term aim to undermine ICFTU, promote East–West contact: 'uncriticially idyllic picture' of East European unions (CGIL Secretary Aldo Bonaccini, 1978).

Latin America

After 1964 closure of Confederation of Latin American Workers (CTAL), WFTU set up Permanent Congress for the Trade Union Unity of Latin American Workers (CPUSTAL), in Chile (HQ moved to Mexico City, March 1978). Latin American Christian Trade Union Organisation (CLASC) and other non-Communist bodies did not cooperate because of CPUSTAL's Communist aims. WFTU-sponsored World Trade Union Conference Against Multinational Companies, Santiago, April 1973. Agreement signed with Latin American Federation of Journalists (FELAP).

Middle East

Soviet line on Arab-Israeli dispute followed in recent years. Set up Joint Working Committee with International Federation of Arab Trade Unions (ICATU), March 1968. President Numeiry outlawed Sudanese (Communist-controlled) union movement 1971.

Pacific Area

United Trade Union Conference of Asia and Oceania projected for 1983 expected by WFTU to increase channel of influence. Represented at South Pacific Regional Conference March 1977, November 1979 (Sydney) and December 1977 (New Zealand); Pat Clancy WFTU Bureau and General Council member (and on Australian CP National Executive) involved in Regional Conferences.

Publications

Monthly *World Trade Union Movement*, published in Mexico City, Prague, Tokyo, East Berlin, Moscow, Bucharest and Almada

(Portugal) (c. 75 000 copies printed in English, French, Russian, Spanish, Arabic, Japanese, German, Portuguese and Romanian). Weekly *Flashes from the Trade Unions* (formerly *News in Brief*) (in English, French, Russian and Spanish). Broadcasting service *WFTU Calling* started in April 1981.

Annex III   Estimate Soviet Subsidies to International Front Organisations, 1979

	US$
Afro-Asian People's Solidarity Organisation	1 260 000
Christian Peace Conference	210 000
International Association of Democratic Lawyers	100 000
International Federation of Resistance Fighters	125 000
International Organisation of Journalists	515 000
International Institute for Peace	260 000
International Radio and Television Organisation	50 000
International Union of Students	905 000
Women's International Democratic Federation	390 000
World Federation of Democratic Youth	1 575 000
World Federation of Scientific Workers	100 000
World Federation of Trade Unions	8 575 000
World Peace Council	49 380 000

SOURCE   Subcommittee on Oversight, US House of Representatives, 6 February 1980.

Annex IV Generals for Peace and Disarmament

The following retired officers were listed as members of this Group in October 1983 at the time of the publication of *Generale gegen Nachrustung*, in Hamburg:

General Gert Bastian (West Germany), former senior officer at the Bundeswehr; elected to the West German Bundestag in 1983 as a member of the Green Party, but resigned from the Party faction in February 1984;
General Johan Christie (Norway), former senior officer in NATO Allied Command Europe;
Marshal Francisco da Costa Gomes (Portugal), former Portuguese President 1974–76, now chairman of the Portuguese Peace Committee and a vice-president of the WPC;
Brigadier Michael Harbottle (Britain), former Chief of Staff of the UN Peace-Keeping Force in Cyprus; director of the Centre for International Peacebuilding, London, Administration;
General Georgios Koumanakos (Greece), former senior officer in NATO's Southern Command; leader of the Greek Committee against Foreign Military Bases, and a WPC Presidential Committee member;
General Michiel von Meyenfeldt (Netherlands), former governor of the Royal Military Academy, Breda; member of the Commission for Problems of War and Peace under the synod of the Reformed Church of the Netherlands, Chairmen of Group;
General Antonios Papaspyrou (Greece), former senior officer;
Admiral Miltiades Papathanassiou (Greece), retired naval officer; president of the Pan-Hellenic Committee for Disarmament;
General Nino Pasti (Italy), former senior NATO officer and president of the superior council of the Italian Armed Forces; senator; president of La Lotta per la Pace; member of the

Italian National Coordinating Committee for Peace; member of the WPC;

Admiral Sanguinetti (France), former deputy chief of staff of the French Navy; member of the French Peace Council; member of the WPC;

General Tombopoulos (Greece), former senior NATO officer; vice-president of the Greek Committee for the Struggle against the American Bases;

General Günter Vollmer (West Germany), signatory of the Krefeld Appeal. Retired 1977. Formerly Commander, Military District, Hannover.

Notes

CHAPTER 1 ADVERSARIES AND CRITICS

1. Henry Kissinger, *The White House Years* (Weidenfeld & Nicolson, 1979) p. 119.
2. Earl Mountbatten's address to the Stockholm International Peace Research Institute, 11 May 1979.
3. *SIPRI Yearbook* for 1982.
4. Lord Strang, *Home and Abroad* (André Deutsch, 1956) p. 137.
5. L. I. Brezhnev, 24th CPSU Congress, 30 Marh 1971.
6. L. I. Brezhnev, 25th CPSU Congress, 24 February 1976.
7. *Pravda*, 21 April 1974.

CHAPTER 2 WESTERN DEFENCE

1. *NATO: Facts and Figures* (1981) p. 14.
2. See account by Sir Nicholas Henderson, *The Birth of NATO* (Weidenfeld & Nicholson, 1982).
3. Dr David Reynolds, 'The United States and European Security', *RUSI Journal*, June 1983.
4. Robert McNamara, 'The military role of nuclear weapons: perceptions and misperceptions', *Survival*, November/December 1983.
5. See Harold Brown's statement of 20 August 1980, (*Survival*, November/December 1980).
6. McNamara, op. cit. p. 263.
7. General Rogers, 'Increasing threats to NATO's security call for sustained response', *NATO Review*, June 1981.
8. *NATO and the Warsaw Pact: Force Comparisons*, NATO, May 1982.
9. *Soviet Military Power*, US Department of Defense, March 1983.
10. International Institute for Strategic Studies (IISS), *The Military Balance, 1983–1984*, London.
11. *NATO and the Warsaw Pact: Force Comparisons*, op. cit. Figures derived from the IISS Military Balance indicate a Soviet increase from 660 to 1070 in the same period.
12. General Rogers, 'NATO: The next Decade', *RUSI Journal*, December 1982.
13. General Rogers, 'Sword and Shield', *NATO's Sixteen Nations*, no. 1 of 1983.
14. *Strengthening Conventional Deterrence in Europe*, Report of the European Security Study, Macmillan, 1983.
15. *NATO and the Warsaw Pact: Force Comparisons*, op. cit., p. 61.

CHAPTER 3 INTERNATIONAL FRONT ORGANISATIONS 1919–39

1. Leonard Schapiro, *The Communist Party of the Soviet Union* (Eyre & Spottiswoode, 1970) p. 198.
2. V. I. Lenin, 'Left-wing Communism: an Infantile Disorder', in *Essentials of Lenin*, vol. II (London, 1947) p. 596.
3. An abridged version of this memorandum, never officially published, is printed in E. Lazitch and Milorad M. Drachkovitch: *Lenin and the Comintern*, vol. 1 (Hoover Institution Press, Stanford, California, 1972) pp. 549–50.
4. *International Press Correspondence* (April 1926) p. 402.
5. *The Communist Solar System*, an IRIS survey (Hollis & Carter, 1957) p. 59.
6. Paul Hollander, *Political Pilgrims* (Oxford University Press, 1981) chs 3 and 4.
7. *Speak Memory* (New York, 1966) pp. 262–3.
8. David Caute, *The Fellow Travellers* (Weidenfeld & Nicolson, 1973) p. 55.
9. Ruth Fischer, *Stalin and German Communism* (Harvard University Press, 1948) p. 610–13.
10. Caute, op. cit., pp. 132–3.
11. Fischer, op. cit., p. 614.
12. Sheila Grant Duff, *The Parting of Ways* (Peter Owen, 1982) p. 91.
13. Caute, op. cit., pp. 138–42.
14. Ibid., pp. 150–1.
15. Ibid., pp. 162–3.
16. Shapiro, op. cit., p. 371.
17. *The Communist Solar System* (Labour Party 1933) p. 1.
18. D. W. Daycock, *The KPD and NSDAP*, a study of the relationship between the political extremes in Weimar Germany, 1923–1933, University of London, Ph.D. Thesis (1980).
19. Shapiro, op. cit., pp. 489–90.
20. Cabinet Paper of 13 March 1943; *Daily Telegraph*, 7 October 1975.
21. Caute, op. cit., pp. 188–92.
22. Ibid., pp. 135–6.
23. Fischer, op. cit., p. 614.
24. *The Communist Solar System*, IRIS Survey, op. cit., p. 6. See also Arthur Koestler, *The Invisible Writing* (Collins, 1954) pp. 204–12.

CHAPTER 4 INTERNATIONAL FRONT ORGANISATIONS – WW II

1. *Labour Magazine*, London, December 1924.
2. *Guardian*, 22 and 24 January 1981.
3. *Observer*, London, 3 February 1957.
4. 'Checklist of Communist Parties and Fronts 1980', in *Problems of Communism* Washington DC, March–April, 1981, p. 92.
5. *The Times*, London, 19 March 1976.
6. *New Statesman*, London, 17 October 1980.
7. *Pravda*, Moscow, 22 August 1973.

8. *Kommunist*, Moscow, No 2, 1979.
9. *Questions of Philosophy*, Moscow, October 1980.
10. The Subcommittee on Oversight, Permanent Select committee on Intelligence, US House of Representatives, Government Printing Office, Washington DC (Oversight Subcommittee) July 1978, pp. 568–9.
11. BBC Summary of World Broadcasts, January 1981.

CHAPTER 5 THE WORLD PEACE COUNCIL

1. *World Marxist Review*, no. 1, January 1981.
2. *WPC Programme of Action*, 1981.
3. CTK, Czechoslovak news agency, 26 June 1983.
4. *Daily Telegraph*, 27 June 1983.
5. *Peace Courier*, June 1982.
6. *World Marxist Review*, Prague, December 1983, pp. 122–6.
7. *ECOSOC Report*, 16 March 1981.
8. *Neues Deutschland*, 9 June 1981.
9. Memorandum by Generals for Peace and Disarmament, to the United Nations Second Special Session on Disarmament, 1982.
10. *Neues Deutschland*, 25 January 1983.
11. *New Times* no. 24, June 1984.

CHAPTER 6 ID OF SOVIET CP AND KGB ACTIVITIES

1. Leonard Shapiro, 'The International Department of the CPSU: Key to Soviet Policy', *International Journal*, Toronto, Winter 1976–77 pp. 41–5.
2. *Lenin and the World Revolutionary Process*, a selection of articles and speeches by Boris Ponomarev (Progress Publishers, Moscosw 1980; (English translation)) p. 20.
3. Oversight Subcommittee, February 1980.
4. John Barron, KGB, *The Secret Work of Soviet Secret Agents* (Hodder & Stoughton, 1974) pp. 164–86.
5. *Morning Star*, London, 5 February 1983.
6. *Sunday Chronicle*, Georgetown, 19 December 1976.
7. Ponomarev, op. cit., pp. 332–3.
8. Oversight Subcommittee, July 1978, pp. 577–8.
9. *Guardian*, London, 31 March 1976.

CHAPTER 7 CAMPAIGNS AGAINST NATO

1. *The Soviet Peace Offensive* (Western Goals, Virginia) pp. 11–14.
2. 'WPC and Disarmament', 8 June 1978, p. 4.
3. *The Soviet Peace Offensive*, op. cit., pp. 33, 76–7.
4. Resolution of the USPC Workshop on Nuclear Power, 9–11 November 1979.
5. John Barron, 'The KGB's Magical War for Peace', *Readers Digest*, October 1982, p. 238.
6. *The Soviet Peace Offensive*, op. cit., p. 55.

7. *Readers Digest*, op. cit., p. 247.
8. Riverside Church Disarmament Programme, 15–16 November 1981.
9. *The Soviet Peace Offensive*, op. cit. p. 84.
10. Ibid., pp. 92–4.
11. Herbert Romerstein, *The World Peace Council and Soviet Active Measures*, (July 1982).
12. *Readers Digest*, op. cit., pp. 253–8.
13. Michael Straight, *After Long Silence* (Collins, 1983) p. 202.
14. See Neal Wood, *Communism and British Intellectuals* (London, 1959).
15. Henry Pelling, *The British Communist Party* (London, rev. 1975) pp. 144–8.
16. *Morning Star*, 28 January 1980.
17. *New Worker*, 2 May 1980.
18. *Morning Star*, 27 June 1980.
19. *Irish Times*, 20 August 1980.
20. *Morning Star*, 21 June 1982.
21. *The Times*, 30 August 1983.
22. *Sunday Telegraph*, 13 September 1981.
23. *Labour Weekly*, 9 July 1982.
24. Oversight Subcommittee, February 1980, pp. 71–2.
25. *New Times*, Moscow, no. 6, February 1981.
26. *New Times*, Moscow, no. 35, August 1983.

CHAPTER 8 PEACE MOVEMENT IN UK, 1930–62

1. Quoted in Bertrand Russell, *Which Way to Peace?* (Michael Joseph, 1936) p. 37.
2. Donald Birn, *The League of Nations Union 1918–1945* (Clarendon Press, 1981) pp. 11 and 130.
3. Ibid.
4. A. J. P. Taylor, *The Trouble Makers* (Panther Books, 1969) p. 156.
5. Birn, op. cit.
6. Sir Austen Chamberlain to Lord Tyrrell, 13 February, 1938.
7. Martin Ceadel, 'The Myths of King and Country', *The Times*, 9 February 1983.
8. Adelaide Livingstone and Marjorie Johnstone, *The Peace Ballot: the Official History* (London, 1935).
9. National Declaration Committee, Yellow Leaflet, London 1935.
10. W. S. Churchill, *The Gathering Storm* (Cassells, 1948) p. 152.
11. C. E. M. Joad, *Journey Through the War Mind* (1940) p. 98.
12. *New Statesman*, 18 July 1936, p. 83.
13. Hayes, *Challenge of Conscience; The Story of the Conscientious Objectors of 1939–1949* (Allen & Unwin, 1949) p. 29.
14. *Report and Manifesto of the World Anti-War Congress* (Amsterdam, 1932) pp. 13–15.
15. A. J. P. Taylor, *The Trouble Makers* (Panther Books, 1969) p. 167.
16. Churchill, op. cit., p. 100.
17. Fenner Brockway, *Inside the Left* (Allen & Unwin, 1942) pp. 339–40.
18. Churchill, op. cit., p. 176.

19. *Partisan Review*, March–April 1941, cited in Orwell and Angus (eds) *Collected Essays* (Seker & Warburg, 1968) pp. ii, 69.
20. See Angus Calder, *The Peoples' War: Britain 1939–1945* (Jonathan Cape, 1969) pp. 57–9; *Communist Party of Great Britain*: Memorandum by the Home Secreetary, WP (43) 109, 13 March, 1943.
21. Canon John Collins, *Faith Under Fire* (Leslie Frewin Publishers, 1966) p. 98.
22. Christopher Driver, *The Disarmers* (Hodder & Stoughton, 1964).
23. *Listener*, 21 March 1968.
24. Peter Worsley, 'Political Style' in John Minnion and Philip Bolsover (Eds) *The CND Story* (Allison & Busby, 1983).
25. Collins, op. cit., p. 326.
26. Data on Polls from the files of the British Institute of Public Opinion.
27. Collins, op. cit., p. 332.

CHAPTER 9   PEACE MOVEMENT IN UK, 1963–83

1. John Cox, *Overkill* (Pelican, 1981) p. 209.
2. *The CND Story*, op. cit., p. 61.
3. *Morning Star*, 14 November 1983.
4. Tony Chater, *The Case for Peace and Disarmament* (CPGB, 1980).
5. Letter to *The Times*, 16 December 1982.
6. *Daily Telegraph*, 29 November 1982.
7. Cox, op. cit., p. 226.
8. E. P. Thompson, *Protest and Survive* (Penguin Books, 1980).
9. *The Times*, 8 September 1980.
10. *The CND Story*, op. cit., Appendix 2.
11. *Observer*, 20 June 1982.
12. *The Times*, 29 November 1982.
13. *Sunday Times*, 3 April 1983.
14. *The Times*, 8 April 1983.
15. MARPLAN Poll, *Guardian*, 22 October 1983.
16. *The Times*, July 1983; *Tribune*, 29 July 1983.
17. *Tribune*, 9 December 1983.
18. *Woman*, 23 July 1983.
19. *The CND Story*, op. cit., pp. 127–8.
20. *The Church and the Bomb* (Church Information Office, 1982), *passim*.
21. *The Times*, 11 February 1983.
22. *The Times*, 27 May 1983.
23. *Sanity*, November 1983.
24. *Daily Telegraph*, 26 January 1984.
25. *Guardian*, 23 February 1981.
26. *New Statesman*, 21 January 1983.
27. *Guardian*, 21 February 1983.
28. *How to Avert the Threat to Europe* (Progress Publishers, Moscow, 1983).
29. *The Times*, 25 July 1984; *The Economist*, 28 July 1984, 'Peace Movements in Western Europe'.

CHAPTER 10 PEACE MOVEMENTS IN WESTERN EUROPE

1. *de Waarheid*, CPN daily, 22 December 1979.
2. *Transaktie*, no. 4, 1979.
3. Advertisement in the Protestant daily *Trouw*, 21 September 1977.
4. *Transaktie*, no. 4, 1979.
5. *de Waarheid*, 8 and 10 April 1978.
6. *Neues Deutschland*, 15 February 1982.
7. *Guardian*, 12 May 1982.
8. Klaus Rainer Röhl *Fünf Finger sind Keine Faust* (Selbstanzeige, S.9–11), Krepenheuer & Witsch, Cologne 1974).
9. *International Herald Tribune*, 6 April 1982.
10. *Scotsman*, 11 June 1982.
11. *Die Welt*, 24 November 1983.
12. *The Times*, 20 June 1983.
13. See Professor Eiling Bjol's *Nordic Security* (Adelphi Paper No. 181).
14. *Lyllands Posten*, 17 May 1981 and 26 July 1981.
15. *Sunday Times*, 4 July 1982.
16. *The Times*, 14 and 20 February 1984.
17. *The Times*, 10 February 1984.
18. *The Times*, 9 August 1983.
19. *The Times*, 26 October 1982.
20. *Le Monde*, 24 October 1981.
21. *Guardian*, 13 January 1983.
22. *Disarmament Campaigns*, May 1983.

CHAPTER 11 CAMPAIGNS IN THE USA

1. Edward Kennedy and Mark Hatfield, *Freeze! How You Can Help Prevent Nuclear War* (Bantam Books, 1982) p. 114.
2. Leon Wieseltier, 'The Great Nuclear Debate', *The New Republic*, 14 February 1983.
3. Kennedy, op. cit., p. 116.
4. Alexander Cockburn and James Ridgway, 'The Freeze Movement Versus Reagan', *New Left Review*, January–February 1983, p. 7.
5. Elaine Potter, 'The Network that aims to stop Cruise', *Sunday Times*, 6 March 1983, p. 13.
6. Cockburn, op. cit., p. 7.
7. *Newsweek*, 21 June 1982.
8. Rob Okun, 'Dr Helen Caldicott: Waking America up to the Nuclear Nightmare', *A New Roots Interview*, No. 377 (The Advocated Press, Newhaven, Conn.).
9. Kennedy, op. cit., p. 120.
10. Ibid., p. 119.
11. Ibid., p. 123.
12. The President's speech to the National Association of Evangelists, *New York Times*, 9 March 1983.

13. *Newsweek*, 21 June 1982.
14. IISS Strategic Survey 1982/83, p. 17.
15. *Major Legislation of the Congress*, 97th Congres, January 1983, Issue no. 10.
16. 'The Nuclear Freeze', *Disarmament Campaigns*, December 1983.
17. Ibid.
18. 'Freeze Hearings', Public Interest Report, Journal of the Federation of American Scientists, vol. 35, no. 9, November 1982.
19. Ibid., vol. 36, no. 1, January 1983.
20. Ibid., vol. 36, no. 4, April 1983.
21. *Congressional Quarterly Weekly Report (CQWR)*, vol. 41, no. 10, 12 March 1983.
22. 98th Congress, 1st Session, H.J. Res. 1.3. Zablocki's Statement was carried by UPI (Washington) on 5 May 1983.
23. *CQWR*, vol. 41, no. 38, 24 September 1983.
24. 'Senate in US Rejects Nuclear Freeze Talks and Raising Debt Limit'. *International Herald Tribune* 2 November 1983.
25. *CQWR*, vol. 41, no. 38. 24 September 1983.
26. L. Bruce van Voorst 'The Churches and Nuclear Deterrence', *Foreign Affairs*, Spring 1983, p. 832.
27. 'Bishops and the Bomb', *Time*, 29 November 1982, p. 45.
28. The full text of 'The Challenge of Peace: God's Promise and our response' is contained in *Origins*: NC Documentary Service, 19 May 1983, vol. 13, no. 1. Unless otherwise indicated, all the quotations which follow are from this source.
29. 'Pastoral Proceeding', *New Republic*, 30 May 1983, p. 15.
30. Pope John Paul II, Message to the UN Special Session, 1982.
31. 'Text of Administration's letter to US Catholic Bishops on Nuclear Policies', *New York Times*, 17 November, 1982.
32. *International Herald Tribune*, 23 November 1982.
33. Jim Lucky, 'The Bishops' Third Draft', *Catholic New York*, 7 April, 1983, p. 5.
34. Kenneth Briggs 'Bishops' letter on nuclear arms is revised to "more flexible" view', *New York Times*, 6 April 1983.
35. Albert Wohlstetter, 'Bishops, statesmen and other strategists on the bombing of Innocents', *Commentary*, June 1983.
36. Kennedy, op. cit., p. 127.
37. Van Voorst, op. cit., *passim*.
38. *The Times*, 4 January 1984.
39. Kennedy, op. cit., p. 131.

CHAPTER 12 UNOFFICIAL PEACE ACTIVITIES IN EASTERN EUROPE

1. John Sandford *The Sword and the Ploughshare* (Merlin Press, 1983) pp. 76–80.
2. Martin McCauley, *Power and Authority in East Germany: the Socialist Unity Party*, ISC Conflict Study no. 132 (1982) pp. 8–9.
3. *Frankfurter Allgemeine Zeitung*, 9 March 1982.
4. *Neues Deutschland*, 21 November 1981.
5. *Frankfurter Rundschau*, 8 January 1982.
6. END Bulletin No. 9, May/June 1982.

7. *Die Welt*, 22 March 1982.
8. *Frankfurter Rundschau*, 23 December 1981.
9. *Financial Times*, 23 April 1982.
10. *The Times*, 24 March 1982.
11. *Frankfurter Rundschau*, 2 February 1982.
12. Keston News Service, no. 143, 25 February 1982.
13. *Financial Times*, 23 April 1982.
14. *The Times*, 13 May 1983.
15. *Financial Times*, 15 April 1982.
16. *Peace News*, 26 November 1982.
17. Disarmament Campaigns, September 1983.
18. Quoted in SIPRI Yearbook, 1983, p. 117.
19. Václav Racek in *Voices from Prague* (Palach Press) p. 15.
20. *Daily Telegraph*, 20 June 1983.
21. *New Statesman*, 24 February 1984.
22. *Sovetskaia Voennaia Entsiklopediia*, vol. 6, Moscow 1978, pp. 252–3.
23. *Izvestia*, 28 January 1982; Radio Liberty Report 103/82, 3 March 1982.
24. *The Times*, 22 April 1982.
25. *Kommunist*, no. 20, July 1981, p. 90.
26. Reuters, 26 February 1982.
27. *Guardian*, 21 May 1982.
28. *Guardian*, 20 April 1982.
29. *Newsweek*, 14 June 1982.
30. Vienna home service, 22 April 1982.
31. *Liberation*, 15 June 1982.
32. *International Herald Tribune*, 2 November 1982.
33. E. P. Thompson, *The Defence of Britain* (1983) p. 27.
34. *Tass*, 14 October 1983.
35. Jaroslav Šabata in *Voices from Prague*, op. cit., pp. 59 and 68.

CHAPTER 13   FUTURE CONDITIONAL

1. *How to Avert the Threat to Europe* (Progress Publishers, Moscow, 1983) pp. 9 and 14.
2. Declaration of Brussels, issued by NATO Foreign Ministers, 9 December 1983.
3. *Political Declaration of the Warsaw Pact Member States*, 5 January 1983, p. 8.
4. Lord Carrington, 'Alastair Buchan Memorial Lecture', *Survival*, July/August 1983, p. 153.

Index of Names

Abernathy, Rev. Ralph   63
Aczél, György   225
Afanasiev, V. G.   92
Aguirre del Cristo, Severo   247
Akkermans, H.   162, 163
Alberz, Pastor Heinrich   169
Aldington, Richard   115
Ali, Aruna Asaf   274
Allende, Hortensia   63, 247
Allende, President   252
Al-Sharkawi, Abdul Rahman   255
Altamimi, Saleem Obaid   277
Alvarez Moreno, Mercedes   274
Al-Wahishi, Ahmed   271
Amorim, Luisa   274
Ana, Marcos   263
Andreev, Kosta   265
Andrei, Evgenia   274
Andriamanjato, Richard   247, 258
Andropov, Pres. Yuri   33, 57, 180, 234, 239
Anh Phan   247, 261
Antonov, Sergei   85
Aptheker, Herbert   95
Arafat, Yasser   63, 70
Aragon, Louis   44, 46, 47, 63
Arbatov, Georgi   80, 81, 99
Arboleda, Nathaniel Hill   247
Arce-Martinez, Prof. Sergio   258
Ariyawasa, Lesturuge   289
Arnot, Robin Page   43
Arteaga, Miguel Angel   265
Attlee, Clement   48, 103, 125, 243
Auden, W. H.   44
Averyanov, Boris   284
Aviles Lopez, Olga   247
Azcarate   88
Aziz, Abdul   255

Badeeb, Ali   247
Bajbouj, Mohammad J.   247
Bakir, Mohammed   271
Bakker, M.   160
Balasova, Milena   269

Baldwin, Stanley   117, 124, 125, 126
Ball, George   195
Balla, Vital   247
Ballantyne, Edith   63, 249
Banfi, Arialdo   263
Barabas, Miklos   66
Barbusse, Henri   45, 46
Barcena, Aurora   274
Barcesat, Eduardo   261
Barnes, Ernest W., Bishop of Birmingham   129
Bartels, Wim   165
Bartha, Bishop Tibor   258, 259
Barthelet, Jean   186
Bassarak, Prof. Gerhard   258
Bastian, General Gert   75, 167, 173, 175, 177, 294
Batovrin, Sergei   231–2, 233, 234, 235
Baudissin, Gen. von   75
Bell, Tom   43
Bentoumi, Amar   261
Berkov, Alexander   95
Berlinguer, Enrico   89, 183
Bernal, J. D.   48
Bernardin, Card. Archbp. of Chicago   202, 203, 204, 206
Bevan, Aneurin   131
Bevin, Ernest   21, 125
Bick, Barbara   95
Biedenkopf, Kurt   169
Bingham, Jonathan   195
Binh, Madame   255
Biswas, Chitta   255
Bloomfield, Jon   140
Böll, Heinrich   169
Bonacchini, Aldo   290
Bonev, Dr Vladimir   263
Booth, Arthur   62
Brack, Jean   263
Braine, John   134
Brandt, Willi   175
Brecht, Bertolt   47, 63
Brezhnev, Pres. Leonid   12, 13, 57, 87, 111, 142, 161, 176, 177, 178, 189, 209, 234

Index of Names

Briones, Ernesto Araneda 284
Brittain, Vera 121
Brockway, Fenner (later Lord) 117, 126, 140
Browder, Earl 47
Brown, Freda 66, 178, 247, 274, 276
Brutents, K. N. 80
Bruyn, Günter de 218
Bubl, Frieder 277
Budtz, Lasse 178
Bukharin 48
Bulányi, György 223
Burgos, Eduardo A. 247
Burhop, Dr Eric 106
Burns, Emile 48
Buschmann, Martha 168, 170, 247
Bush, Vice-Pres. George 174
Busha, Hanna 275

Caldicott, Dr Helen 194
Camp, Katherine 96
Campbell, J. R. 48, 123
Carillo, Santiago 89
Carter, Henry 119
Carter, Pres. Jimmy 142, 162, 167, 189, 191, 192
Castillo, Francisco 288
Castillo, José 271
Cecil, Lord Robert 118, 119, 121
Celano, Leonardo Cardieiro 271
Cezanne, Jörg 277
Chamberlain, Austen 119
Chamberlain, Neville 11, 50, 121, 127
Chandra, Romesh 64, 65, 73, 74, 89, 91, 95, 96, 97, 99, 100, 101, 104, 111, 161, 247, 249, 268
Chater, Tony 139–40
Chazov, Evgeny 99
Chebotok, Stanislav 86
Checa, Genaro Carnero 267
Checinski, Andrzej 277
Chernenko, Pres. Koustantin 79
Chernyaev, A. S. 80
Cheysson, Claude 184
Chicherin, Grigorei 41
Christie, Gen. Johan 75, 294
Churchill, Sir Winston 3, 6, 127, 243
Cirera, Daniel 247
Clancy, Pat 290
Clark, William 205, 206
Clifford, Clark 208
Coates, Ken 152
Cohen, Senator 201
Colby, William 208

Collick, Percy 124
Collins, Canon John 130, 131, 133, 134
Conte, Silvio 195
Conyers, John 97, 100
Corneanu, Nicolae 258
Coss, Manuel 271
Covet, Alain 287
Cox, John 139, 140
Croasdell, Florence 70, 104
Cserveny, Vilmos 277
Cyrankieviez, Josef 247

Dajka, Ferenc 287
Dalton, T. W. F. 126
Damantang, Camara 247
Daniel, Yuli 266
Daravoinea, Nicolae 271
Davies, Thomas 195
Deakin, Arthur 103, 285
Debu-Budel, Jacques 263
Deile, Rev. Volkmar 170, 173
Denis, Jacques 184, 185, 247
Dickel, Helga 275
Digne, René 287
Dimitrov, Georgi 49, 51
Divilkovsky, Sergei 101
Djaghroud, Fatma-Zohra 274
Dominguez, Pablo Reyes 277
Domsch, Kurt 220
Donnepp, Inge 169
Draganu, Tudor 261
Drefahl, Günter 165, 247
Dreibrodt, Heinz 168
Dreiser, Theodore 44, 46
Du Bosch, Jean 186
Duff, Peggy 131
Duhamel, Georges 45
Dumov, Alexei 86
Duschek, Maria 275
Dutton, Dr John 106, 281

Echeverria, Luis 247
Edelman, Fanny 274
Eden, Anthony 121
Ehrenberg, Ilya 93
Einstein, Albert 46
Eisenstein, Sergei M. 48
Elias, Khalil 277
Ellis, Havelock 46
El-Sibai, Yusuf 256
Ellsberg, Daniel 230
Eppelmann, Pastor Rainer 219, 220
Eppler, Erhard 168, 169
Espir de Castro, Vilma 274

Index of Names

Faber, Mient Jan 158, 164, 225
Fadeyev, Alexander 93
Falin, Valentin 81
Faulkner, Stanley 95
Federov, F. K. 66
Feinglass, Abraham 96
Feld, Bernard 192
Fernandez, Leopoldo Vargas 265
Fimmen, Edo 46
Fleischgakker, Vladimir 233
Fomin, Sergei 258
Foot, Michael 131
Forgács, Eva 224
Forsberg, Randall 190, 191, 193–4, 197–8
Forster, Edward M. 47
France, Anatole 45
Francis, Harry 104
Franco, Gen. Francisco 44
Frank, Waldo 47
Friedlander, Ben 95
Friedlander, Eva 95
Frunza, Ilie 288
Frye, Dr Alton 198
Fuchs, Georg 268
Fuchs, Klaus 218
Fucikova, Gusta 247
Fuller, Gen. J. S. F. 115
Funke, Otto 263

Gadaffi, Pres. 107
Gailan, Abdul Galil 255
Gaitskell, Hugh 103, 135, 137
Gallagher, John 271
Ganguli, Dev Kumar 288
Gaspar, Sandor 284, 286
Gaulle, Gen. Charles de 184
Geiger, Michael 271
Georges, George 247
Gerhardt, Andrzej 277
Gide, André 44, 45, 47
Gil, Elena 249
Giorgis, Dawit Wolde 247
Gollan, John 48
Gollancz, Victor 48, 51
Gomes, Marshal Francisco da Costa 75, 247, 294
Gonzales, Franklin 277
Gonzales, Oscar 277
Goodlett, Dr Carlton 95, 96
Goor, Canon Raymond 63, 109
Gorky, Maxim 46
Gornicki, Wieslaw 68
Görög, Rev. Tibor 258

Grass, Günter 218
Graves, Robert 115
Gray, Rev. Charles 258
Gregotios, Met. Paulus Mar 258
Gromon, András 223
Gromyko, Andrei 79
Groot, Paul de 159
Guha, Ranajit 277
Gumbleton, Thomas, Bishop of Detroit 203
Gupta, Indrajit 284
Gutierren, Olga 275
Guyot, Raymond 280
György, Karoly 271
Gysi, Klaus 216

Habre, Elias el 284
Hadi, Issam Abdul 274
Hager, Sabine 275
Haig, Gen. Alexander 84
Hajek, Dr Jiri 227
Haldane, J. B. S. 48
Harbottle, Brig. Michael 294
Hardy, Thomas 45
Harriman, Averell 208
Hartling, Peter 218
Hatfield, Mark 194, 195
Hauseladen, Georg 168
Havemann, Robert 219, 227
Hawkins, Geoffrey 133
Hayes, Denis 122
Hayes, Dorothy 95
Hegedüs, Andras 225
Hellstern, Heinrich 247, 258
Hemingway, Ernest 44, 47
Hempel, Johannes, Bishop of Saxony 220
Hermann, Jean-Maurice 265
Hernandez, Manuel 277
Herrera, Gerardo 271
Heym, Stefan 218
Hidalgo, Norma 275
Hilaly, Ahmed el 261
Hinds, Lennox 261
Hislam, Laurie 122
Hitler, Adolf 11, 44, 52, 117, 125
Hoare, Samuel 116, 126
Hockstra, H. 161
Hoffman, Karel 284
Hoffmann, Gen. Heinz 220
Holtom, Gerald 133n
Honecker, Erich 215, 222
Hromadka, Prof. Joseph 55, 259
Hussain, Nuri Abdul Razzaq 66, 255

Huxley, Aldous 47, 121
Huxley, Sir Julian 131

Ibarruri, Dolores 247
Ibragimov, Mirza 255
Insunza, Sergio 261
Ispanovits, Maron 263
Issakhodjaev, Abdel Rashid 255
Ivanov, Kosta 247
Ivanov, Semion 261

Jackson, Senator 195
Jaeglé, André 281
János, László 224
Jaruzelski, Gen. 68
Jin Bom Kim 277
Joad, Prof. C. E. M. 119, 121–2, 129
Joan, Ivan Nicolai 277
John, Augustus 134
John, Helen 149
John Paul II, Pope 204
Johnson, Dr Hewlett 44, 48, 51, 63
Johnson, Pres. L. B. 189
Jokai, Lorand 261
Joliot-Curie, Fréderic 51
Joliot-Curie, Irène 51
Junior, Alfredo 277

Kade, Prof. Gerhard 268
Kaldor, Mary 225
Kalmyk, Valeria 275
Kaminski, Leszek 271
Kandelaki, David 50
Kantorowicz, Alfred 47
Kapralov, Yuri 99, 100
Karaganov, S. A. 97
Karam, Bahia 255
Karamfilov, Dimiter 271
Karmel, Babrak 106
Karpov, Anatoly 93
Kassai, Akira 277
Kaur, Surjeet 275
Kehler, Randall 192
Kekkonen, Matti 248
Kekkonen, Pres. Urho 176
Kelly, Petra 167, 172, 173, 175
Kennan, George 208
Kennedy, Edward 194, 195, 209
Kennedy, Pres. J. 243
Kent, Mgr Bruce 56, 139, 140, 141, 146, 147, 148, 152
Kenyon, A. 266
Kharkhardin, Oleg 62, 91, 161, 249
Khronopulo, Yuri 233

Kierulff, Helge Theil 263
Kim Gwang Hub 271
Kimmel, Bruce 98
Kiraly, Andras 265
Kissinger, Dr Henry 6
Klaczkow, Sergiusz 265
Knapp, Helena 194
Kohl, Chanc. Helmut 174, 205
Koivisto, Pres. Mauno 180
Kokoshin, Andrei 101
Kone, Ravane 271
Konieczny, Jan 288
Konrad, György 224
Kopteltsev, Valentin 231
Kornilenko, Vladislav 76
Kornilov, Yuri 234
Köszegi, Ferenc 224, 225
Kotsakis, Spyros 263
Koumanakos, Gen. Georgios 75, 294
Kovács, László 223
Kovalenko, I. I. 80
Krakhmanlikova, Zoya 266
Kriz, Jan 288
Krusche, Bishop Werner 221
Kubka, Jiri 66, 265
Kunalan, Srinivasan 271
Kushida, Fuki 274
Kushner, Sylvia 95, 96
Kusnierik, Jan 284
Kuusinen, Hertta 275
Kuusinen, Otto 41–2, 49
Kuznetsov, Valentin 85
Kwadjo, Johnny 271
Kyriakou, Andreas 287

Lamond, James 96, 104, 106, 248, 249
Langignon, Michael 184
Lanoue, Georges 288
Lansbury, George 124, 125
Laski, Harold 44, 48, 51
Lauko, Karoly 247
Laval, Pierre 126
Lavigne, Pierre 261
Lawther, Will 103
Layzell, James 104
Lee, Adm. 75
Legay, Jean-Marie 106, 281
Leinen, Josef 174
Lékai, Card. László 223
Lenin, Vladimir 39, 40, 41, 42, 45, 214, 229
Lens, Sidney 95
Leonhard, Rudolf 47
Leonov, Vadim Vasilyevich 86

Index of Names

Le Rocque, Adm. Gene 100
Lewis, Cecil Day 51
Lhote, Alix 263
Lindner, Lothar 287
Lis, Ladislav 227
Litvinov, Maxim M. 49, 50
Lomas, Alfred 104
Louis, Victor 93
Lopez, Alan 277
Lorenz, Hans 288
Lothian, Lord 127
Lukas, Karel 247
Luns, Dr Joseph 84
Luther, Martin 215, 217
Lützkendorf, Rolf 247
Luvualu, Pascal 248
Lysenko, Dr Trofin 60
Lyssarides, Vassos 255

Mabassy, Leonard 277
Macaulay, Rose 131
MacBride, Sean 62, 63, 249, 255
MacDonald, Ramsay 117
Macmillan, Harold 243
McGovern, James 123
McNamara, Robert 26, 27
Malek, Ivan 281
Malraux, André 44, 47
Manchka, P. I. 80
Mann, Heinrich 46, 47, 51
Mannhardt, Klaus 170
Marchais, Georges 89
Marchenko, Anatoly 229
Maresiev, Alexei Petrovich 263
Markey, Edward 195
Marshall, Gen. George C. 21
Maslennikov 141
Masri, Walid 277
Mastikov, Vesselin 277, 278
Matveer, Vikenti 140
Medvedev, Zhores 151
Medvedkov, Yuri 233, 234, 235
Medvedkova, Olga 150, 235
Mekdad, Faysel 271
Meinhof, Ulrike 168
Meizer, Abdul Mohsen Abu 255
Merkulov, Vladimir 85, 179
Mertes, Alois 205
Meyenfeldt, Gen. Michiel 75, 294
Michalatos, Panayotis 277
Michalko, Dr Jan 258
Milovidov, Maj. Gen. A. S. 58
Minyerski, Nelly 261
Mirejovsky, Lubomir 258

Mitterrand, Pres. François 184
Mnumzana, Susan 275
Moabi, Max 247
Mochalin, D. N. 161
Mochalski, Dr Herbert 258
Mogensen, Thomas Bo 277
Mohei El-Din, Khaled 248
Moiane, Salome 274
Molnari, Sandor 277
Molotov, Vyacheslav 50
Mondale, Walter 209
Morales, Gilberto 288
Morgan, John Hanley 248
Morrison, Chaplain 202
Mosley, Oswald 128
Mostovets, Nikolai 101
Mountbatten of Burma, Earl 8
Mroue, Azza el Horr 275
Munzenberg, Willi 42, 45, 46, 49, 51, 60
Muskie, Edmund 208
Mussolini, Benito 44, 125, 126
Myerson, Michael 98, 100

Nabokov, Vladimir 45
Nakhodin, Vsevolod 277
Napoleone, Roberto 183
Nassar, Bahig 247
Natoli, Ugo 261
Navarro, Ana-Maria 275
Nawrocki, Witold 271
Neagu, Andrei 263
Nemoudry, Jan 284
Newport, Gus Eugene 248
Nguyen Thi Dinh 274
Nichols, Beverley 116
Nielsen, Knud 62
Niemöller, Pastor Martin 63, 167, 247, 259
Niggemeier, Horst 168–9
Nikodim, Met. of Leningrad 259
Nikolayeva-Tereshkova, Valentina 274
Nixon, Pres. Richard 189
Noel-Baker, Philip, Lord 56, 124
Nordenstreng, Kaarle 265
Nordmann, Joe 261
Numeiry, Pres. 290
Nunn, Senator Sam 201
Nzo, Alfred 248, 255

O'Connor, John, Bishop of New York 203
Oestreicher, Canon Paul 148, 149
Ogarkov, Marshal Nikolai 229

Index of Names

Ondra, J. 259
Ong Dung 271
Orwell, George 48, 128
Osborne, John 134
Ovchinnikov, Leonid 86

Page, Bertrand 288
Palme, Dutt 48, 50
Palme, Olof 180
Papandreou, Andreas 180, 181, 182
Papaspirou, Gen. Antonios 75, 294
Papathanassiou, Adm. Miltiades 294
Paramonov, Sergai 101
Pardo, Antonio 271
Pasti, Gen. Nino 75, 99, 162, 178, 184, 294
Pastukhov, Boris 230
Paul VI, Pope 202
Pavett, Jean 104
Pecs, Bishop of 223
Pelikan, Jiri 272
Pera, Mauri 287
Perez, Camilo O. 248
Petersen, Arne 179
Peytcheva, Jesselina 275
Pezely, Rudolf 168
Phem Quang Phuoc 258
Phillipe, Francisco 277
Pieck, W. (later Pres.) 51
Pierson-Mathy, Paulette 255
Pietraroia, Rosario 288
Pimen, Patriarch 165
Pinochet, Pres. 252
Platts-Mills, John 252, 261
Polevoi, Boris 56
Pollitt, Harry 50, 102, 130
Ponomarev, Boris 58, 78, 79, 80, 86, 87, 88, 90, 92, 96, 183
Ponsonby of Shulbrede, Lord 121, 123, 127
Popov, Anatoli 165
Popov, Dr Oleg 233
Porkkale, Veikko 287
Pouchol, Alain 288
Price, Brian 285
Priestley, J. B. 47, 131, 132
Prigoshin, Jorge 277
Primakov, E. M. 66, 248
Pritt, Denis N. 44, 51
Proektor, Daniel 81
Provance, Terry 97, 99
Pudovkin 48

Radzinski, Oleg 233, 235

Randle, Michael 130
Ratebzad, Anahita 255
Rathjens, George 192
Reagan, Pres. Ronald 35, 142, 165, 172, 183, 191, 192, 195, 202, 209
Retureau, Daniel 289
Ribbentrop, Joachim von 50
Rinser, Luisa 218
Ritsos, Yannis 247
Roberts, Allan 106
Rodriguez, Arsenio 247
Rogers, Gen. Bernard 28, 30, 31
Röhl, Klaus Rainer 167
Roosevelt, Pres. Franklin D. 44, 47
Rosa, Rev. Christie 258
Rosenoer, Sergei 233, 234
Rossaint, Dr Josef 263
Rosschou, Carl 247
Rostow, Eugene 203
Rowney, Edward 203
Ruddock, Joan 141, 146
Rümpel, Werner 97, 163, 165
Rusk, Dean 205
Russell, Bertrand 46, 121, 129, 131, 134
Rusza, Ferenc 224, 226

Sacco 46
Sadek, Gen. Frantisek 263
Saillant, Louis 285
Saito, Kazuyoshi 261
Sakharov, Andrei 92, 232
Sakharov, Boris 265
Sako, Mamdou 247
Salisbury, Bishop of 149
Samad, Nadim Abdul 248
Samrin, Heng 74
Sanguinetti, Adm. 75, 185, 294
Santana, Daniel 277
Sarnoff, Irving 95, 96
Sartre, Jean Paul 63
Sassoon, Siegfried 115
Scargill, Arthur 104
Schaffer, Gordon 104
Schell, Jonathan 193
Schlesinger, James 203
Schmidt, Chancellor Helmut 34
Schmidt, Petrus 271
Schouten, Nico 97, 160, 161, 162, 164, 166
Scoville, Herbert 195, 203
Schultz, George 236
Sebestyen, Ilona 248
Seghers, Anna 47
Seguillon, Pierre-Luc 184

Index of Names

Sendov, Blagovest 248
Shakra, Sana Abu 247
Shaposhnikov, Vitaly 66, 80, 91, 248
Sharif, Aziz 255
Sharma, Jitendra 261
Shaw, George Bernard 44, 46, 51
Shelepin, Alexander 159
Sheppard, Canon Dick 121, 122
Sherif, Aziz 248
Shustov, Vladimir 101
Silone, Ignazio 44
Silva, Bernardine 258
Simon, Alain 288
Sims, Joe 277
Sinclair, Upton 45, 46
Sinyavsky, Andrei 266
Sissoko, Filifing 248
Sitwell, Osbert 121
Smith, Gerard 208
Sokorski, Wlodzimierz 263
Solzhenitzyn, Alexander 266
Sommer, Reinhard 288
Soper, Rev. Donald (later Lord) 119, 121, 129
Spooela, Markku 277
Soswinski, Dr Ludwig 263
Spender, Stephen 51
Spregel, Jack 95
Springhall, D. F. 50
Sriwastava, Krishna 284
Stalin, Joseph V. 19, 44, 48, 49, 51, 57, 64
Stamate, Victor 265
Steinbruner, John 195
Stepan, Miroslav 66, 271
Stephen, I. L. P. 123
Stern, Alain 288
Stone, Dr Jeremy 195, 198, 199
Strachey, John 46, 48, 51
Straight, Michael 102
Stürman, Werner 170
Suarez, Ernesto 277
Subasinghe, T. B. 248
Sun Yat Sen, Madame 46
Suslov, Mikhail 79, 161
Swift, Frank 247

Tairov, Tair 247
Talbot, Karen 96, 247
Taneva, Maria 275
Tatarnikov, Gen. 140–1
Taylor, A. J. P. 118, 132
Ternzi, Amerigo 248
Terracini, Umberto 263

Thampy, Abraham K. 258
Theodorakis, Mikis 248
Thiele, Ilse 274
Thompson, E. P. 143, 145, 151, 154, 155, 215, 224, 225, 233, 234, 238
Thorez, Maurice 48
Thuy Grang Hoang 277
Tito, Pres. J. B. 60, 64
Toeplitz, Heinrich 261
Tombopoulos, Gen. Michaelis 75, 294
Torres, Emma 248
Tosek, Ruth 56
Tost, Ulrich 172
Toth, Dr Karoly 66, 258
Trachtenberg, Alexander 47
Travnicek, Tomas 70, 71, 248
Trenchard, Marshal of the RAF Lord 115
Trevelyan, Charles 124
Trotsky, Leon 48, 49
Truman, Pres. Harry S. 21
Tschiche, Pastor Hans-Jochen 219
Tümmers, Peter 168
Tycner, Wanda 275
Tyrluk, Ryszard 247

Ulbricht, Walther 51, 215
Ulcak, Dusan 272
Ullmann, Richard K. 259
Ulyanovsky, R. A. 80

Valanidou, Christina 271
Van Agt, Andries 161, 164
Vanzetti 46
Varela, Alfredo 248
Vas, Janes 288
Vasiliev, Viktor 268
Verga, Roberto 284
Vetter, Heinz Oskar 165
Vilon-Guezo, Romain 284
Vire-Tuominen, Mirjam 274
Vlasov, Gen. 83
Vokrouhlicky 272
Vollet, Robert 263
Vollmer, Gen. Günter 75, 294

Walde, Werner 217
Warner, Senator 195
Warnke, Paul 195
Watson, Thomas 208
Webb, Beatrice 43, 44, 51
Webb, Sidney 43, 44, 51
Weinberger, Caspar 179
Wells, H. G. 45

Wesker, Arnold   134
Weyl, Roland   261
Wiegand, Manfred   265
Wilkinson, Ellen   46
Wilmot, John   125
Wilson, Edmund   44
Wilson, Harold   243
Wilson, William   106
Wohlstetter, Albert   207
Wolff, Joop   159, 165
Woolf, Leonard   51
Worsley, Peter   133

Yakovlev, Alexander   80
Yepishev, Gen. Alexei   230

Young, Ronald   95
Youssouf, Mohammad Haji   277

Zablocki, Clement   200
Zagladin, Vadim   80, 86, 88, 92, 154, 161, 163, 183
Zakaria, Ibrahim   248, 284, 286
Zamyatin, Leonid   81
Zharikov, Alexander   271
Zhivkov, Todor   181
Zhukov, G. A.   66, 93, 141, 152, 153, 182, 213, 248
Ziartides, Andreas   284
Zidar, Ferdinando   266
Zinoviev, Gregory   40
Zweig, Stefan   45

General Index

AALAPSO 256
AAPSO 55, 62, 65, 66, 246, 251, 254–7, 292
AATUF 289
ABPLG 104
AFF 174
AFSC 97, 100, 190, 192
AGDF 169
ASF 169, 170, 173, 174
Action Group for Peace and Reconciliation—*See* ASF
Action Group Service for Peace—*See* AGDF
Addis Ababa, AAPSO international conferences 65, 255, 257
Aden, IUS international seminar 273
WPC seminar 253
Afro-Asian Peoples' Solidarity Organisation—*See* AAPSO
Agitprop 79
Aldermaston Marches 132, 138
Algiers, IADL international conference 262
All-African Trade Union Federation 289
All-Britain Peace Liaison Group 104
All-Indian Peace and Solidarity Organisation 110
American Friends 188
American Friends Service Committee—*See* AFSC
American Friends of the Soviet Union 51
American League against War and Fascism 46
Amsterdam Pleydel Movement 46
Anglican Pacifist Fellowship 122
Anti-Nazi League 107
Anti-Apartheid Movement 107
Anti-Ballistic Missile Treaty 138
Art for Peace 86
Artists for Peace 103
Association of Citizens Initiative Groups 174

Association des Ecrivains et Artistes Révolutionnaires 47
Association of the Victims of the Nazi Regime – League of Anti-Fascists 171
Association of World Federalists 62–3
Athens: AAPSO international conference 257
Conferences on nuclear free zones 181, 225
IUS international student conference 273
WPC international conference 252
Atlantic Alliance 3, 8, 22, 23, 24, 30, 31, 32, 33, 237, 241, 242
Atom Weapons Research Establishment 132
Austrian Peace Council 71
Authors' World Peace Appeal 103

BASW 106
BPA 70, 104, 249
BPC 43, 103, 104, 130, 134
BSFS 104, 106
Baltic Area, WPC workers conference 178
Basle, WPC international conference 252
Bausoldaten 216, 222
Belgian Union for the Defence of Peace 186, 187
Berlin Appeal 218–20, 227
END convention 71, 152
Bertrand Russell Peace Foundation 150, 152, 154
Biological Weapons Convention 138
'Blue Streak' missile 135
Bologna, WPC international conference 252
Brazzaville, AAPSO international seminar 257
British Anti-War Movement 123
British Association of Scientific Workers 106

British Cultural Committee for
  Peace 103
British Movement Against War and
  Fascism 123
British Peace Assembly—*See* BPA
British Peace Committee—*See* BPC
British Polaris force 245—*See also* Polaris
  missiles
British-Soviet Friendship Society 43, 44
British Union 128
British Vietnam Association 104, 106
Brussels; END conference 152
  IADL international Colloquium 262
  ICESC contacts 178
Budapest: CPC consultation 260
  WPC World conference 253
  Youth Peace Festival 226
Buenos Aires, international
  conference 252
Bundestag vote on INF 174, 175
Burghfield, CND demonstrations 146

CALC 95, 100, 192
CBS 193
CDA 158, 161, 164
CDFT 186
CDU 169
CDU/FDP coalition 173
CENYC 278, 279
CESC—*See* ICESC
CGIL 183, 285, 290
CGT 185, 285
CIO 285
CNAPD 186, 187
CND 56, 107, 129, 131-6, 137, 138-49,
  157, 233, 234, 240
CODENE 185, 186
CPC 55, 246, 257-60, 292
CPGB 48, 50, 102, 104, 106, 107, 133,
  138-9, 140
CPN 63, 158, 159, 161, 162, 166
CPSU 52, 62, 64, 65, 66, 78, 161, 183
  Central Committee 14, 78, 79, 81, 93
  Congress 57
  International Department—*See* ID
  International Information
    Department—*See* IID
CPUSA 95, 98, 100
CSCE 6, 89, 163
CTB 191
Cadres Abroad Department 81
Campaign for Nuclear Disarmament—*See*
  CND

Campaign for the Special Session on
  Disarmament 100
Catholic Trade Union Association,
  France 186
Central Committee of the Soviet
  Communist Party—*See under* CPSU
Central Council of Polish Trade
  Unions 286
Charter 77 226, 227, 228, 235
Chevaline Project 243
Chicago Peace Council 95
Chile Solidarity Campaign 107
Christian CND 148
Christian Democratic Party,
  Netherlands—*See* CDA
Christian Peace Conference—*See* CPC
Christians for Socialism 160
Clergy and Laity Concerned—*See* CALC
Cohen-Nunn proposal 202
Colombo, AAPSO international
  conference 65
Cominform 78
Comintern 13, 14, 39, 45, 48, 49, 78
  Third Congress 41
*Comité National d'Action pour la Paix et la
  Developpement* 186, 187
Committee of 100 134, 135, 138
Committee for Nuclear Disarmament in
  Europe—*See* CODENE
Committee for Peace, Disarmament and
  Cooperation 171
Committee for a Sane Nuclear
  Policy 188
Committee for Workers Defence 228
Communist Information Bureau
  (COMINFORM) 78
Communist Party of Great Britain—*See*
  CPGB
Communist Party of the Netherlands—*See*
  CPN
Communist Party of the Soviet
  Union—*See* CPSU
Communist Party of the USA 95
Communist Youth International 45
Comprehensive Test Ban 191
Confederation of Latin American
  Workers 290
Conference on Security and Cooperation
  in Europe—*See* CSCE
Cooperation Committee for Peace and
  Security 85, 177
Council of European National Youth
  Committees 278, 279
Council of Foreign Ministers 20

General Index

Cruise Missiles—*See* GLCM
DAC   130, 132, 134
DEMYC   54, 278
DFG-VK   171, 174
DFU   167, 168, 171
DGB   168
DKP   117, 168, 169, 170, 171, 172
DP   182
Damascus: AAPSO international conference   257
  IUS international student conference   273
  IUS international student forum   273
Dancers for Disarmament   196
Datteln Petition   168–9
Democratic Initiative for Women   99, 171
Democrat Youth Community of Europe—*See* DEMYC
Democrazia Proletaria   182
Deterrence   23, 24
Dortmund, Krefeld Appeal rally   170, 171
Double-Track Decision   23, 32, 112, 156, 176, 190, 215, 238
Dresden, Lutheran rally   223
  Peace Forum   219, 220
Dublin Committee   112, 249
  IUS Forum   273
Dutch Communist Party—*See* CPN
  Labour Party   164

EBU   269–70
ECOSOC   55, 68, 71, 72
END   17, 71, 144, 150–5, 166, 185, 215, 233, 234
ERW   108, 109, 110, 141, 167
ETUC   283, 287
East Berlin: peace demonstration   217
  regional church synod   221
  WFDY-IUS world youth festival   170
  WFSW conference   282
  WPC world assembly of peace   95
East German: Lutheran Church   220–1
  Peace Council   165, 186, 222
  Protestant peace week   222
  RC Bps pastoral letter   222
  Socialist Unity Party—*See* SED
Ecumenical Youth Council of Europe   278
Emergency Committee for Direct Action Against Nuclear War—*See* DAC
Enhanced Radiation Weapons—*See* ERW

European Broadcasting Union   269–70
European communist parties conference   88
European Nuclear Disarmament—*See* END
European Trade Union Confederation—*See* ETUC

FAO   55
FAS   195, 197, 198
FIR   54, 246, 263–4, 292
FISE   62, 287
FOR   99, 122, 192
Fabian Society   43
Federation of American Scientists—*See* FAS
Federation of East German Churches, synod   221
Fellowship of Reconciliation—*See* FOR
Flexible Response   26–8
Frankfurt: FIR coordinating committee   264
  FIR international symposium   264
  IADL peace conference   262
Freie Deutsche Jugen   220
French Communist Party   220—*See* PCF
French nuclear deterent   184, 240
Friedensdienst   216, 217, 218, 219
Friends of Afghanistan   106
Friends of the Soviet Union   106

GLCM   34, 36, 108, 111, 139, 142, 144, 145, 147, 155, 157, 167, 175, 199, 200, 240, 241
General Synod of the Church of England   149
General Union of Workers of Black Africa   289
Generals for Peace and Disarmament   75, 99, 141, 185, 293–4
Geneva, WPC emergency conference   251
  World disarmament conference   117
German Communist Party (KPD)   45, 46, 49—*See also* DKP
German Greens—*See* West German Green Party
German Peace Society   99
German Peace Union—*See* DFU
Greenham Common   146, 149
Greenpeace   230
Grenoble, AAPSO colloquium   257

Group for Establishing Trust between the USSR and the USA 150, 231–5

Hanoi, AAPSO conference 257
WPC special conference 251
Hanover, Protestant Church debate 174
Helsinki: Final Act 60, 226
human rights monitoring group 234
IUS world forum 273
WPC: HQ 246
Hungarian Centre for Peace Research 225
Hungarian National Peace Council 224, 225
Hungarian Peace Group for Dialogue 224, 225, 226
Hyde Park CND rally 144
Hydrogen Bomb National Campaign 130

IADL 54, 74, 95, 246, 260–2, 292
ICATU 112, 290
ICBM 190, 191
ICESC 63, 92, 109, 163, 176
ICFTU 62, 105, 112, 285, 286, 287, 290
ICSA 251, 255
ID 77, 78–82, 89, 90, 92, 96, 101, 161
IID 81, 82
IIP 55, 246, 250, 268–9, 292
IKV 157, 158–9, 160, 164, 165–6, 169, 173
ILF 62, 91, 111, 178, 249
ILO 67, 286–7
IMEMO 80, 81
INF 16, 23, 32–5, 60, 111, 174, 190, 245
IUS 53, 66, 91, 105, 246, 270–4, 292
IUSY 278, 279
Independent Labour Party 48, 123
Indian Communist Party 65
Indian Society for Cultural Relations with the USSR 110
Initiative Group: Stop the Neutron Bomb 97, 160, 161, 162, 163
Institute for Defence and Disarmament Studies 190
Institute for the US and Canada 80
Institute of World Economy and International Relations 80, 81
Interchurch Peace Council, Netherlands—*See* IKV
Intermediate Range Nuclear Forces—*See* INF
International Association of Democratic Lawyers—*See* IADL

International Bureau of Tourism and Exchanges of Youth 277
International Commission of Enquiry into Crimes of the Racist Regimes in Southern Africa 62
International Committee Against Apartheid, Racism and Colonialism in Southern Africa 62
International Committee for European Security and Cooperation —*See* ICESC
International Committee on South Africa 251, 255
International Confederation of Arab Trade Unions 112, 290
International Confederation of Free Trade Unions—*See* ICFTU
International Congress of Jurists 54
International Congress of Writers for the Defence of Culture 46, 47
International Disarmament Week 144
International Federation of Former Political Prisoners of Fascism 264
International Federation of Journalists 266
International Federation of Liberal and Radical Youth 278–9
International Federation of Resistance Fighters—*See* FIR
International Forum Against the Neutron Bomb 161
International Institute for Peace—*See* IIP
International Labour Office 67, 286–7
International League Against War and Fascism 46
International Liaison Forum of Peace Forces—*See* ILF
International Organisation of Journalists 54, 55, 66, 74, 246, 265–8, 292
International Peace Coordination Centre 159
International Physicians for the Prevention of Nuclear War 99
International Radio and TV Organisation—*See* OIRT
International Socialists 107
International Symposium Against the Neutron Bomb 162
International Trade Union Committee for Peace and Disarmament 112, 249
International Transport Union 46
International Union of Resistance and Deportee Movements 264

General Index

International Union of Socialist
  Youth 278, 279
International Union of Students—*See* IUS
International Workers' Aid 45
Italian Communist Party 182
Italian Communist Youth
  Organisation 182
Italian Radical Party 182

Jeunesse Ouvriere Chrétienne 185
Joint Committee: Stop the Neutron
  Bomb, Stop the Nuclear Arms
  Race 163–6

KFAZ 170, 171
KGB 78, 82, 214, 230, 233, 235, 266
  Disinformation Department 82–4
KOR 228
Kabul: AAPSO solidarity
  conference 257
  international conference 253
Kennedy-Hatfield resolution 195, 201,
  202
Kingston, Jamaica, international
  seminar 249
Konsomol 230
Krefeld Appeal 167, 169, 219

LAW 47, 51
LNU 117–22
LRD 42, 43, 107
Labour Party (GB) 46, 48, 123–6, 128,
  130, 131, 134, 135, 137, 146
  Research Department—*See* LRD
Latin American and Caribbean
  conference 110
Latin American Federation of
  Journalists 267, 290
Latin American Institute for
  Transnational Studies 267
League Against War and Fascism 48
League of American Writers 47, 51
League of Anti-Fascists 99
League of Nations 46, 117
League of Nations Union 117–22
League for Peace and Democracy 48, 51
League of Yugoslav Socialist Youth 270
Left Book Club 48, 51
Liaison Committee for the Defence of
  Trade Unions 107
Liberal Party (GB) 48
Liberation movement 107
London CND rally 144
Lotta per la Pace 184

Luanda, IUS conference 272
Lutheran Church in East
  Germany 215–16

MBFR 167
MDP 184, 185, 186
MFS 97, 99, 100
MIRVs 33, 190
MX missiles 190, 198, 200, 205, 206,
  209
Madrid: European Security Review
  Conference 232
Manchester City Council resolution 148
Marshall Plan 78
Massive Retaliation 25
Mecklenburg, church synod
  resolution 217
Medical Association for the Prevention of
  War 104
Methodist Federation for Social
  Action 95
Methodist Peace Fellowship 119, 122
Mexican Peace Movement 110
Mexico City: IADL multi-disciplinary
  conference 262
  WPC world conference 253
Militant Tendency 107
Minuteman 190
Mobilisation for Survival—*See* MFS
Mogadishu, WFDY and PAYM
  international conference 279
Moscow: CPC world conference 260
  CPC with WPC international peace
  conference 260
  Group for Establishing Trust 154, 238
  IADL international conference 262
  World Conference of Peace
  Forces 178
  World Conferences of Religious
  Leaders for Peace 251
  World Congress of Peace Forces 170
Mouvement National Judiciaire 54
Mouvement de la Paix—*See* MDP
Movement for Colonial Freedom 107
Munzenburg Trust 46—*See also*
  International Workers' Aid
Musicians Organisation for Peace 103
Mutual Assured Destruction 26

NATO 15, 26–36, 94, 108–12, 130,
  132, 135, 142–9, 156, 157, 163, 174,
  175, 238–42
  Council 111
NCANWT 130, 131, 134

NCY 279
NGOs 63, 67, 71
  Committee on Disarmament 110
NPC 119, 141
NTS 83
NUIS 270
NVV 285
National Mobilisation Committee to End the War in Vietnam 95
National Peace Campaign 97
National Peace Council 119, 141
National Committee for the Abolition of Nuclear Weapon Tests—*See* NCANWT
National Committee for a Sane Nuclear Policy—*See* SANE
National Coordinating Commission of the Branch Trade Unions of Poland 286
National Freeze Campaign 192
National Freeze Clearing House 192
National Union of Students 107
National Lawyers Guild 95, 97
Nazi–Soviet Pact 48–51
Netherlands: Committee for European Security and Cooperation 166
  Communist Party—*See* CPN
  Congress Against Nuclear Armaments 159
Neutron bomb—*See* ERW
New Delhi: IADL International Lawyers' conference 262
  IUS conference 272
  WPC-AAPSO international conference 65
New Left 107
New Mobe 95, 96
New York Central Park rally 196
Nicosia: AAPSO international conference 257
  IUS international seminar 273
  IUS Round Table 273
No Conscription Fellowship 117
No More War Movement 117
Non-aligned Movement 68
Non-aligned Students Organisations 278
Non-Governmental Organisations—*See* NGOs
Non-Proliferation Treaty 138
Nordic Centre Youth 279
Nordic Women's Peace Marches 178–9, 230

North Atlantic Alliance—*See* Atlantic Alliance
North Atlantic Treaty 3, 19, 21–2
  Organisation—*See* NATO
Nuclear Freeze Foundation 194
Nuclear Weapons Freeze Advertising Campaign 147
Nuclear Weapons Freeze Campaign 194
Nuremburg rally 47
Nurses for a Non-Nuclear Future 196

OATUU 289
OGPU 44, 83
OIRT 54, 246, 269, 292
Olaf Palme Commission on Disarmament and Security Issues 81
Organisation of African Trade Union Unity 289
Outer Space Treaty 137

PASOK 180
PAYM 279
PCF 90, 184, 186
PCI 182–3
PDUP 182
PLO 68
PPU 117, 121–2, 128, 130
PSR 194
Palestine Liberation Organisation 68
Pan-African Youth Movement 279
Paris: IADL symposium 262
  IUS international youth and student conference 272
  WPC-AAPSO international conference 65
  WPC international campaign committee 252
  WPC international conference 252
Parliamentarians for Peace 104
Partial Test Ban Treaty 9, 137
Partito di Unita Proletaria 182
Pax Christi 158, 192, 202
Peace Group for Dialogue 224, 225, 226
Peace Pledge Union—*See* PPU
People's Coalition for Peace and Justice 95
People's Convention 128
People's Front for the Liberation of Oman 72
People's Petition against Enhanced Radiation Weapons 160

General Index

Permanent Congress for the Trade Union Unity of Latin American Workers 290
Pershing II missiles 34, 146, 154, 155, 157, 167, 175, 199, 200, 218, 241, 242
Phnom Penh, AAPSO international conference 257
Physicians for Social Responsibility 194
Polaris missiles 142, 243, 245
Polisario Front 68
Politburo 80
Popular Front against fascism 42, 46, 48, 123
Popular Labour Alliance 83
Prague: Christian Peace conference 160–1
  Warsaw Pact summit meeting 76
  World Assembly for Peace and Life 68, 70, 155, 166, 227
Pugwash Conferences 192

RSL 107–8
Rank and File movement 107
Rapacki Plan 225
Red Aid 45
Revolutionary Socialist League 107–8
Revolutionary Workers League 95
Right to Work Campaign 107
Rome, FIR world conference 264
Rostock Appeal 223

SALT 9, 23n, 33, 88, 96, 98, 138, 142, 189, 190, 198, 199, 208, 245
SANE 95, 188, 200
SDAJ 170
SDP 167
SDS 47
SED 160, 163, 168, 215, 217, 219
SIPRI 190
SPD 168, 169, 171, 178
SSOJ 270
SS-20 143, 146, 147, 153, 183, 184, 199, 217, 218, 240, 241
START 23n, 96, 196, 199, 200, 202, 209, 245
Saxony: Church Synod resolution 217
  Lutheran Peace Forum 220
Scarborough, Labour Party conferences 135
Schutzverband deutscher Schriftsteller 47
Sea Bed Treaty 137–8
Sheffield, annual CND conference 145
Sheppard Peace Movement 121
Slovakia, RC bishops' pastoral letter 228
Social Democratic Party of West Germany 167
Socialist League 48, 123–4
Socialist Workers Party 107
Society of Friends 139
Sofia, World Parliament of People for Peace 170
Sojourners 192
Solidarity 228, 286
Soviet Academy of Sciences 80
Soviet Communist Party—*See* CPSU
Soviet Peace Committee 56, 62, 91, 140, 141, 150, 152, 166, 222, 231, 232
Soviet Peace Fund 56, 93
Soviet Young Communist League 230
Special NGOs Committee on Disarmament 63
Spontaneous Peace Groups, Hungary 223
Stockholm: conference on disarmament 236
  International Institute for Peace Research 190
  Peace Appeal 59, 60, 130
  WPC conferences on Vietnam 95, 251
Strategic Arms Limitation Talks—*See* SALT
Strategic Arms Reduction Talks—*See* START
Student Christian Movement 105
Students for Peace, *Détente* and Disarmament 54
Struggle for Peace 184
Swedish Peace Committee 178
Swiss Peace Committee 63
Sydney, WPC conference 251

Teachers for Peace 104
Ten Power Disarmament Committee 134
Third (Communist) International—*See* Comintern
Thor missiles 131
Trade Unions International 287–9
Trades Union Congress 135, 285
Trafalgar Square, CND rally 144
Transport and General Workers Union 135
Traprock Peace Center 192
Trident missiles 139, 142, 145, 147, 190, 244
Tripoli, WPC world conference 253

Trust 83
12 June Disarmament Coalition 100
UBDP 186, 187
UK nuclear deterrent 35, 239, 243-5
UN 10, 59, 67, 68, 71
  Disarmament Commission 67
  General Assembly 15, 59, 181
  Special Committee Against
    Apartheid 272
  Special Session on Disarmament—*See*
    UNSSOD
  Youth Association 105
UNCTAD 67, 68
UNEP 67
UNESCO 55, 67, 68
UNIDO 55, 67, 68
UNSSOD 75, 97, 100, 101, 141, 196, 204, 209, 232
Union des Femmes Françaises 54, 275
Union des Intellectuels Français 51
Union of German Students'
  Organisations 174
Union of Italian Women 275
Union of Opponents of Military
  Service 171, 174
Union of Shop Distributive and Allied
  Workers 135
United Church of Christ 200
United Nations—*See* UN
United Nations Association 134
United Nations Atomic Energy
  Commission 7
US: Bishops' Pastoral Letter 203-7
  Peace Council 92, 98, 99, 100
  Strategic Air Command 214
WFDY 53, 66, 103, 105, 111, 159, 246, 272, 276-80, 292
WFSW 54, 106, 246, 281, 292
WFTU 53, 62, 74, 91, 103, 104, 105, 109, 111, 112, 246, 283-91, 292
WIDF 54, 66, 95, 109, 178, 241, 274-6, 292
WILPF 63, 95, 96, 249
WPC 13, 14, 43, 53, 55, 56, 60, 61, 62, 64-76, 91, 92, 93, 94, 95, 96, 97, 109, 110, 111, 161, 163, 170, 177, 182, 246, 250, 292
War Registers League 188
War Resisters International 65
Warsaw Pact 18, 29, 63, 109, 145, 227, 240
Washington, WPC conference 96
Weimar, IUS world forum 273

West Berlin, second END
  convention 152, 154
West German Committees for Peace,
  Disarmament and
  Cooperation 170, 171
West German Green Party 157, 167, 171-2, 173, 175
West German Socialist Party—*See* SPD
Women for Life on Earth 149
Women for Peace 178, 222
Women Strike for Peace 95
Women's International Democratic
  Federation—*See* WIDF
Women's International League for Peace
  and Freedom—*See* WILPF
Women's Peace Foundation—*See* AFF
Workers Revolutionary Party 107
World Anti-War Congress 123
World Assembly for Peace and Life,
  Against Nuclear War 68, 70, 112
World Committee for the Struggle
  Against War 46
World Committee of Partisans for
  Peace 64, 250
World Conference Against Apartheid
  Racism and Colonialism in South
  Africa 255
World Confederation of Labour 112, 286
World Congress of Intellectuals for
  Peace 64, 93, 250
World Congress of Peace Forces 65
World Federation of Democratic
  Youth—*See* WFDY
World Federation of Scientific
  Workers—*See* WFSU
World Federation of Teachers'
  Unions—*See* FISE
World Federation of Trade Unions—*See*
  WFTU
World Forum of Peace Forces 92
World Forum of Youth 54
World Information Service on Energy 99
World Parliament of People for
  Peace 61, 70 , 72, 74, 111
World Peace Council—*See* WPC
World Peace Fund 56
World Peace Congress 63
World Veterans' Federation 264

Young Communist League 84, 105
Young Socialist German Workers 170
Youth CND 140

Zhukov letter 152, 215, 238